IMAGES
of Rail

Summit County's Narrow-Gauge Railroads

ON THE COVER: **ENGINE 265.** Well-oiled and carrying a full load of coal and water, Denver, Leadville & Gunnison engine 265, built in 1886 by the Rhode Island Locomotive Works, pauses with another helper engine south of the Breckenridge depot before beginning its climb over Boreas Pass. In this 1898 photograph, the crew and guests pose for the photographer before tackling the snow awaiting them along the High Line. (Photograph by Dr. Clinton H Scott, courtesy of the Ed and Nancy Bathke collection.)

IMAGES of Rail

SUMMIT COUNTY'S NARROW-GAUGE RAILROADS

Bob Schoppe and Sandra F. Mather, PhD

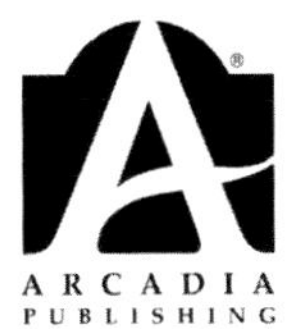

ISBN 978-1-4671-1685-5

Published by Arcadia Publishing
Charleston, South Carolina

Printed in the United States of America

Library of Congress Control Number: 2016947307

For all general information, please contact Arcadia Publishing:
Telephone 843-853-2070
Fax 843-853-0044
E-mail sales@arcadiapublishing.com
For customer service and orders:
Toll-Free 1-888-313-2665

Visit us on the Internet at www.arcadiapublishing.com

The authors dedicate this book to the men who built and worked on the railroad and their families who endured daily hardships as well as to those who keep the legacy alive for future generations.

Contents

Acknowledgments 6

Introduction 7

1. Como 9
2. The High Line to Breckenridge 19
3. Breckenridge, North to Dickey 47
4. Dillon and Keystone 65
5. Frisco and the Ten Mile Canyon 71
6. On to Leadville 111
7. Preserving the Legacy 119

About the Organizations 127

ACKNOWLEDGMENTS

The authors wish to thank a number of people who made this publication possible, including Simone Belz of the Frisco Historic Park & Museum and Tom Klinger, who reviewed the manuscript. Photographs came from a wide variety of sources: the Denver, South Park & Pacific Historical Society; the Summit Historical Society; the Frisco Historic Park & Museum; the Bill Fountain collection; the Bill and Nancy Bathke collection; the Clair Dungan collection; the Maureen Nicholls collection; the Todd Hackett collection; the Dave Cattani collection; the Town of Breckenridge; the Breckenridge Heritage Alliance; and Rick Hague. The authors are indebted to these sources for providing the valuable historic photographs.

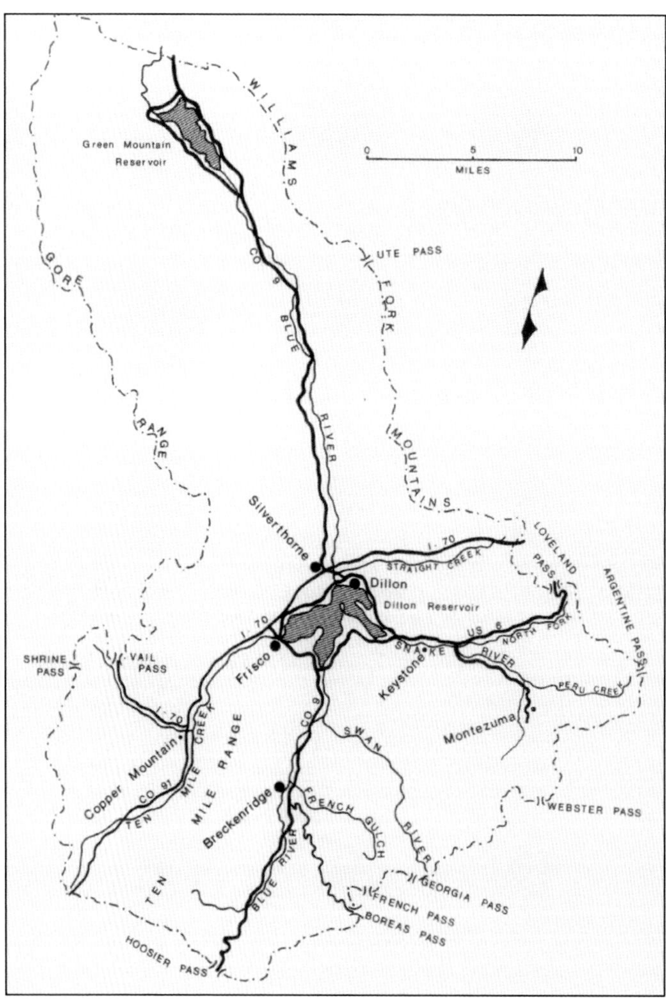

MAP OF SUMMIT COUNTY, COLORADO. Summit County, located approximately 75 miles west of Denver, is home to sixty mountain peaks over 11,000 feet, four ski resorts, two huge reservoirs, and numerous high-altitude mountain passes. Dillon and Frisco are located on Lake Dillon, while Breckenridge lies to the south along the Blue River. Montezuma overlooks the Snake River in the eastern part of the county. (Reproduction by Sandra F. Pritchard Mather.)

INTRODUCTION

The development of the mining and agricultural economies of Summit County required cheap, efficient transportation. From the spring of 1859 on, when gold was discovered in what became Summit County, adequate, reliable transportation meant the difference between economic advantage and stagnation. Without it, ore, hay, timber, sheep, and cattle could not reach local or distant markets, and food, clothing, and mining and agricultural equipment and supplies would not be available for those needing them.

Although pack trains and wagons carried a staggering tonnage of merchandise and ore to and from Summit County, some pieces of equipment for the mines proved far too heavy and bulky to be carried by wagon and sled. Stockpiled ore had to be moved more quickly and at cheaper rates to be profitable. Merchants and miners required something that could carry larger loads faster and at less expense—that something was the railroad.

Two narrow-gauge railroads served Summit County: the Denver & Rio Grande and the Denver, South Park & Pacific. The word "Pacific" told of the company's desire to reach the Pacific Ocean. Investors and entrepreneurs created both as a means of efficiently moving the mineral wealth of the county, thus tying their fortunes to the mining economy; when it died, so too did the railroads.

The president of the Denver & Rio Grande, William Jackson Palmer, felt that "a population engaged in mining is by far the most profitable of any for a railroad." Therefore, he built the Leadville, Ten Mile & Breckenridge Railroad (officially the Leadville & Ten Mile Narrow Gauge Railroad), which ran from Leadville through the Ten Mile Canyon, serving Robinson and Kokomo by December 1880, Wheeler by September 1881, and Dillon by November 1882, a distance of 36 miles. A hoped-for extension along the Blue River to Breckenridge, which would have been called the Blue River Branch of the Denver & Rio Grande Railroad, was never built. Keeping all of its options open, the company also surveyed an alternate route to Breckenridge over Hoosier Pass. Despite the ambitious plans, lack of money halted the line at Dillon.

Another plan that never materialized included a route to Kremmling that would have tapped the ranches lining the lower Blue River. Rumors flew in May 1902 that the Denver & Rio Grande would finally build its extension north. The railroad graded along the waterway and laid track about a mile north of Dillon. A train ran over the short extension each day to maintain the right-of-way. Eventually even this stopped. After workers removed the rails and ties, the grade became a county road.

The Denver, South Park & Pacific (DSP&P), created by Gov. John Evans in 1872, became part of the Union Pacific rail system in 1880. Led by Jay Gould, the railroad wanted its own line to Leadville rather than share one as it had been doing with the Denver & Rio Grande. Railroad surveyors arrived in the county in June 1881. Feeling that the county's mineral resources, especially in the Snake River valley, warranted its attention, the railroad decided to begin work at once on a main line that would fully control passenger and freight service in the county. The company planned to build spurs to mines off the main track. The newspaper editor crowed that with the coming of the railroad, Breckenridge would "be lifted into the list of cities within the pale of civilization. It [Breckenridge] would have distribution facilities almost equal to Denver."

The "South Park" began laying track from Como in 1881, reaching Boreas Pass by the end of the year. The tracks extended to Breckenridge by September 1882 and Dillon by December 1882. The Keystone Branch began service in January 1883. The line continued through the Ten Mile Canyon, arriving in Leadville in 1884.

The mountain railroads of Colorado laid their tracks three feet apart. Railroads in the East and on the plains used standard gauge, meaning four feet, eight and one-half inches between the rails. Narrow-gauge tracks offered advantages. Sharp turns so necessary in the mountains required less blasting. It proved cheaper to go around objects than going through them. The shorter ties saved money, as did the smaller, lighter engines and cars. Narrow-gauge track could be laid faster. Rather than cut and grade new beds, the railroads bought rights-of-way from wagon companies. Crews laid iron rails on untreated ties of spruce and yellow pine spaced 18 inches apart, using approximately 3,000 ties per mile. Rocks blasted from the bed and, later, cinders from passing engines became ballast. Ashes from the firebox, dumped along the tracks, added to the ballast. Work crews did little true grading as the companies rushed to complete their lines. Tracks bent and sagged in the middle, causing the cars to sway sideways and lurch forward and backward. Maximum speeds for passenger trains reached less than 22 miles per hour in the county and less than 12 miles per hour for freight trains in the Ten Mile Canyon and over Boreas Pass. Passengers did not enjoy a speedy, comfortable ride. Instead, the Denver, South Park & Pacific earned the nickname "Damn Slow Pulling and Pretty Rough Riding."

At the turn of the century, financial problems dictated corporate changes. Reorganizing to avoid bankruptcy, the Denver, South Park & Pacific (commonly referred to as just "the Denver, South Park") became the Denver, Leadville & Gunnison Railway Company in 1889. Faced with continuing fiscal instability, the newly formed company was purchased first by the Colorado & Southern (C&S) in 1898 and then by the Chicago, Burlington & Quincy in 1908. These owners had little interest in maintaining the narrow-gauge line because of high operating expenses. Little high-grade ore filled the cars. Most of the ore was low grade, as was true throughout the entire mining era of Summit County. The newest concentration methods resulted in even less to carry. In addition, electricity, available in Breckenridge in 1898 and in Frisco and Dillon in 1909, reduced the need for coal, which had always been a big part of the tonnage carried on incoming trains. The inability to integrate narrow- and standard-gauge rolling stock created further difficulties for the company. To compound the problem, cars, trucks, and buses began replacing the railroad as the primary carrier of people and freight.

The Denver & Rio Grande ended service in the county in 1911. After many years of trying, beginning in 1910–1911, the Colorado & Southern abandoned its lines in 1937. Engine 9 carried the last passengers and freight from Como to Leadville and back on April 9–10, 1937. The *Denver Post* on Friday, April 9, 1937, reported:

> The Last Train leaves Denver on Famous Leadville Line.
>
> Return on Saturday will end traffic on road closely linked with romantic period in history of Colorado.
>
> One coach, one baggage car, and a tiny locomotive stood in the frosty shadows of two big modern trains at the Union Station, early Friday morning, loading a few passengers and some small freight, mostly groceries for the last trip out of Denver on one of the most romantic railroads in the west.

Crews removed rails and ties the following year. Only the 14 miles of narrow-gauge track running from Climax to Leadville remained to carry the mineral molybdenum. The Colorado & Southern converted them to standard gauge on August 25, 1943.

One

Como

The story of the High Line to Breckenridge begins in Como, in Park County (elevation 9,796 feet [2,985 meters]). The town, named for Lake Como in Italy, became the central staging area for the railroad when the company bought land and sold lots to the workers starting in 1879. Single men lived in bunkhouses, while married men and their families could purchase larger homes.

Tents first provided shelter for visitors, but on January 1, 1881, Benjamin Gilman opened the two-story brick Gilman Hotel, later becoming part of the Pacific Hotel (1885). The hotel quickly became the social headquarters of the town. Train schedules allowed passengers on east- and west-bound trains 20 minutes for lunch. A fire on November 9, 1896, totally destroyed the structure. The Como Hotel and Eating House, slightly smaller than the original structure, opened in fall 1897 on the original site and served visitors until it closed in November 1910, only to reopen four years later.

Women played an important role in the lives of the railroading families in Como. While the men endured long hours, delays sometimes hours and sometimes days long, the uncertainty of assignments, and the lack of a daily routine, the women kept the families going. Though they adjusted to the assignments and delays, often preparing meals in the middle of the night, many never adjusted to the constant dangers facing their husbands in their work. Isolation and the harsh winter took a toll on the women, as did the wide open spaces around Como and the long distances to anywhere. Cooking, cleaning, and baking were daily chores done in cold houses with freezing temperatures, swirling winds, and blowing snow outside during the long winter.

Workers built a large six-bay stone roundhouse in 1881. The need for more room resulted in the addition of 13 wooden bays in the 1890s. With this addition, locomotives could receive needed repairs without being sent to the main shops in Denver. The original stone portion of the roundhouse became a well-equipped machine shop and office. On March 25, 1935, the wooden portion burned completely. The stone portion was rebuilt so that repairs could still be done in Como. Following the fire, the machinery filled the original stone portion of the roundhouse; a caboose served as the office.

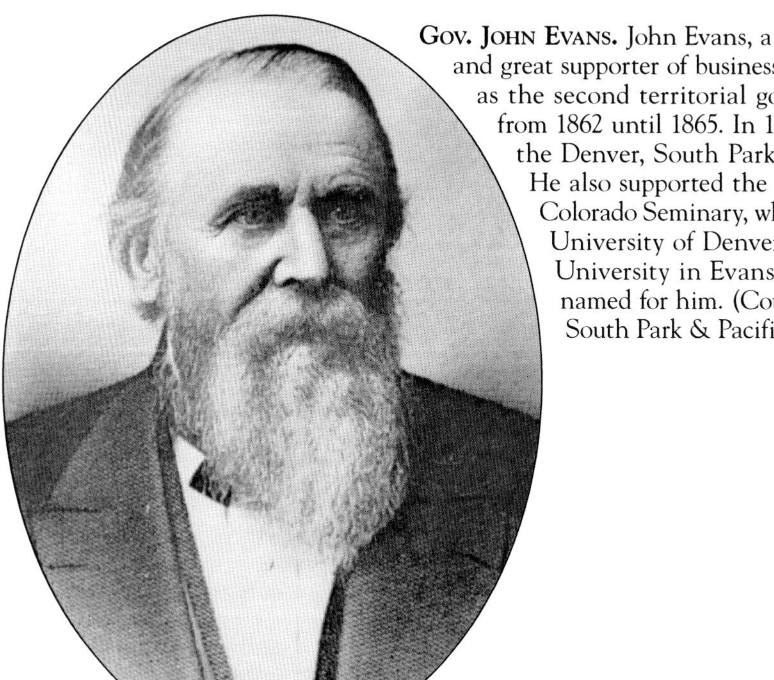

Gov. John Evans. John Evans, a politician, physician, and great supporter of business in Colorado, served as the second territorial governor of Colorado from 1862 until 1865. In 1873, he helped found the Denver, South Park & Pacific Railroad. He also supported the establishment of the Colorado Seminary, which later became the University of Denver, and Northwestern University in Evanston, Illinois, a town named for him. (Courtesy of the Denver, South Park & Pacific Historical Society.)

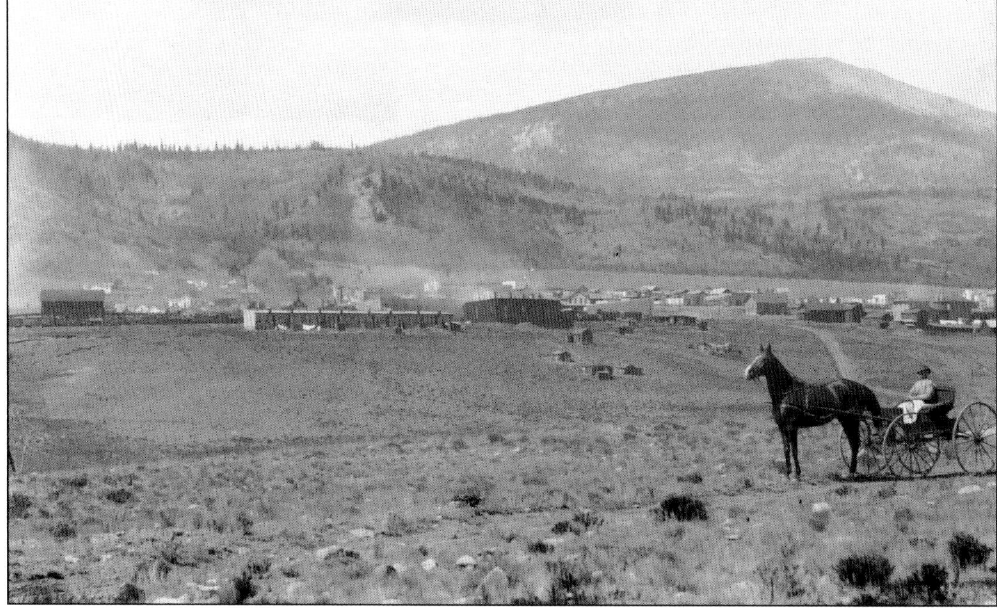

Railroad Facilities in Como. While his driver waits, Clinton H Scott took this photograph in 1897 of the railroad facilities in Como. From left to right are the coal dock, a tenement building that housed railroad workers, the roundhouse, the dispatcher's building, the depot, and the Como Hotel and Eating House. The shacks on the hillside provided shelter for train crews laying over in Como between trips. (Photograph by Dr. Clinton H Scott, courtesy of the Ed and Nancy Bathke collection.)

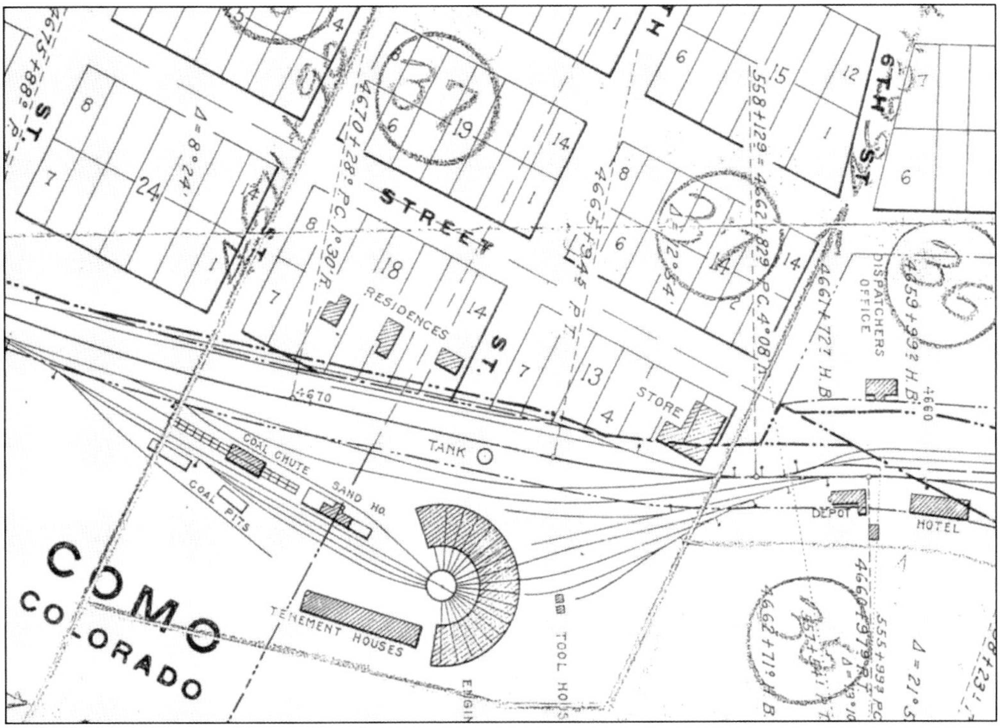

MAP OF RAILROAD FACILITIES IN COMO. This 1918 Interstate Commerce Commission map shows the roundhouse with all 19 stalls, coal dock, sand house, water tank, tenement building to house employees, and coal pits. The rail yards could hold several hundred cars. At first, Como was simply a stop on the way to the coal deposits near Gunnison. But by 1881, it had become a major division point on the High Line to Breckenridge and Leadville. (Courtesy of the Denver, South Park & Pacific Historical Society.)

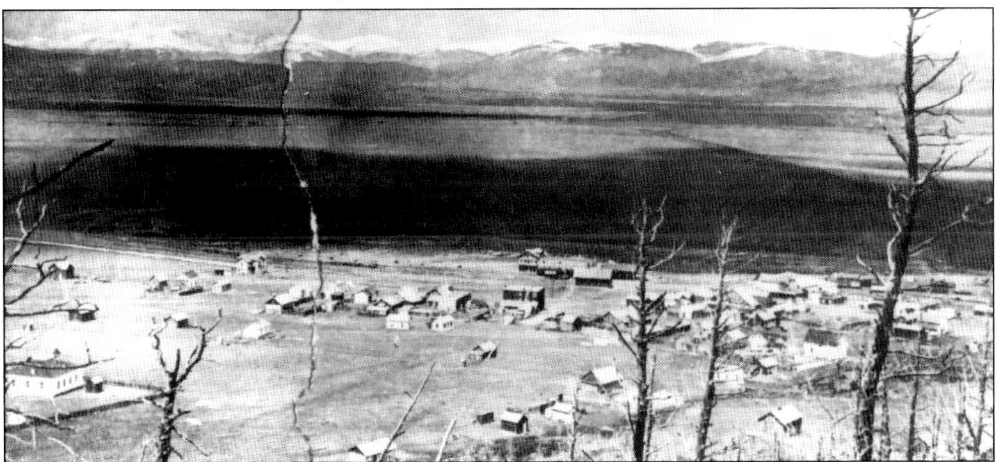

OVERVIEW OF COMO. Taken from the hill just west of town, this c. 1884–1885 photograph shows early Como. The original Gilman Hotel with extension and the depot appear in the center distance. Both the Gilman Hotel and the extension became the Pacific Hotel in the fall of 1885. In front of those buildings on the near side of the tracks stands the newly constructed dispatcher's/superintendent's office, built in the spring of 1884. (Photograph by Alex Martin, courtesy of the Denver, South Park & Pacific Historical Society.)

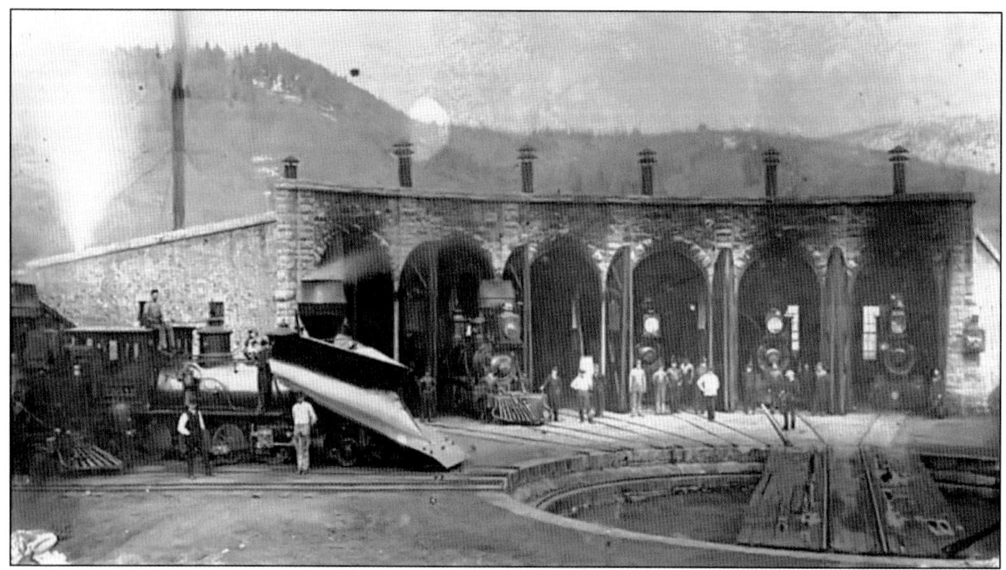

Roundhouse in Como. Six locomotives fill the six-bay roundhouse. In the 1890s, railroad employees added 13 more wooden bays to the right in the photograph to service the engines arriving and departing daily. An engine with a huge bucking snow plow sits to the left. Today, the Denver, South Park & Pacific Historical Society continues to assist owner Dr. Charles Brantigan in restoring both the roundhouse and the turntable. (Courtesy of the Denver, South Park & Pacific Historical Society.)

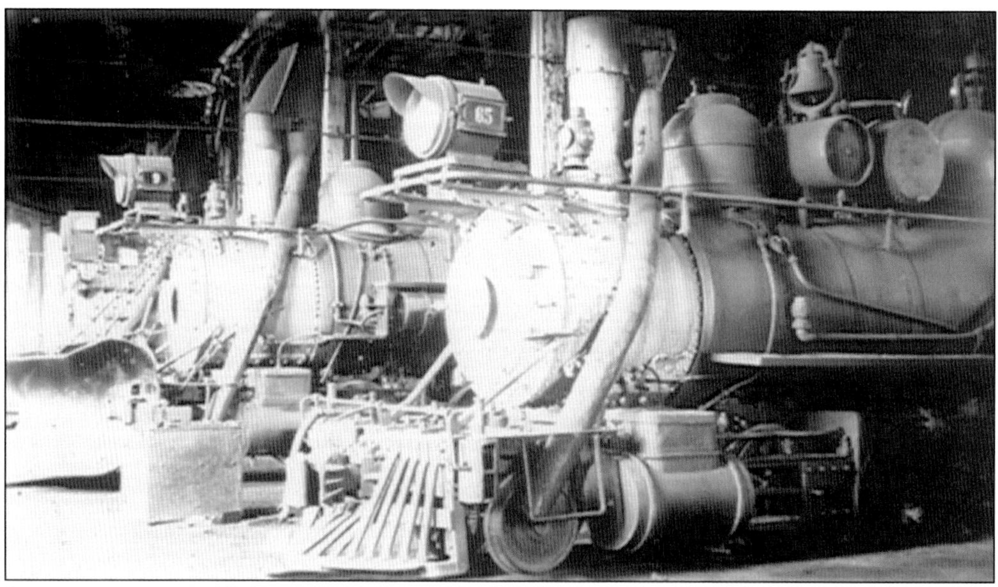

Locomotives in the Roundhouse. Locomotives wait in the roundhouse for maintenance that might range from a quick lubrication to a major overhaul. The building provided critical warmth and shelter from blowing snow, strong winds, and biting temperatures during ferocious South Park winters. Workers built the original six-stall stone roundhouse pictured here in 1881. Maintenance needs required that 13 more stalls be constructed. Today, only the original stone roundhouse remains. (Courtesy of the Bill Fountain collection.)

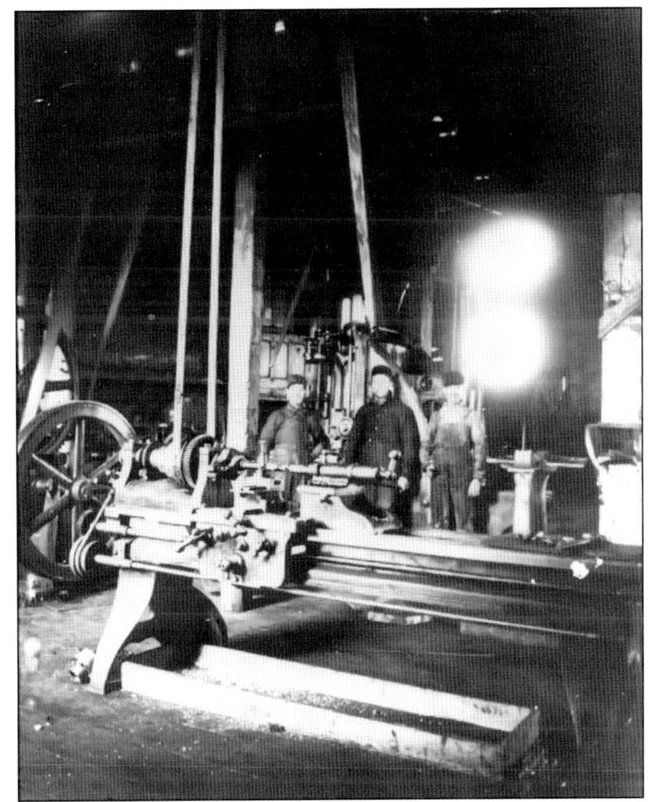

Workers in the Como Roundhouse. After the construction of the 13 wooden stalls, the original stone roundhouse became a machine shop for locomotive repairs. Workers utilized the belt-driven machines to fashion and repair the necessary parts. The belts on each machine extended upwards to a system of rods and pulleys in the ceiling powered by a stationary steam boiler that provided power before electricity arrived in Como. (Courtesy of the Denver, South Park & Pacific Historical Society.)

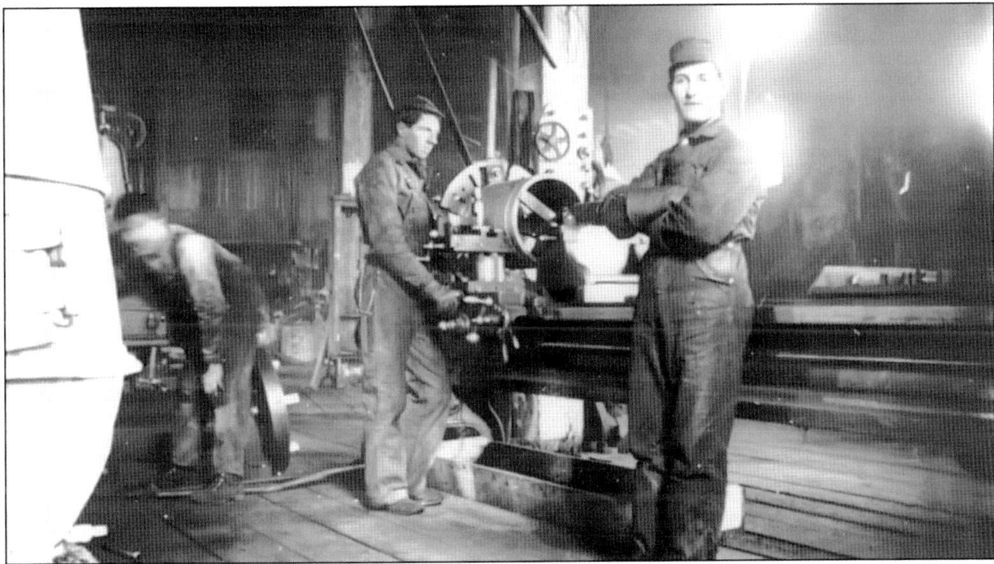

Working a Lathe in the Como Roundhouse. Members of the roundhouse crew pose beside a belt-driven lathe. On the immediate left can be seen one of the large pot-bellied stoves that attempted to keep the roundhouse machine shop warm during the winter months. The lathe and other machines enabled railroad employees to make major repairs to the locomotives rather than sending them to the main repair shops in Denver. (Courtesy of the Denver, South Park & Pacific Historical Society.)

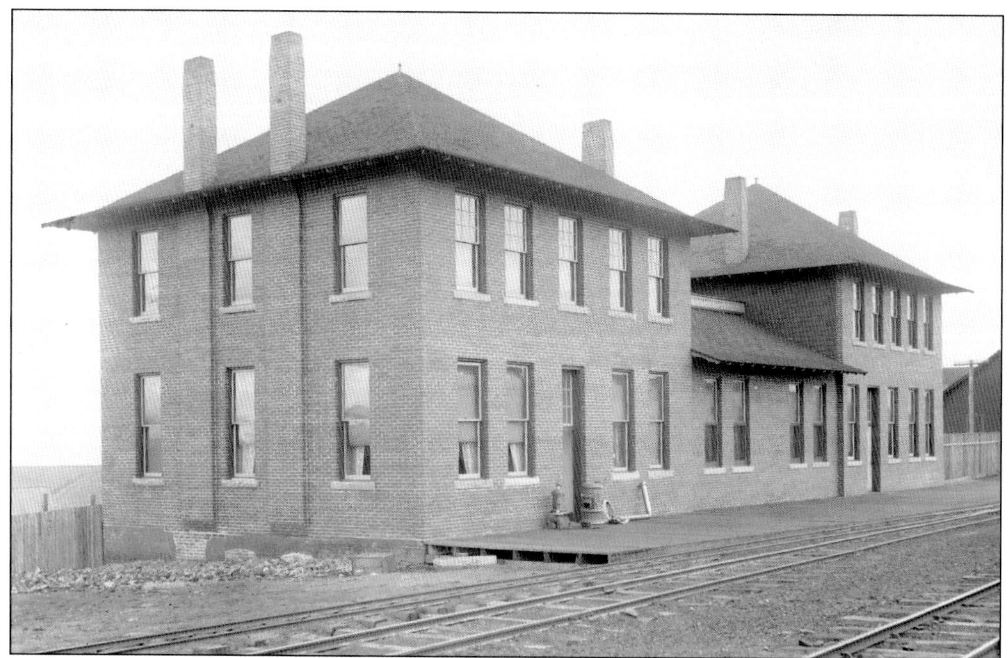

Como Hotel and Eating House. On January 1, 1881, Benjamin Gilman opened his two-story brick hotel to serve Como residents and train passengers. In 1885, the Pacific Hotel Company acquired the property and extensively renovated it. In November 1896, the building burned to the ground, and the following year, the current hotel opened on the foundation of the original Gilman Hotel. In this view of the brand-new hotel taken in the fall of 1897, debris from the fire can be seen on the ground to the left. (Photograph by Dr. Clinton H Scott, courtesy of the Todd Hackett collection.)

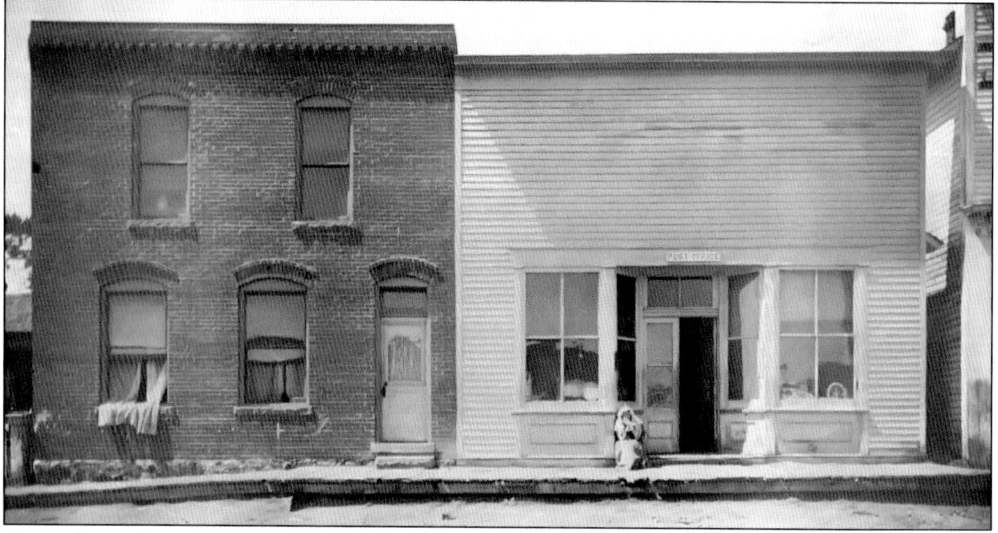

Como Post Office. The Como Post Office, on the right, handled probably the most precious freight arriving each day in Como—letters from home. Virtually all mail arrived by train. Railroads dedicated special cars to mail service, calling them RPOs—railway post office cars. Women often planned their days around the arrival of the mail train. (Photograph by Dr. Clinton H Scott, courtesy of the Ed and Nancy Bathke collection.)

RESTORED DEPOT IN COMO. When the railroad abandoned Como in 1937, the depot became a three-car garage. By the summer of 2008, the 129-year-old building clearly showed the ravages of time and neglect. Close to total collapse, the front face had sunk nearly two feet; the building leaned at nearly 20 degrees. In August 2015, the Denver, South Park & Pacific Historical Society, along with owners David Tomkins and Moya Cleaver, opened the restored depot as a museum. (Courtesy of the Denver, South Park & Pacific Historical Society.)

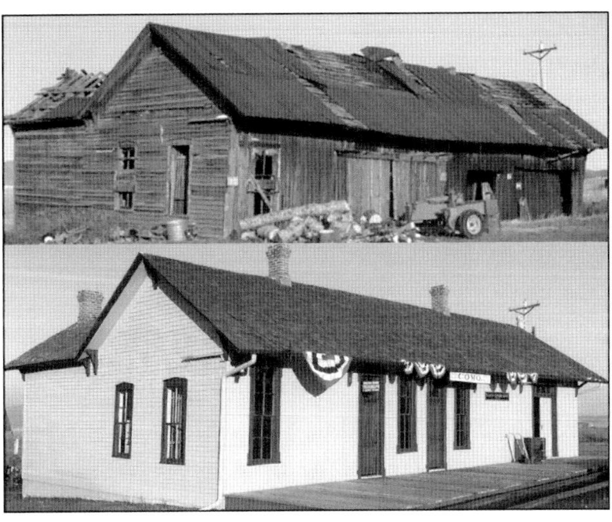

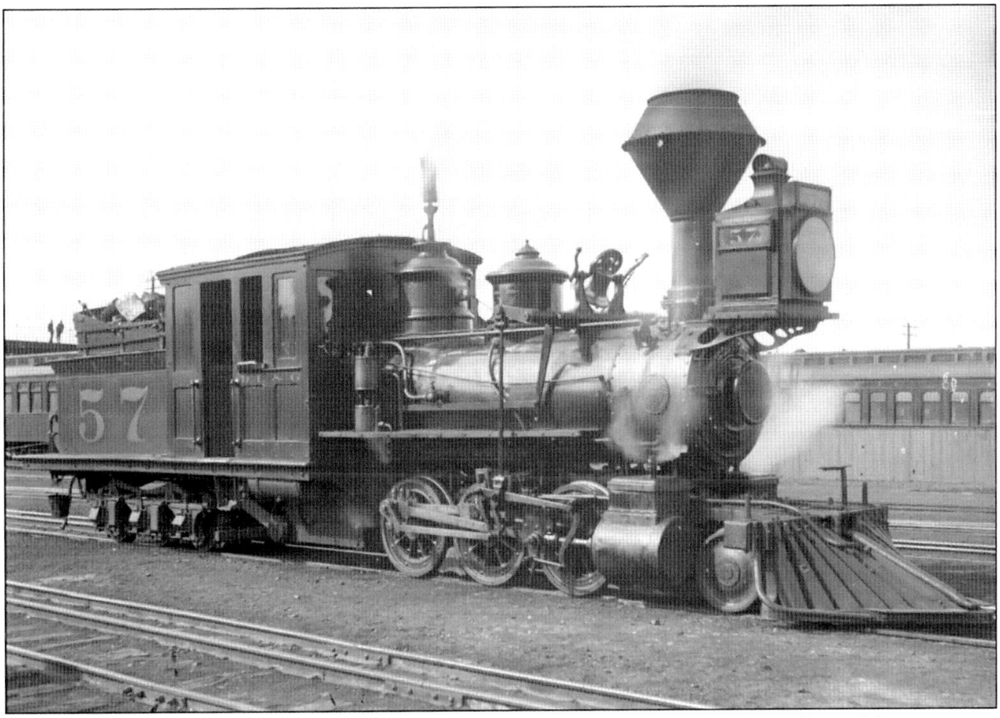

ENGINE 57, C. 1898. Denver, Leadville & Gunnison engine 57, a Mason "Bogie" locomotive, enjoyed a long career. The last of its type operating on the old South Park line, it ran on Colorado & Southern tracks for nearly a year before being sold in 1899 to a logging company in the Midwest. Subsequently, it sat idle on the University of Iowa campus in Ames until becoming part of a scrap drive in World War II. (Photograph by Dr. Clinton H Scott, courtesy of the Todd Hackett collection.)

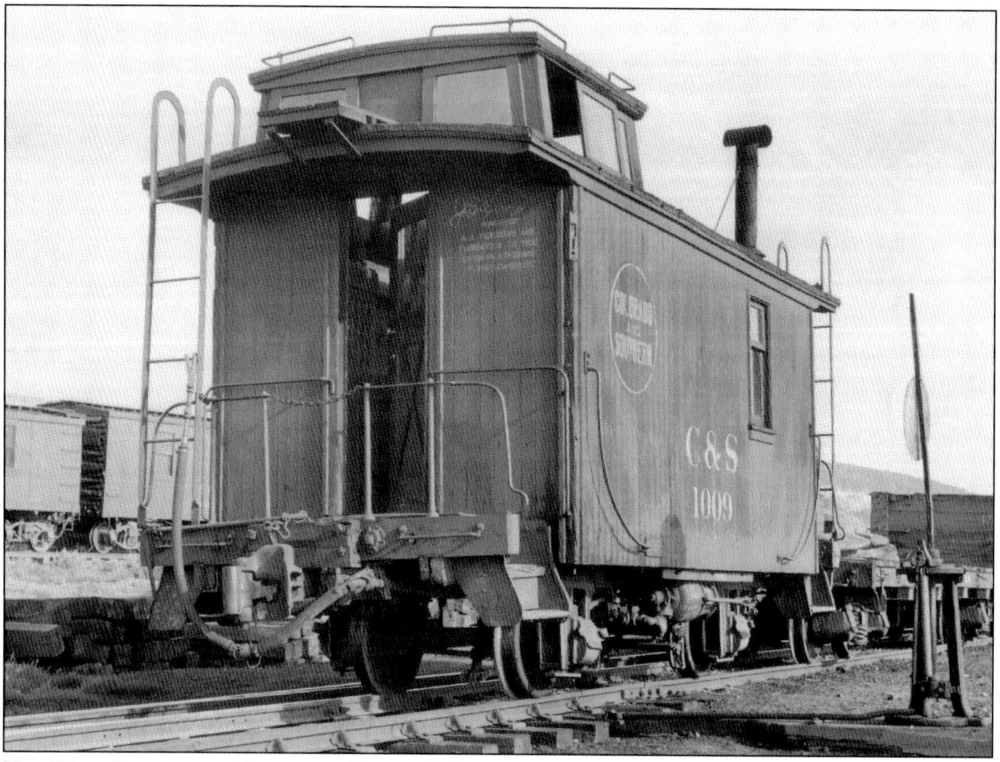

THE VERY IMPORTANT CABOOSE. Originally known as a "waycar," the first caboose on the South Park line entered service around 1882. The cupola, standard on later cabooses, allowed the conductor a view in every direction. Just over 12 feet long, these wooden cabooses were nicknamed "bouncing betties" because of the bouncy ride at the end of the train. Today, just three of the original South Park cabooses survive, including 1009. (Courtesy of the Denver, South Park & Pacific Historical Society.)

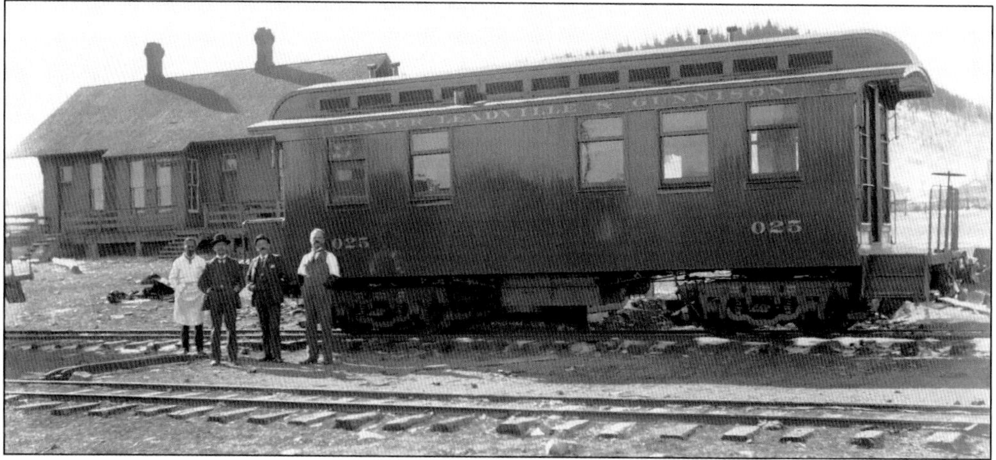

DENVER, LEADVILLE & GUNNISON BUSINESS CAR. Crew and passengers pose for the camera in front of this business car that previously served as a boxcar. Management used these cars when traveling the rails. Later it was converted to a maintenance-of-way car. The dispatcher and superintendent shared the wooden building behind the railroad car. Notice the reflection of one of the men on the side of the car behind him. (Courtesy of the Bill Fountain collection.)

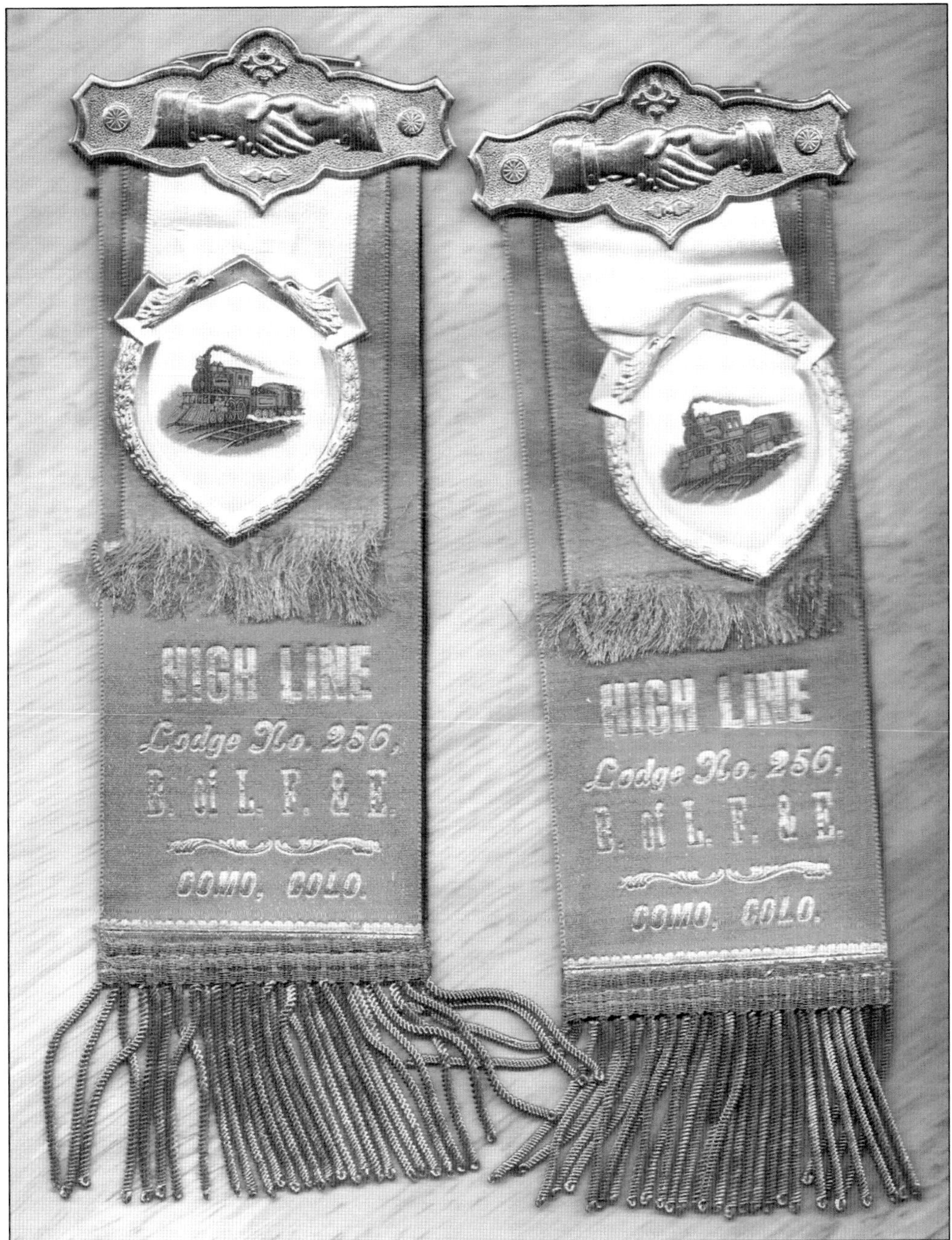

High Line Lodge No. 256. Most railroad employees belonged to unions such as the Brotherhood of Locomotive Firemen and Engineers, who issued these ribbons to each individual chapter. Members of the High Line Chapter, Lodge No. 256, in Como, wore these ribbons at official functions and parades. The back of each ribbon was black so that the ribbon could be reversed to wear at funerals. (Courtesy of the Denver, South Park & Pacific Historical Society.)

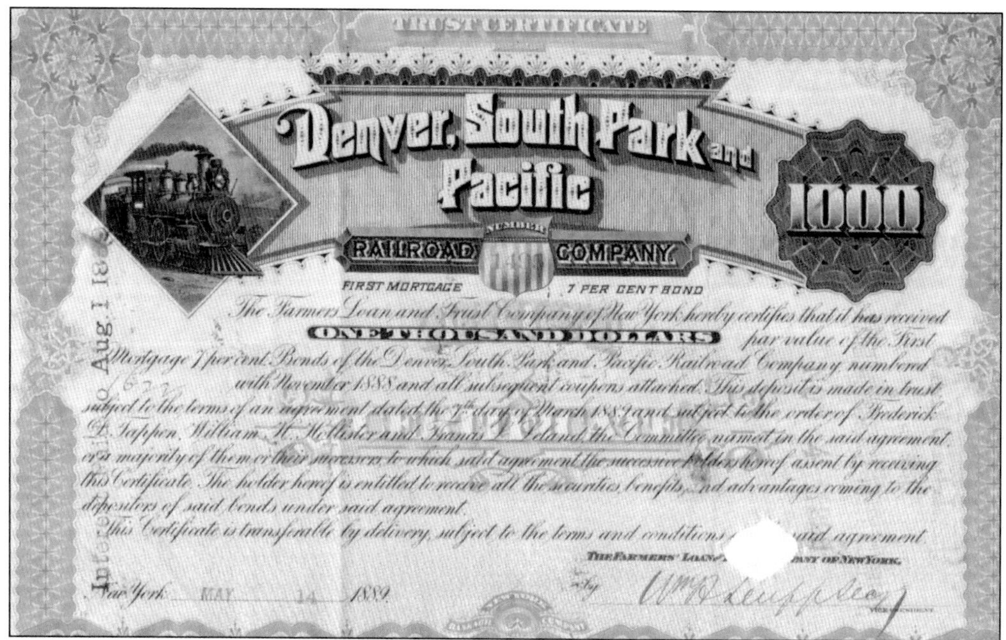
TRUST CERTIFICATE

Denver, South Park and Pacific Railroad Company

1000

FIRST MORTGAGE 7 PER CENT BOND

The Farmers Loan and Trust Company of New York hereby certifies that it has received ONE THOUSAND DOLLARS par value of the First Mortgage 7 per cent. Bonds of the Denver, South Park and Pacific Railroad Company numbered with November 1888 and all subsequent coupons attached. This deposit is made in trust subject to the terms of an agreement dated the 7th day of March 1889 and subject to the order of Frederick D. Tappen, William H. Hollister and Francis L. Leland, the Committee named in the said agreement or a majority of them or their successors, to which said agreement the successive holders hereof assent by receiving this Certificate. The holder hereof is entitled to receive all the securities, benefits, and advantages coming to the depositors of said bonds under said agreement.

This Certificate is transferable by delivery, subject to the terms and conditions of said agreement.

THE FARMERS' LOAN AND TRUST COMPANY OF NEW YORK.

New York MAY 14 1889.

Interest paid to Aug 1 18

DENVER, SOUTH PARK & PACIFIC TRUST CERTIFICATE. The Farmers Loan and Trust Company of New York City issued this $1,000 certificate in 1889. In return for the investment, the holder received all the securities, benefits, and advantages coming to the investor under the terms of the agreement at the time of the purchase. (Courtesy of the Denver, South Park & Pacific Historical Society.)

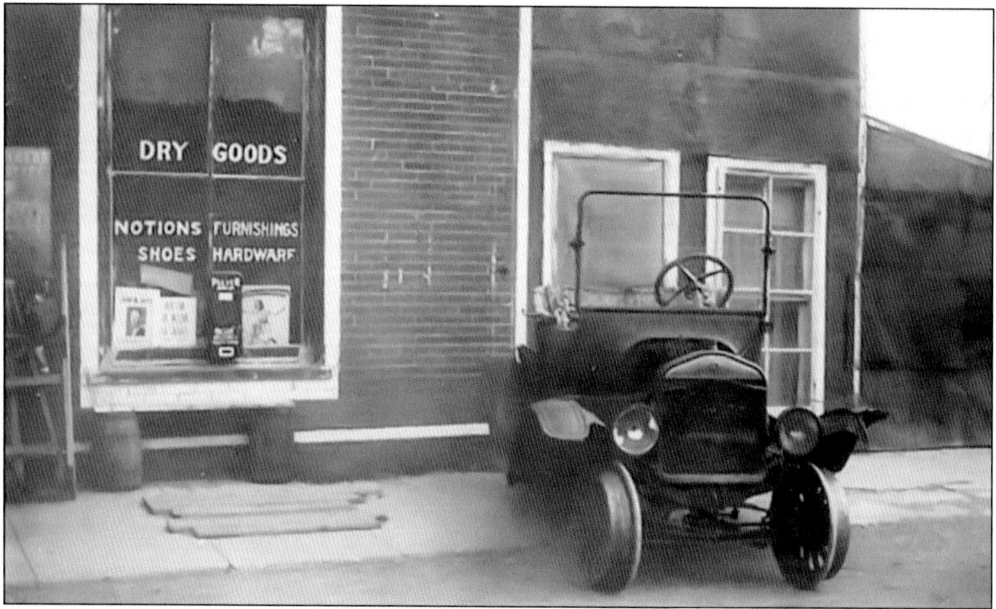

CONVERTED FORD MODEL T. In the summer of 1938, Como residents John Riedesel and Claire and Gene Duggan converted a Ford Model T to run on the Colorado & Southern narrow-gauge rails that had been abandoned the previous year. Before the railroad removed the rails that summer, they traveled over Boreas Pass, through Breckenridge and Frisco, and along the Ten Mile Creek almost to Fremont Pass. (Courtesy of the Denver, South Park & Pacific Historical Society.)

Two

The High Line to Breckenridge

The Denver, South Park & Pacific planned to enter the county from two directions. From the north, the Georgetown, Breckenridge & Leadville Railroad would extend its Clear Creek line over Loveland Pass and follow the Snake River to its confluence with the Blue River in Dillon. Branches would then be built to Breckenridge and Leadville. From the south, the railroad could enter Summit County from South Park in three different ways: over Georgia Pass and down French Gulch to Breckenridge; over Boreas Pass and down Indiana Creek to Illinois Gulch and Breckenridge; or over Hoosier Pass and down the Blue River valley to Breckenridge.

Whichever route the railroad selected, Leadville was the primary destination, not Breckenridge. The company chose the second option, the route over Boreas Pass. Despite being 21 miles shorter, at a lower elevation, and making use of a graded wagon road, some railroad historians feel strongly that other unnamed factors influenced the decision.

Construction began on October 30, 1880. The town of Boreas, constructed in 1882 by railroad workers and named for the wind that constantly blows at 11,481 feet (3,499 meters), was the highest rail station in the United States. The town included a depot, a storehouse with dirt roof, a telegraph house, and a section house east of the tracks. The storehouse and section house still stand. On the west side of the road, the foundation for the stone engine house with coal bin and water tank fed by springs remains. The 1883 structure included a turntable. The main line ran down the middle of today's road. A snow shed built in 1885 covered 600 feet of track. When it burned in 1899, crews rebuilt it and lengthened it to 997 feet. Another snow shed protected a wye and 1,566 feet of sidetrack. The grade for the wye extended west of the engine house foundation. Ties from a spur east of the road lie among the willows. In 1898, crews built a depot, attaching it to the snow shed. The wooden foundation can be seen next to the road.

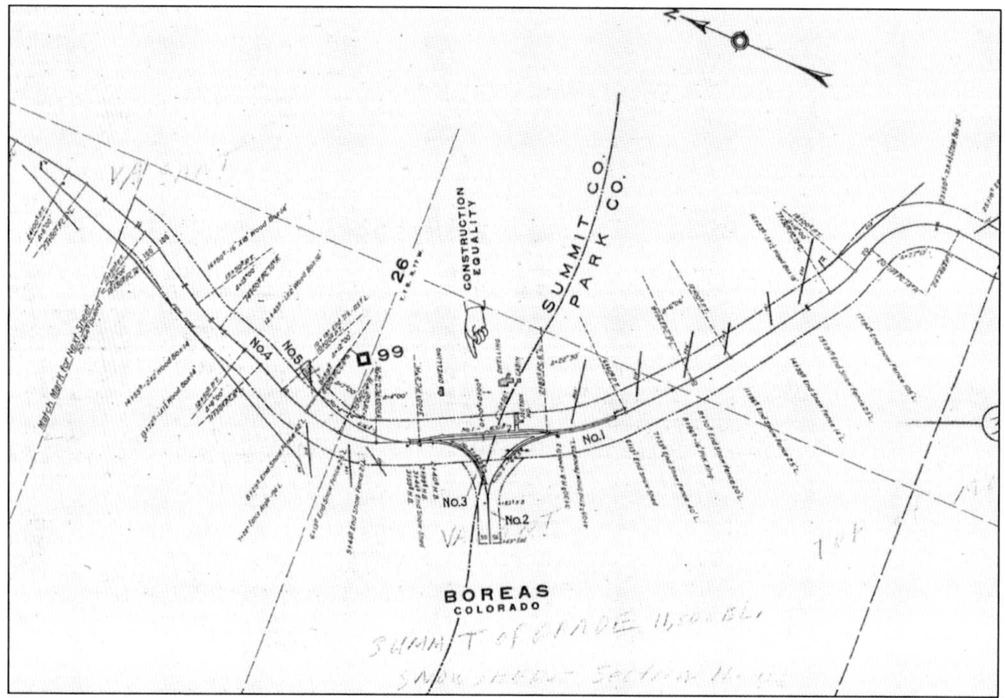

Denver, South Park & Pacific Map of Boreas. The map shows the main line from Como to Breckenridge. Markers indicate the northern and southern ends of the snow shed that covered the main line and much of the wye to the west. The depot is incorrectly identified as the section house. Snow fences line the tracks to redirect the blowing snow. (Courtesy of Denver, South Park & Pacific Historical Society.)

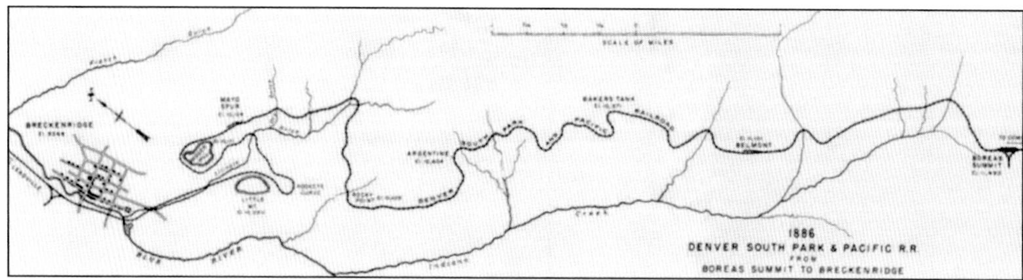

Denver, South Park—Boreas to Breckenridge. The railroad crossed Boreas Pass at 11,493 feet (3,503 meters) and dropped to 9,568 feet (2,916 meters) at Breckenridge. From Boreas to Breckenridge, a distance of 6.5 miles, crews laid slightly more than 11 miles of track. Trains rounded 108 curves of between one and 25 degrees; 82 percent of the 11 miles had a four-percent grade, meaning a drop or rise in elevation of four feet for every 100 feet of horizontal distance. (Courtesy of the Bill Fountain collection.)

BOREAS PASS—RAILROAD AND TOWN. The engine house, with its coal bin, water tank, and turntable, sat between the main line and wye. The combination depot and post office was attached to the snow shed covering the main line. The storehouse, section house, and several dwellings stood to the east of the tracks. (Reproduction by Sandra F. Pritchard Mather.)

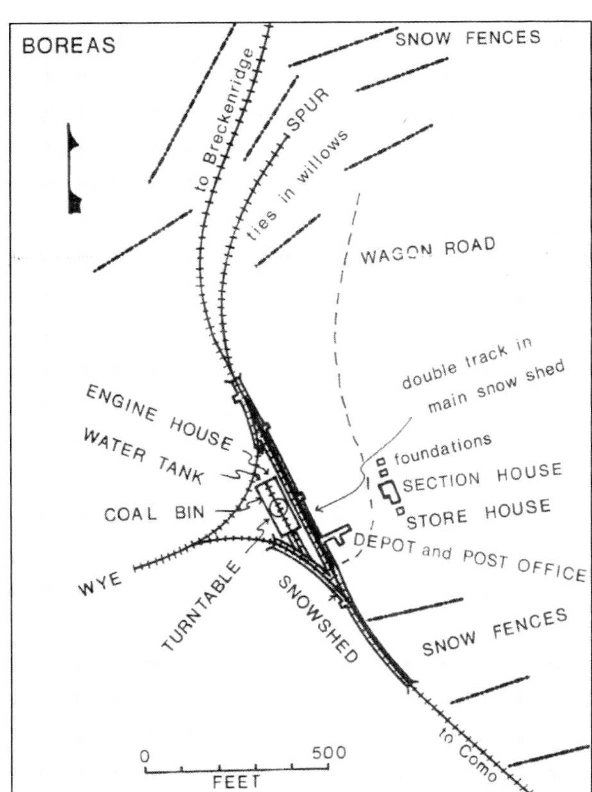

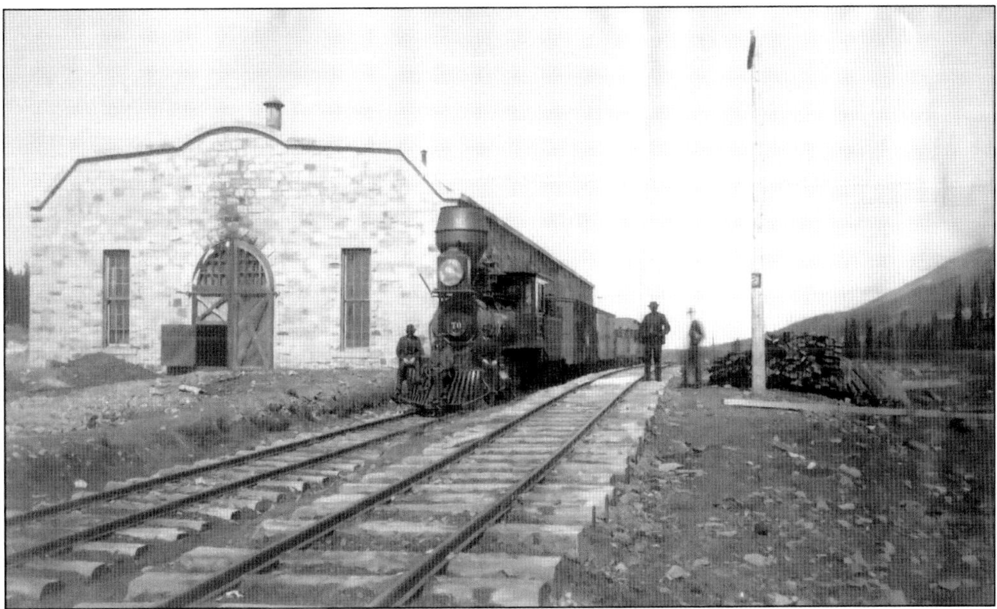

STONE ENGINE HOUSE. To service its engines at the top of Boreas Pass, the railroad built a stone engine house with a spring-fed water tank, coal bin, and turntable to reverse the direction of the helper engines required on some trips. The Continental Divide, which serves as the boundary between Summit and Park Counties, ran east-west through the center of the engine house. (Courtesy of the Summit Historical Society.)

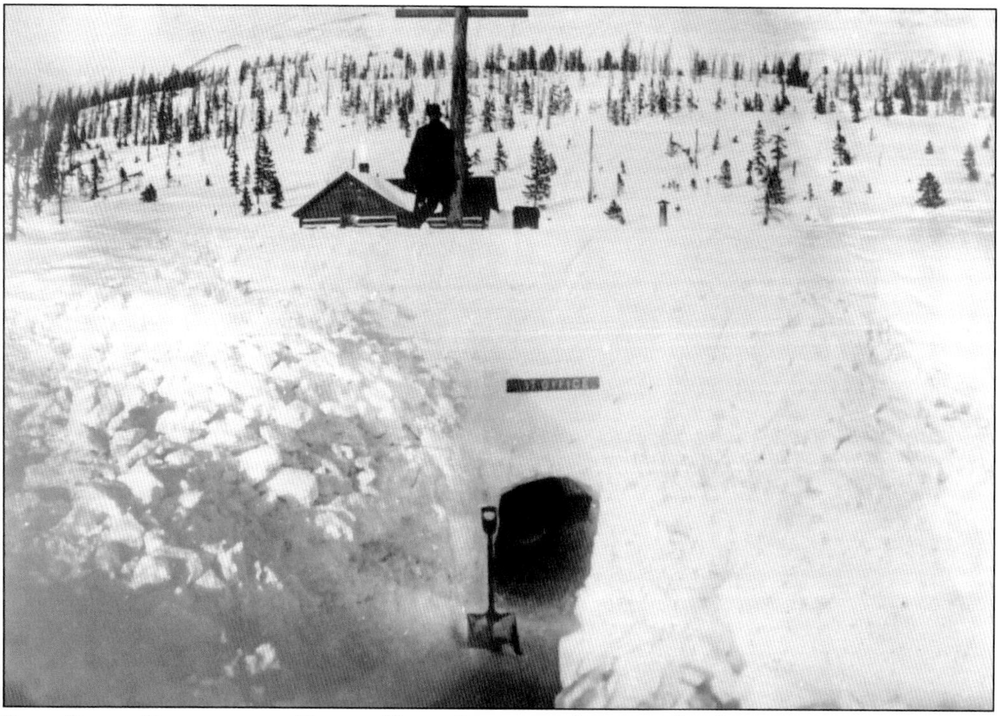

POST OFFICE ENTRANCE AT BOREAS PASS. Constructed in 1882 by the railroad and named for the North Wind, the town of Boreas, at an elevation of 11,481 feet, was the highest rail station in the United States. In winter, when snow depths reached many feet, people entered the post office through a snow tunnel. The section house appears in the background. (Courtesy of the Summit Historical Society.)

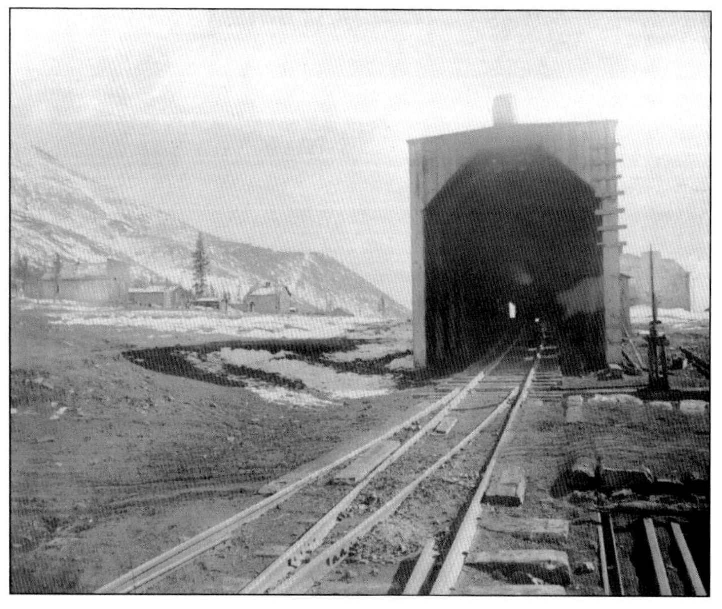

SNOW SHED. In order to load and unload people and freight more easily, workers constructed a snow shed over the track at Boreas Pass. This meant loading and unloading in relative darkness. Sparks from the trains often set the shed ablaze. One fire in December 1903, which burned the shed and ties, created enough heat to twist the rails. At one point, the snow shed covered 997 feet of track. (Courtesy of the Bill Fountain collection.)

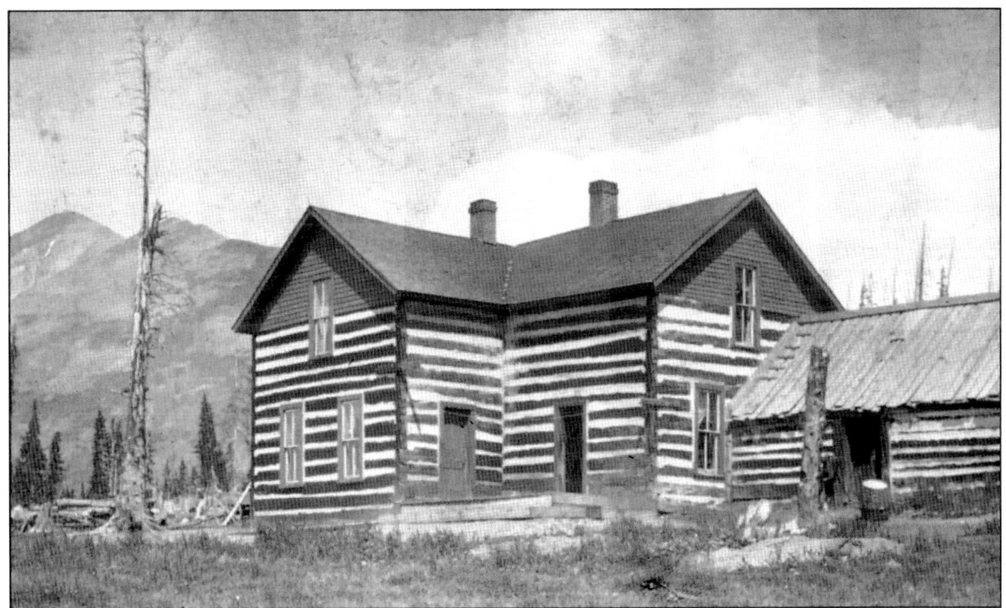

Boreas Section House, 1880s. Railroad employees who maintained the tracks and worked in the stone engine house lived in this section house. Winter weather proved a real challenge, especially at this altitude. Storms often isolated the residents and their families. Men worked constantly to maintain heat in the section house when temperatures dipped far below zero and gale force winds whipped the snow into mountainous drifts. (Courtesy of the Denver, South Park & Pacific Historical Society.)

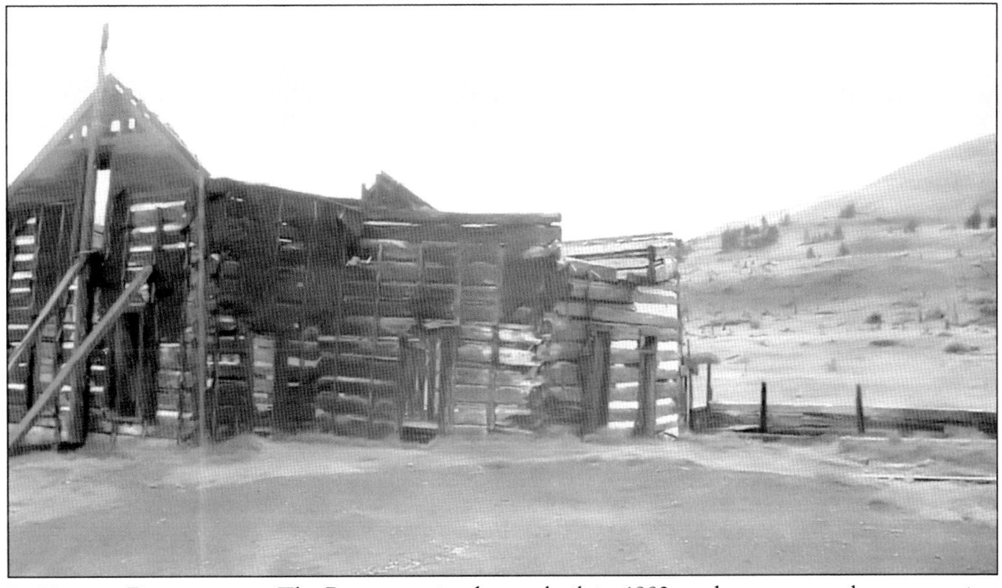

In Need of Restoration. The Boreas section house, built in 1882, underwent complete restoration between 1992 and 1997. Now open to as many as 12 overnight guests at a time, the building has a wood-burning stove for heat, a cook stove, solar- and wind-powered lights, and antique furnishings. It is maintained by the Summit Huts Association. Dogs are not permitted because of potential interaction with abundant nearby wildlife. (Courtesy of the Denver, South Park & Pacific Historical Society.)

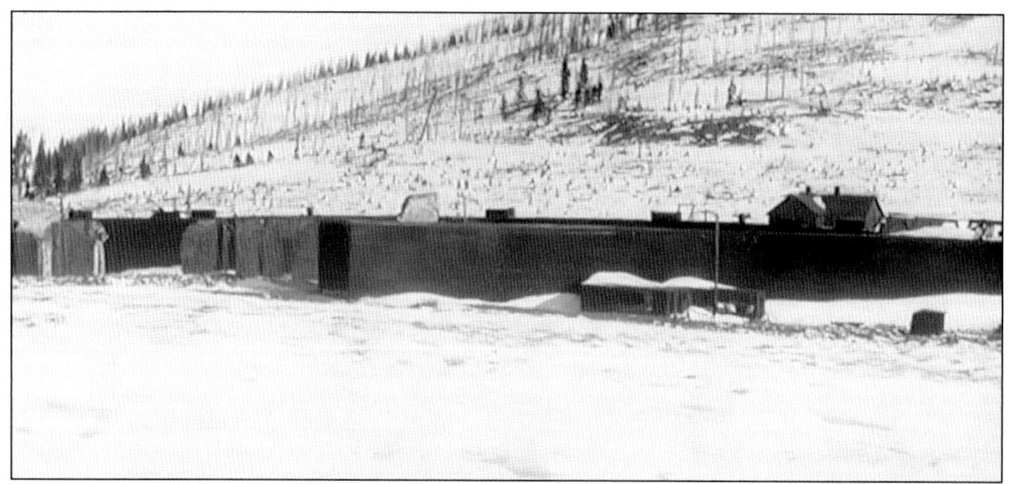

Boreas Snow Shed. One of the longest snow sheds built by the Denver, South Park & Pacific covered the track over Boreas Pass. When the original 600-foot-long 1885 snow shed burned in 1899, crews rebuilt it and lengthened it to 997 feet. A snow shed also covered the wye and 1,566 feet of sidetrack at the pass. (Courtesy of the Denver, South Park & Pacific Historical Society.)

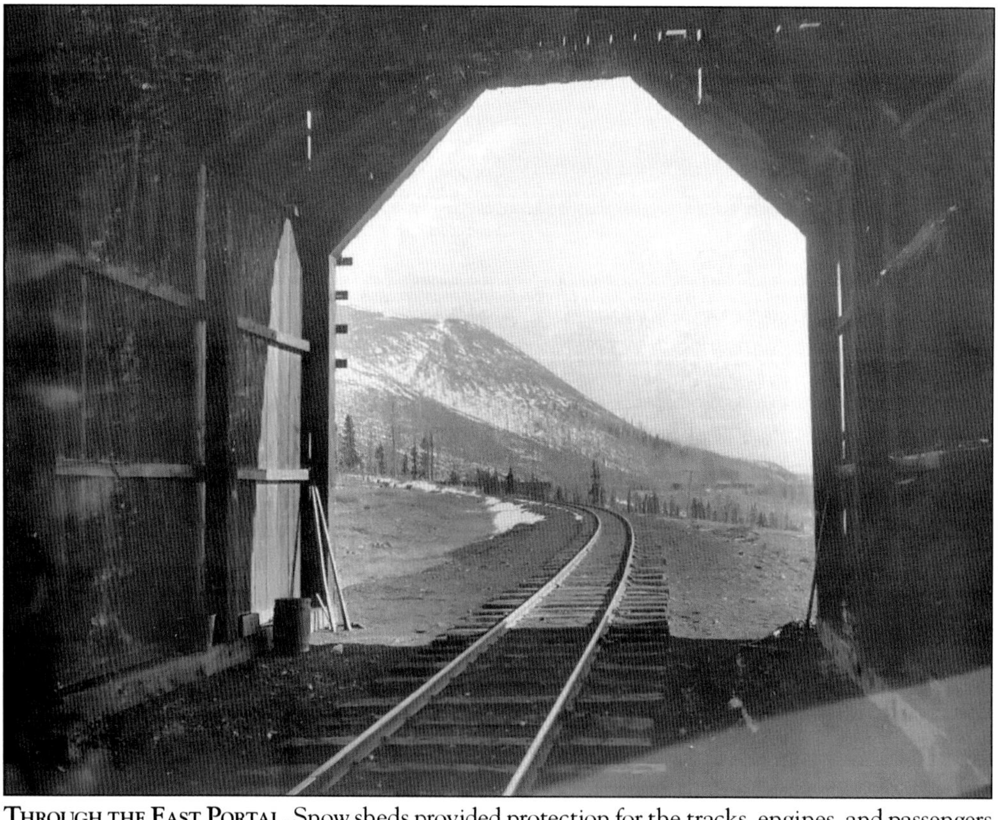

Through the East Portal. Snow sheds provided protection for the tracks, engines, and passengers as they crossed Boreas Pass. In the earliest days of the Denver, South Park, snow sheds covered many miles of track throughout the system. In the distance are two wooden snow sheds. Cinders from the engines often caused fires in the snow sheds, requiring expensive repairs. (Photograph by Otto Westerman, courtesy of the Maureen Nicholls collection.)

LEAVING THE SNOW SHED. With no doors to prevent the blowing snow from entering the snow shed at Boreas Pass, deep snow and ice at the entrances could derail a train. Crews worked constantly to keep the tracks clear. Because there was little room between the tracks and the walls of the snow shed, the snow and ice had to be carried outside for disposition. (Courtesy of the Bill Fountain collection.)

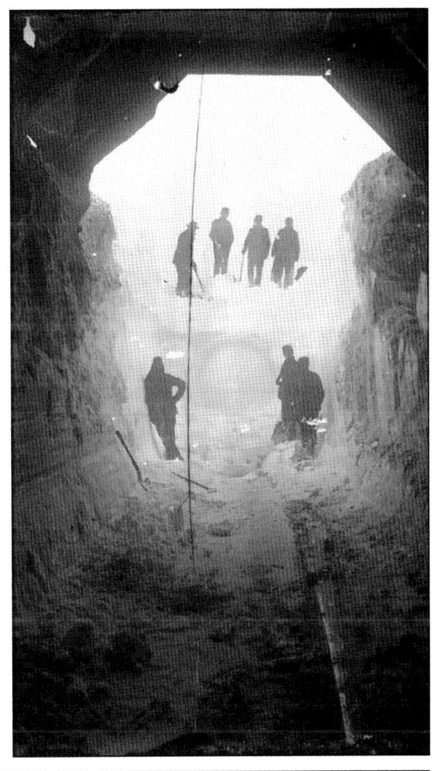

A HELPER ENGINE AT ROCKY POINT. The railroad located helper engines at Como and Dickey to augment the pulling power of the locomotives crossing Boreas Pass. Here, engine 271 pauses on its return to Breckenridge. At the top of Boreas Pass, the engines used the wye to turn around. Railroaders said a train with no cars was "running light." (Photograph by Dr. Clinton H Scott, courtesy of the Ed and Nancy Bathke collection.)

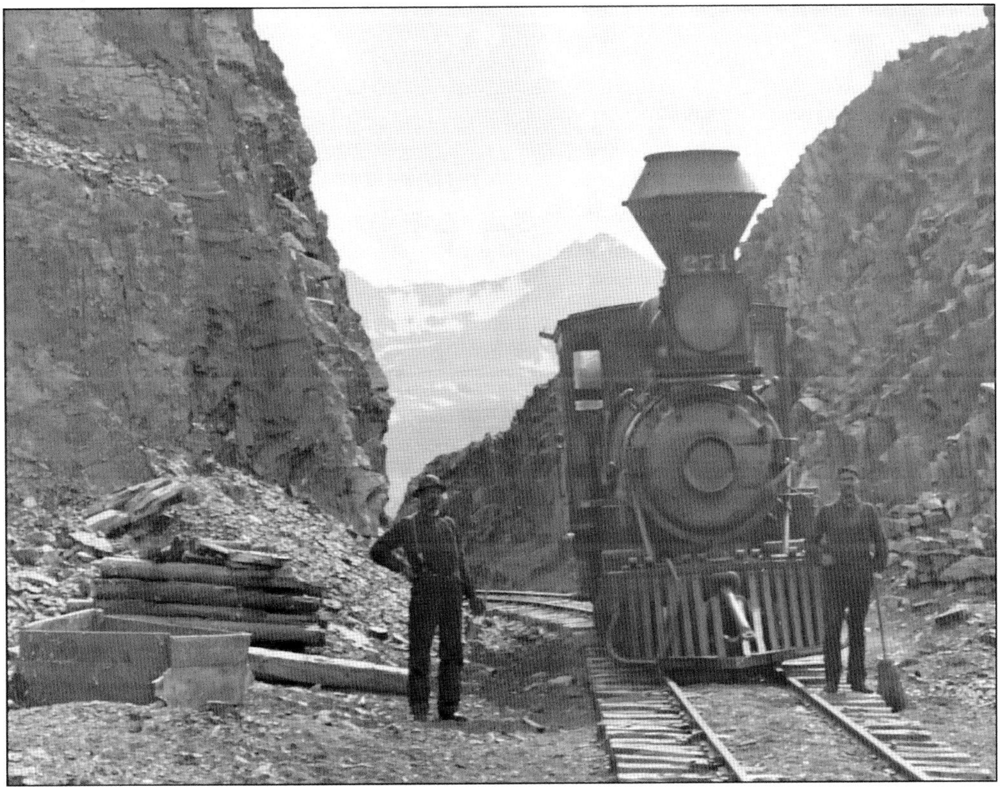

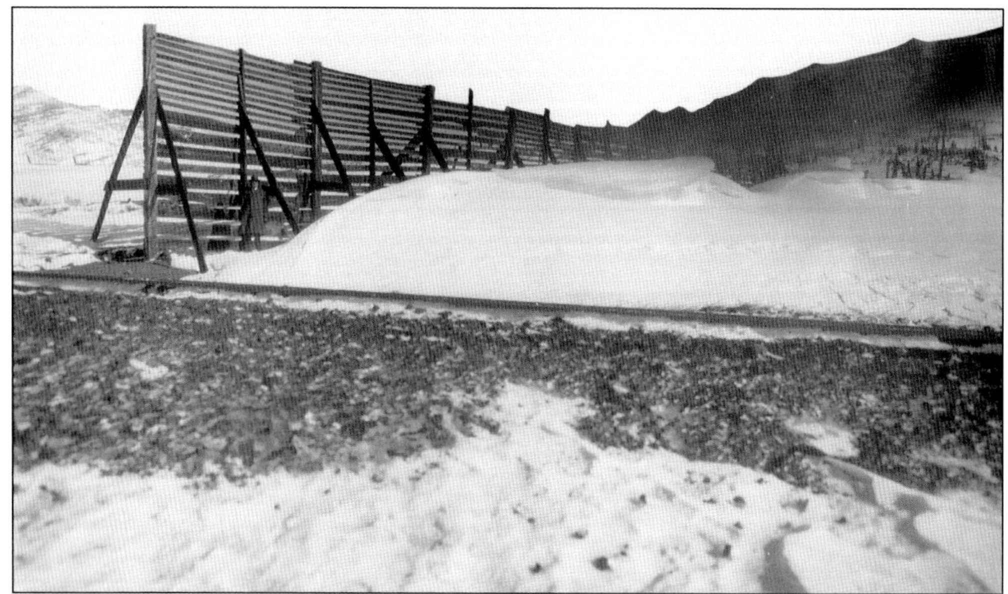

Snow Fences at Boreas Pass. The snow reached such huge depths that the company built tall snow fences on both sides of the tracks at Boreas Pass in an attempt to prevent snow from covering the tracks. In the early 1900s, the company announced plans to raise the tracks on a trestle so that the snow would blow off the raised tracks. The plan never materialized. (Courtesy of the Denver, South Park & Pacific Historical Society.)

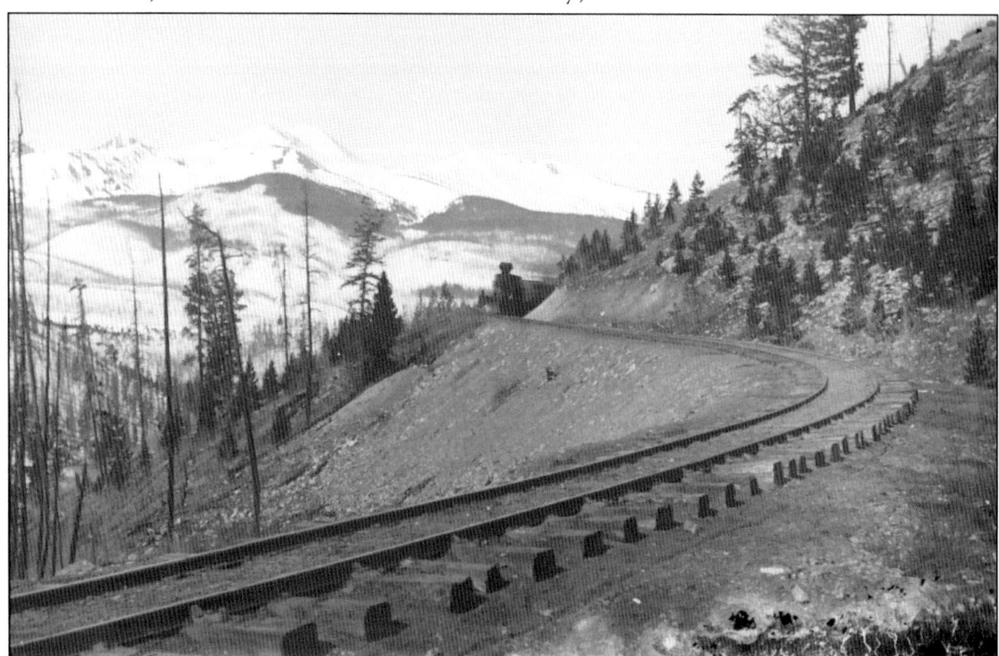

Ties and Track. With the snow-covered Ten Mile Range in the background, an engine heads to Boreas Pass. To save money, the Denver, South Park purchased the already-graded toll road. Crews laid untreated spruce or yellow pine ties 18 inches apart. The weight per yard of track varied from about 40 pounds per yard to 58 pounds per yard. Fish plates bolted the rails together, and the rails were spiked to the ties. (Courtesy of the Denver, South Park & Pacific Historical Society.)

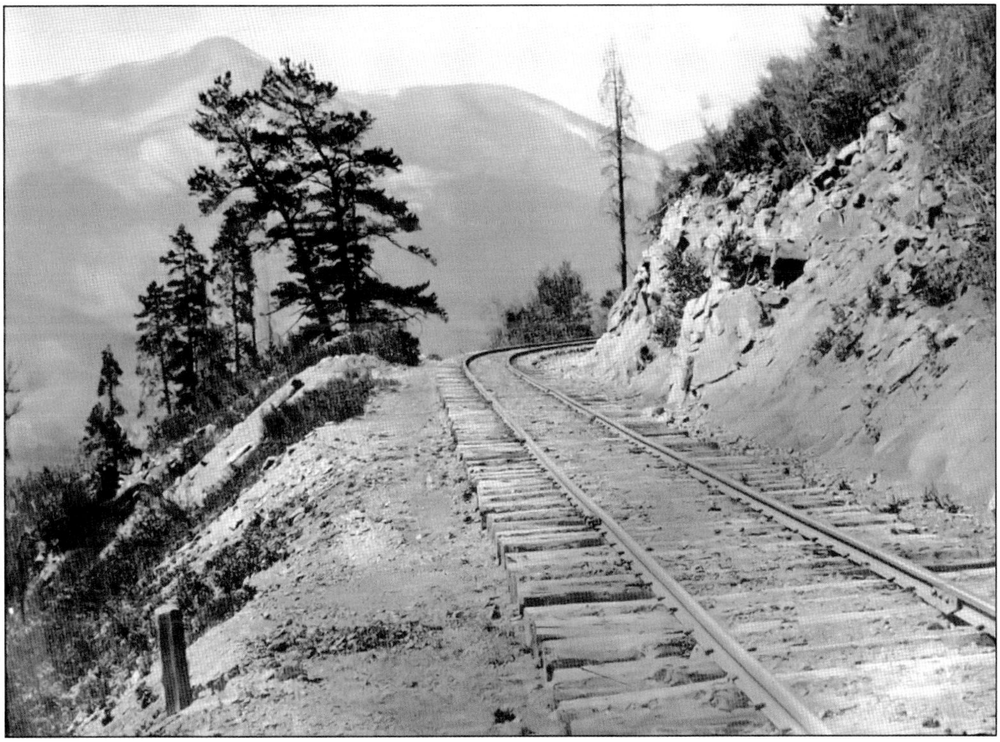

DENVER, SOUTH PARK & PACIFIC NARROW-GAUGE. Narrow-gauge tracks had advantages. Sharp turns so necessary in the mountains required less blasting. Shorter ties saved money, as did the smaller, lighter engines and cars. Narrow-gauge track could be laid faster. Track men earned $2.25 per day in 1882. Rock men earned $2.50. Room and board cost $5 per week. (Courtesy of the Summit Historical Society.)

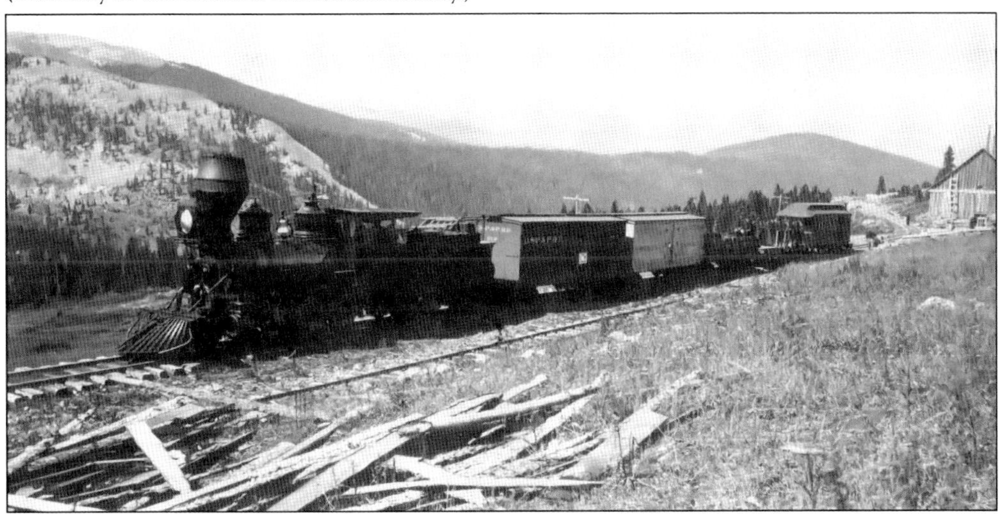

MIXED TRAIN AT FARNHAM IN 1884. Engine 70, pulling a mixed freight and passenger train up to Boreas Pass, pauses at Farnham, just over one mile west of the pass, to allow the passengers to pose for their portrait on the flatcar. A Tiffany Summer and Winter car follows the first boxcar. Interior ice bunkers at both ends of the car kept the contents cold during transport. (Photograph by Alex Martin, courtesy of the Denver, South Park & Pacific Historical Society.)

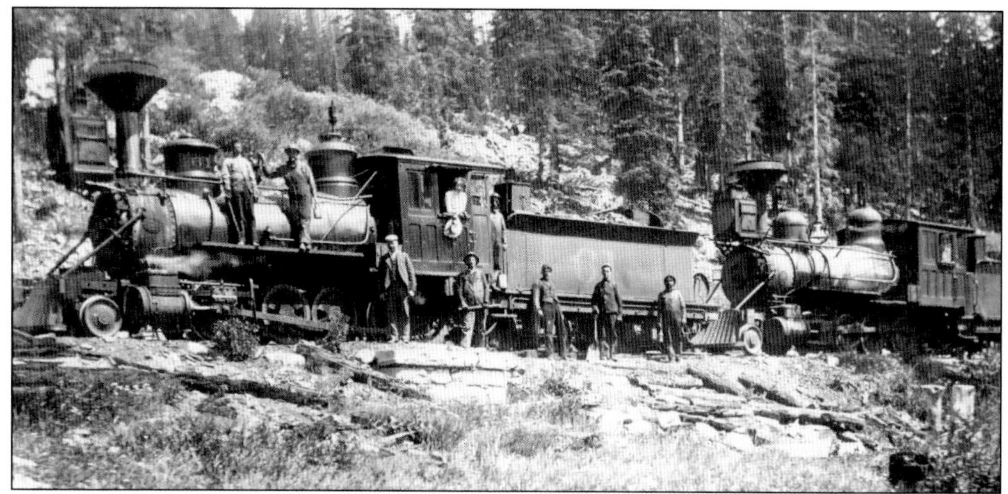

A Woman Engineer? The woman, perhaps accompanied by the man in a business suit, smiles from the cab of engine 61 in this c. 1899 photograph. The lumber next to the tracks indicates that the work crew found it necessary to replace some of the ties beneath the tracks. Winter weather, spring snowmelt, and summer storms caused the untreated ties to rot quickly. (Courtesy of the Denver, South Park & Pacific Historical Society.)

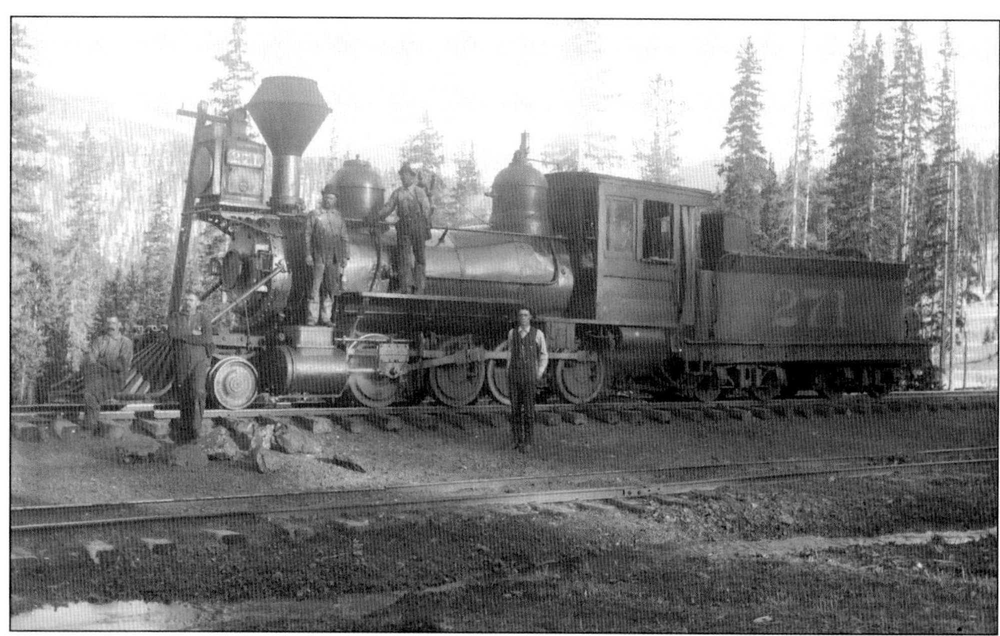

A Dirty Job. The crew of Denver, Leadville & Gunnison engine 271 poses for Dr. Scott. The crew's dirty coveralls attest to the grimy job of operating a coal-fired steam locomotive. The conductor, who stays clean, stands in the center. The words "Union Pacific" on the steam chest indicate that the company acquired the engine while the Union Pacific still controlled the South Park line. (Photograph by Dr. Clinton H Scott, courtesy of the Denver, South Park & Pacific Historical Society.)

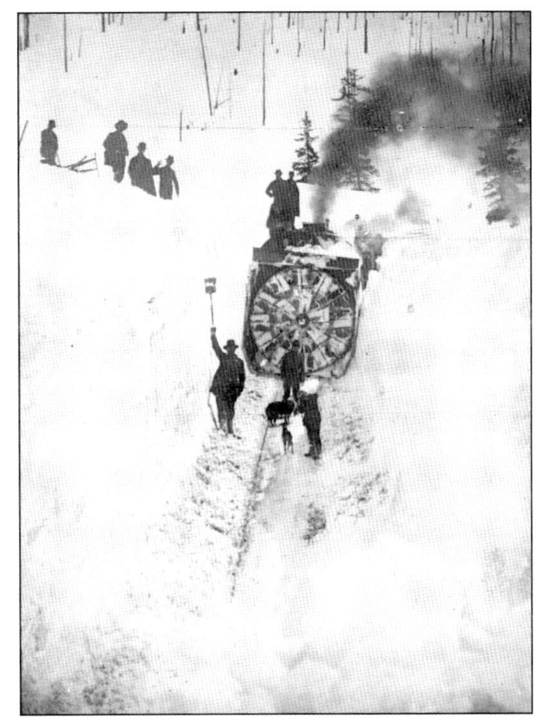

Deep Snow. Deep snow over Boreas Pass and in the Ten Mile Canyon required using the rotary snow plow to clear the tracks. Because it was not self-propelled, between four and six helper engines pushed the rotary. Snow and ice that remained on the tracks after the rotary cut through the drift could easily derail the plow train. (Courtesy of the Summit Historical Society.)

Rotary Snow Plow. When the snow became too deep for bucking plows, the rotary snow plow attacked the drifts, throwing thc snow as much as 30 feet away from the tracks. A coal-fired boiler in the car provided the power to move the blades. The tender carried the coal and water for the boiler. Several locomotives pushed the plow and its tender. (Courtesy of the Bill Fountain collection.)

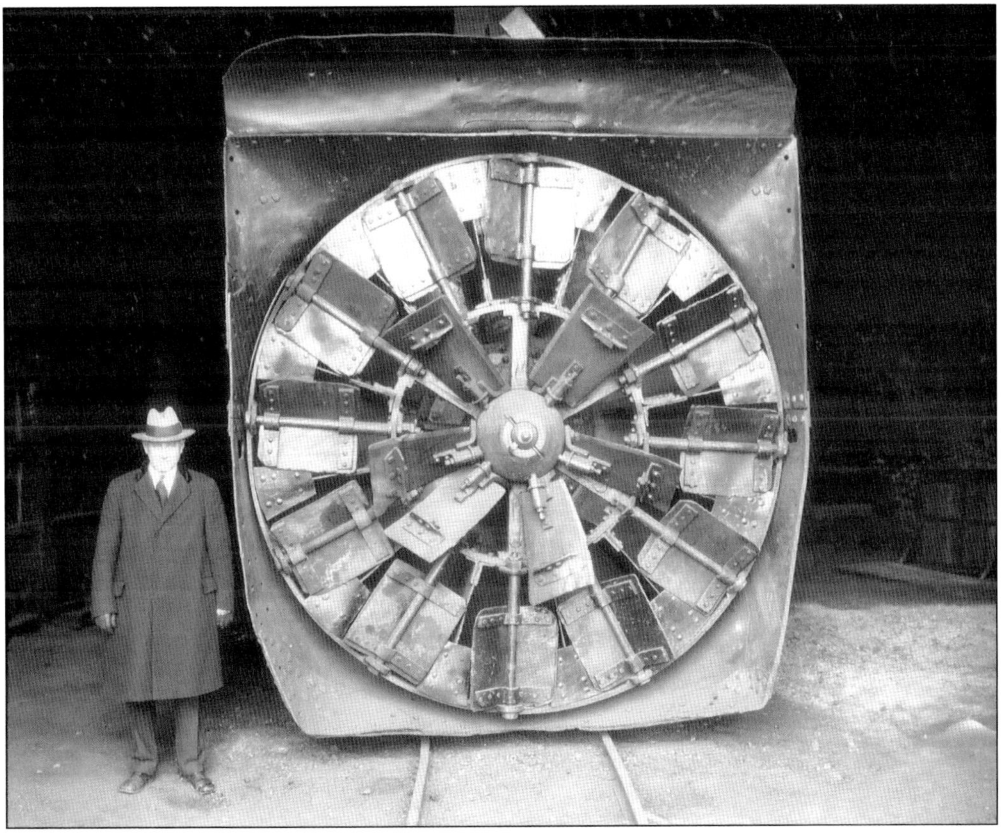

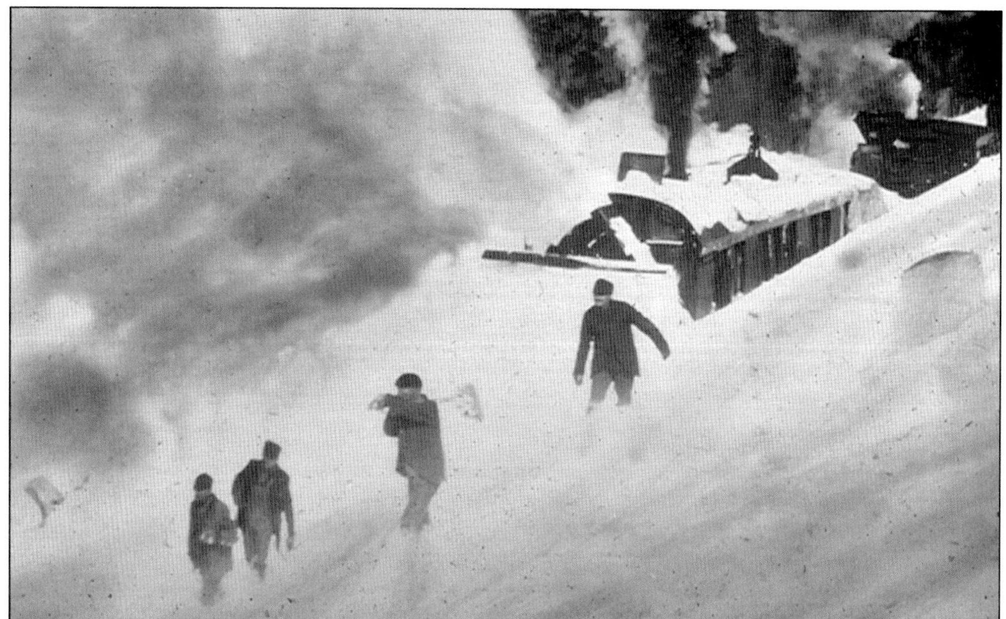

BRRRR! In this c. 1899 photograph, several engines push the rotary snow plow through deep drifts. The rotary makes good progress, much to the relief of the shovelers who must dig out any boulders or tree trunks hidden under the snow before they damage the blades on the rotary. Steep slopes created a dangerous environment for the shovelers walking across the snow. (Courtesy of the Denver, South Park & Pacific Historical Society.)

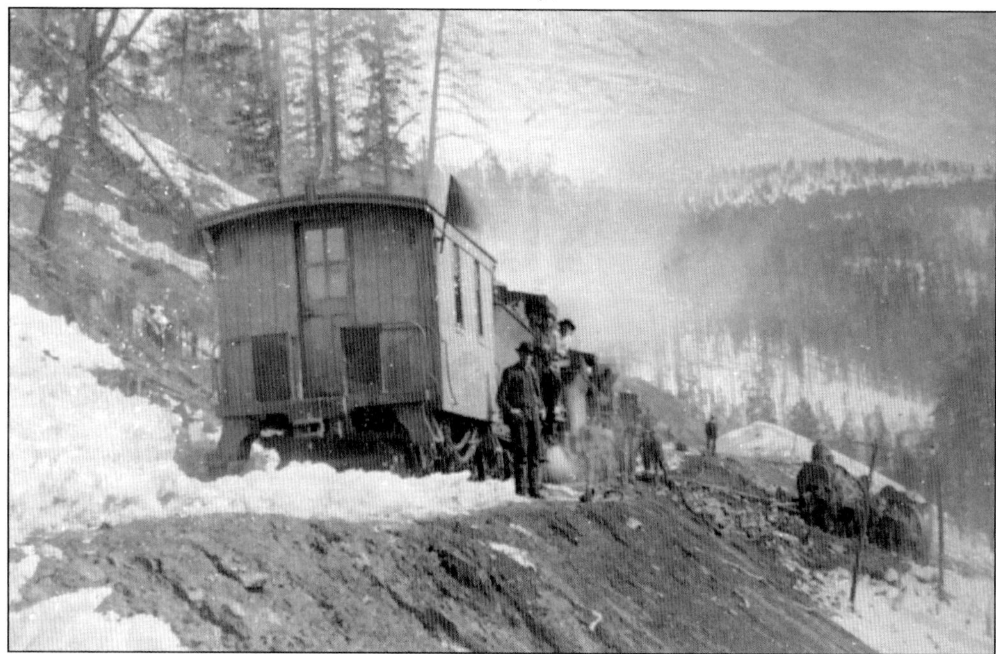

AN EXTRA TRAIN. The flags on the upper rear corner of the waycar (caboose) indicate that this is an extra or unscheduled train. This is a wreck train sent to retrieve the rotary snow plow that came to grief down the hill near Baker tank on Boreas Pass. (Courtesy of the Ed and Nancy Bathke collection.)

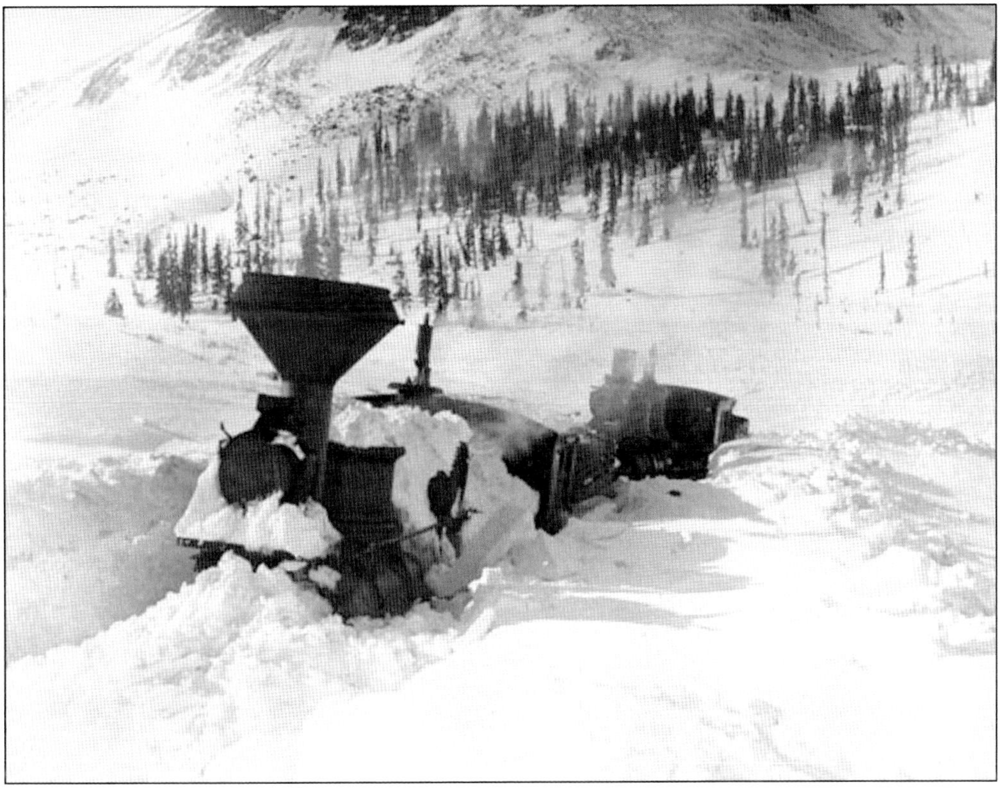

Bucking Snow. Occasionally trains bucking snow became stuck. In this 1904 photograph, these two engines, probably helper engines returning to Leadville after pulling a train to the top of the pass, became stuck in a deep drift. Shovelers might dig out the engines, but the rotary snow plow will be needed to clear the tracks. (Courtesy of the Denver, South Park & Pacific Historical Society.)

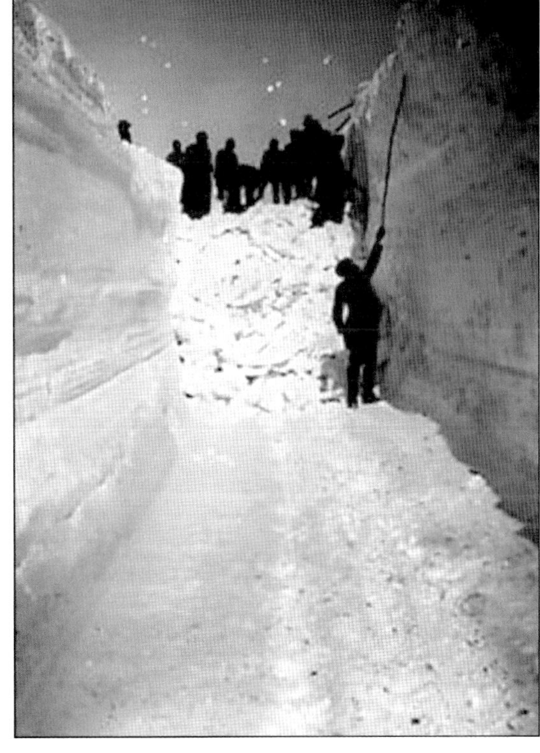

How Deep? The tops of some drifts reached far above the roof of the rotary snow plow. The rotary would clear as far as possible before retreating. Shovelers would throw snow from the top of the drift onto the track for the rotary to blow away on its next cut. The exposed side walls show the depths of the various storms that created the huge drifts. (Courtesy of the Bill Fountain collection.)

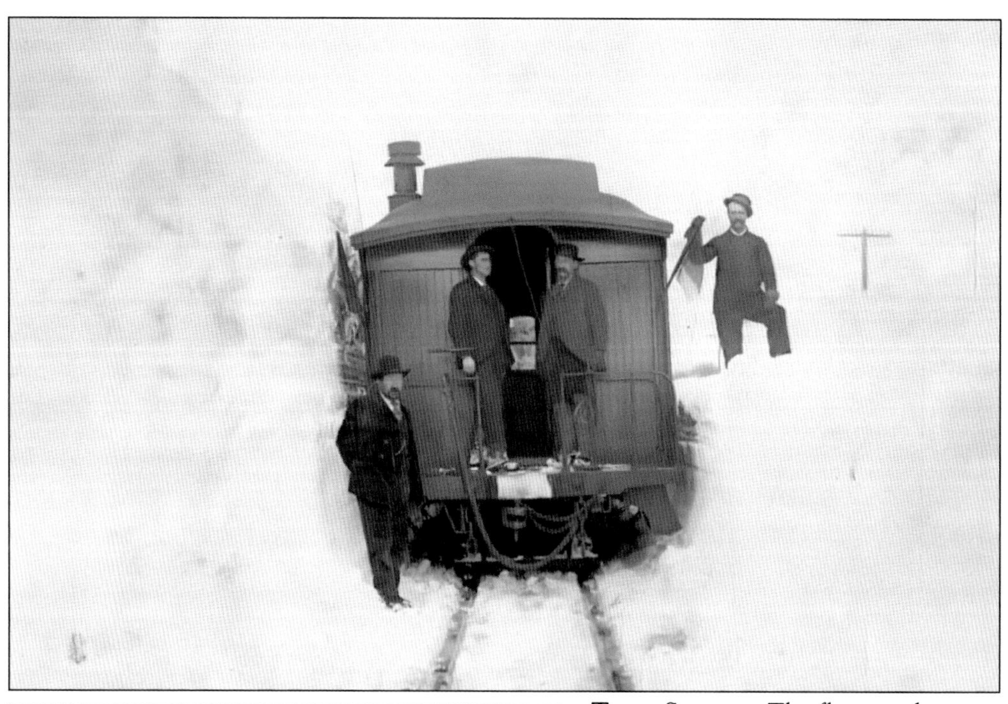

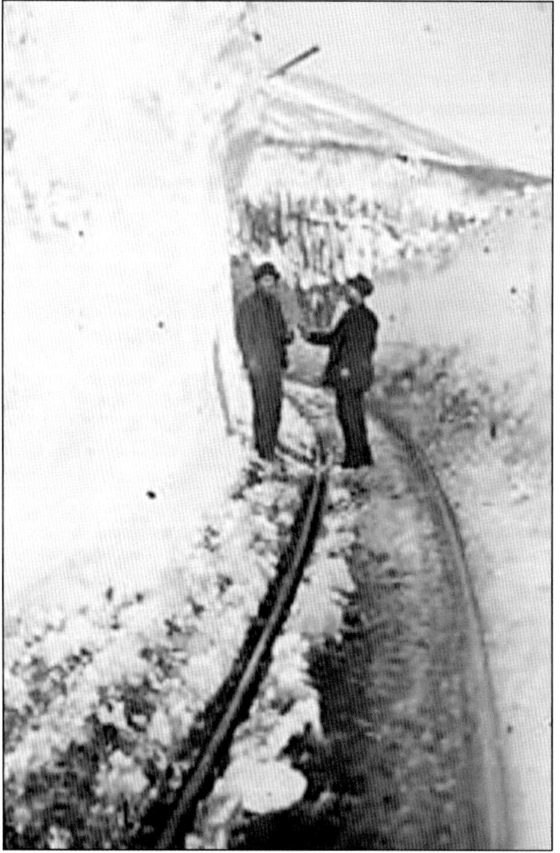

Tight Squeeze. The flags on the rear corners of this Denver, Leadville & Gunnison business car mark the train as an extra. The freshness of the cuts in the snow indicates that the locomotive at the front might be pushing the rotary through a snow slide. The depth of the snow to the left of the business car tells how deep snow slides in this area of the Ten Mile Canyon can be. (Courtesy of the Bill Fountain collection.)

After the Rotary. Two men inspect the cut made by the rotary snow plow. After the rotary moved down the tracks, men checked to see if the shovelers needed to clear space around the tracks. Ice and snow could remain after the rotary passed. If enough ice and snow remained on the tracks, the next train could derail. (Courtesy of the Bill Fountain collection.)

Priest Flanger. This view of the front of Colorado & Southern engine 4 shows the right side priest flanger and raising/lowering linkage. Essentially two steel plates, one in front of each pilot truck wheel and notched for the rail, they were lowered to knock the ice off of the rails and had to be raised again for each switch that was crossed. (Courtesy of John Manley collection.)

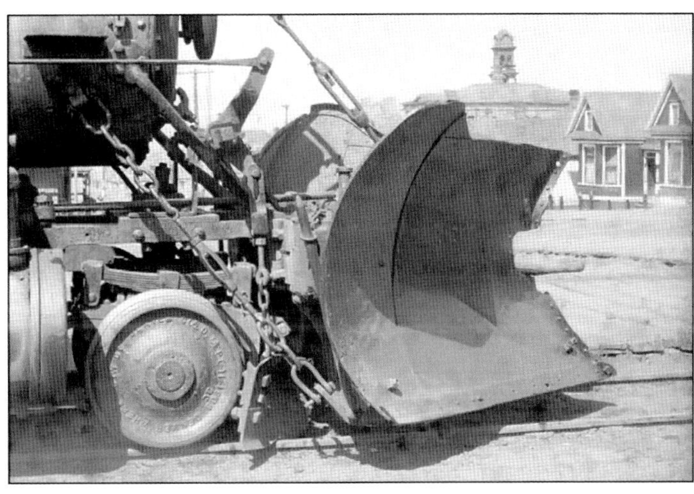

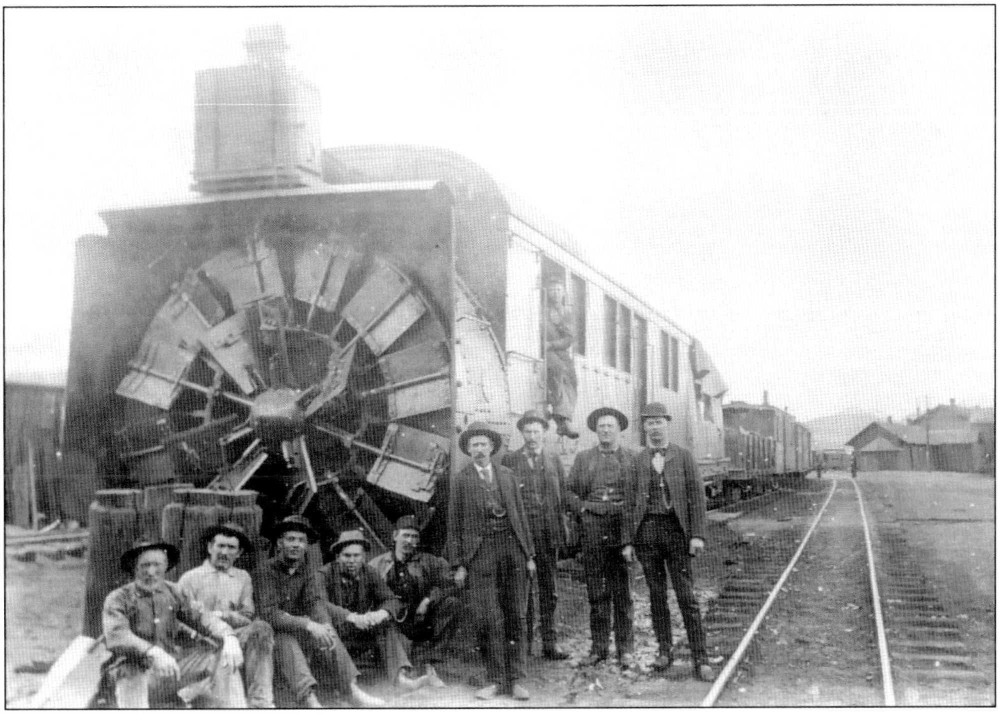

Rotary Crew, c. 1896. Four men operated a rotary snow plow. The pilot sat above and behind the blades, giving him an unobstructed view forward. Using whistle signals, he communicated with the engineers of the pushing locomotives. He used bells and hand signals to relay instructions to the others on his crew, an engineer and two firemen. They decided how fast the rotary should push into the drift and, if necessary, when to reverse direction. (Courtesy of the Denver, South Park & Pacific Historical Society.)

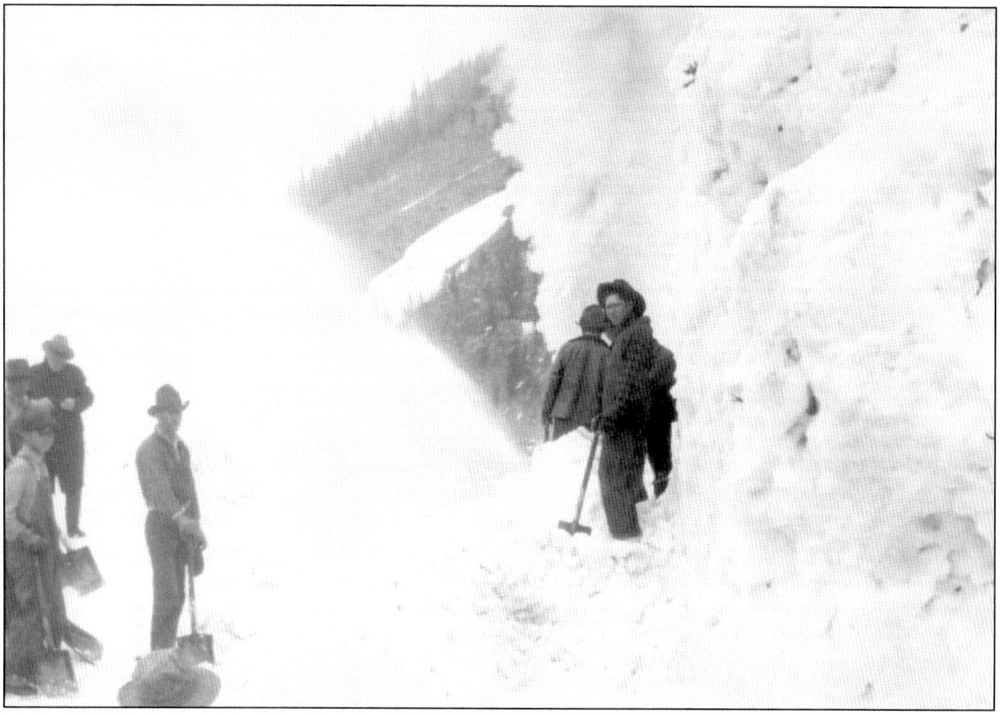

WAITING FOR THE ROTARY. Shovelers wait for the rotary snow plow to clear the snow they have shoveled back onto the tracks. Note the heavy clothing the men wore to protect themselves from blowing and drifting show. (Courtesy of the Denver, South Park & Pacific Historical Society.)

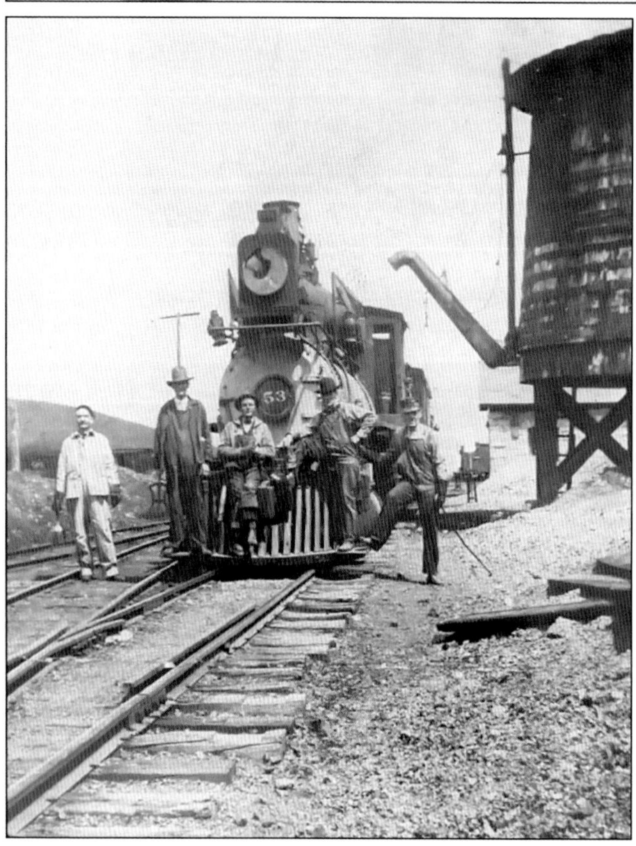

FILLING THE WATER TANK. Water tanks stood beside the tracks, providing the large quantities of water consumed by the steam engines. Especially in winter, the fireman took great care in opening the valve on the water tank to start the water flowing so that the spout did not swing upward, spilling water over the coal in the tender and himself. (Courtesy of the Bill Fountain collection.)

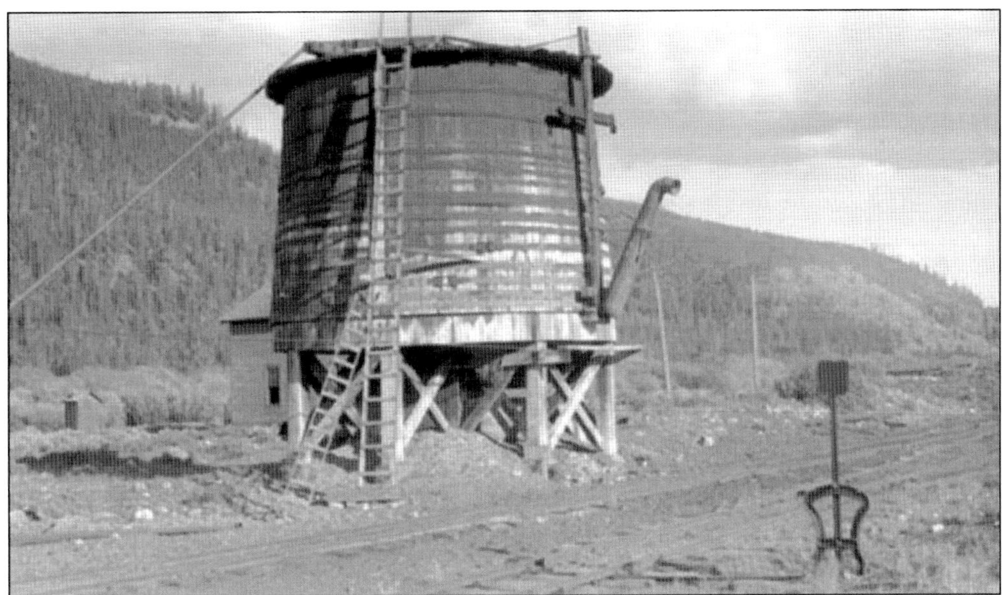

Dickey Water Tank. The huge wooden water tanks could hold thousands of gallons of water. The tanks at Dickey and Kokomo held 47,500 gallons. A variety of methods kept the tanks filled. A two-inch pipe 1,830 feet long supplied the 9,516-gallon tank at Boreas with water from a nearby spring. A six-inch pipe 782 feet long brought water from the Blue River to a standpipe in Breckenridge. (Courtesy of the Bill Fountain collection.)

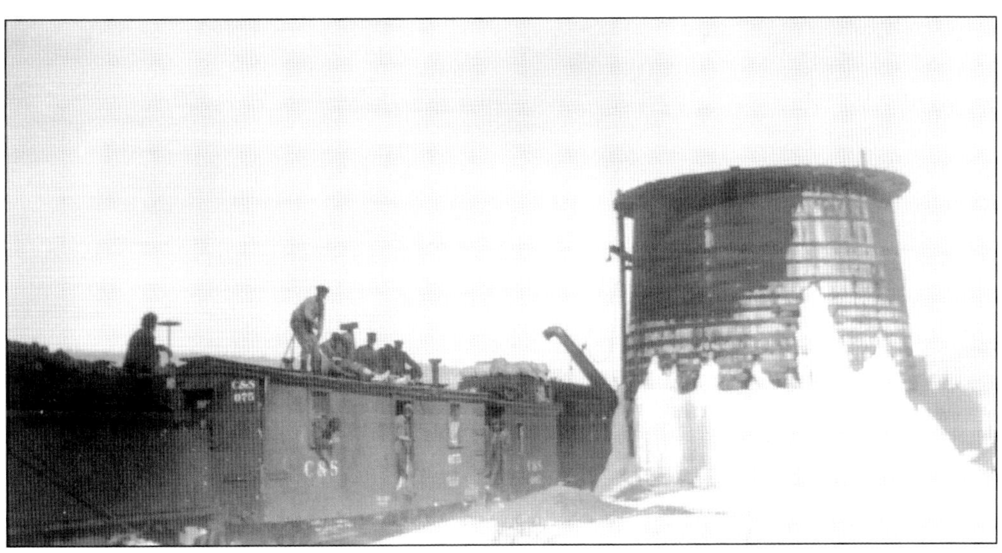

Ice-Covered Water Tank at Dickey. Despite low temperatures, the water in the tanks rarely froze. Instead, leakage from the tanks created spectacular ice falls that often covered the tracks, creating hazardous conditions. To prevent the water in the tender from freezing, the fireman diverted some of the hot water from the engine into the tender. (Courtesy of the Bill Fountain collection.)

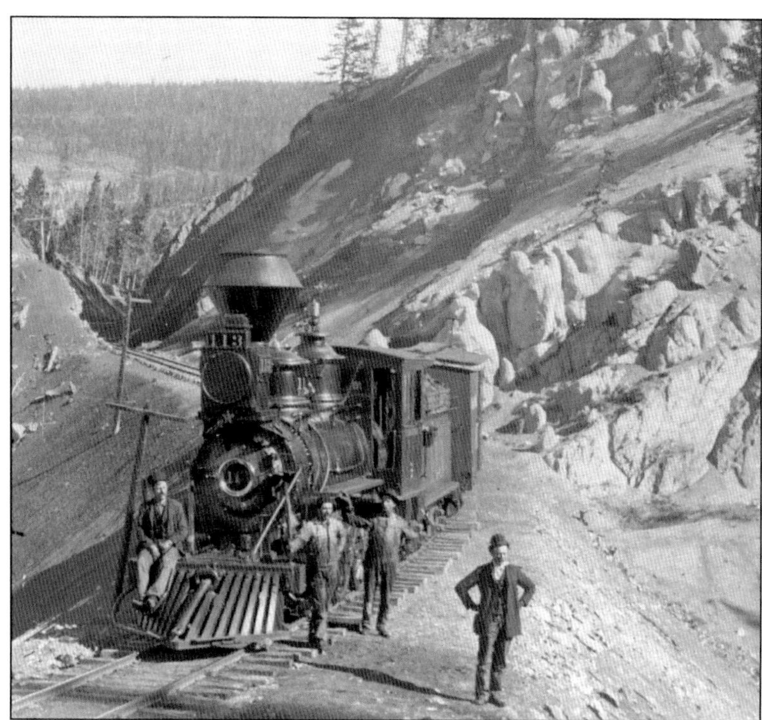

ENGINE 113 AT ROCKY POINT. This engine, built in 1884 and weighing 58,300 pounds, hauled freight and passengers over Boreas Pass. Still working in 1938, it was scrapped in December of that year. Maximum speeds in the mid-1880s for passenger trains reached less than 22 miles per hour in the county and less than 12 miles per hour for freight trains over Boreas Pass. (Courtesy of the Summit Historical Society.)

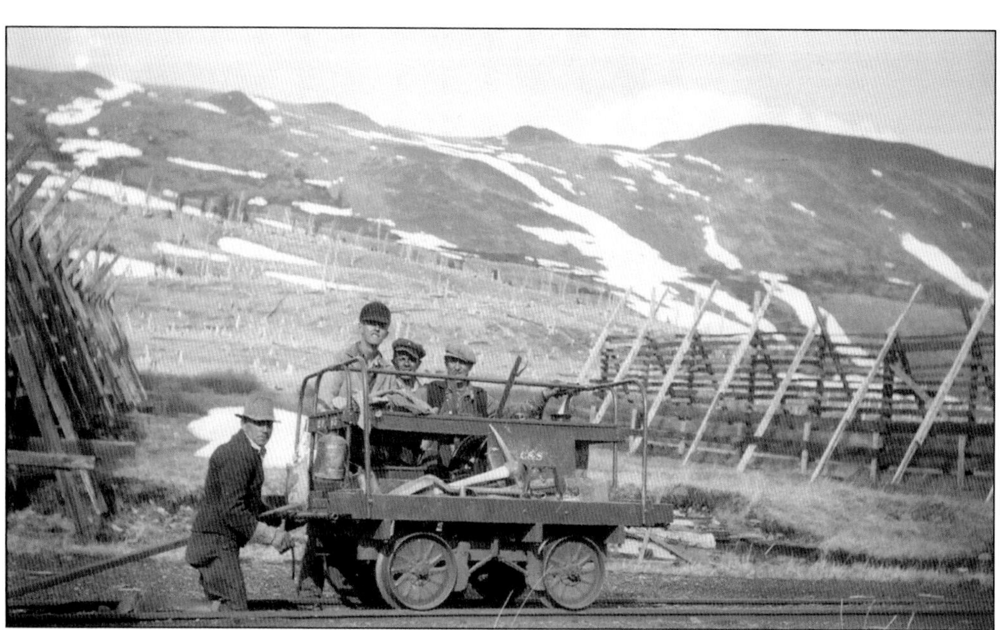

PUTT-PUTT AT BOREAS PASS. Nature worked against the railroads. Crews living in section houses along the tracks inspected the rights-of-way constantly for dangerous conditions. In early versions of the putt-putt, the men provided the power by pumping the handle up and down, strenuous work on steep mountain grades at high altitude. This mechanized version made life much easier for the crews as they inspected the tracks. (Courtesy of the Denver, South Park & Pacific Historical Society.)

Trailer at Rocky Point. Using these self-powered conveyances, variously called a motorcar, speeder, popcar, or putt-putt, maintenance crews rode the rails checking for problems. At Rocky Point, where many trains stopped for photographs, this group of men, obviously not railroad workers, pose for a picture on their trailer. In the background, workers have stockpiled replacement ties. (Courtesy of the Bill Fountain collection.)

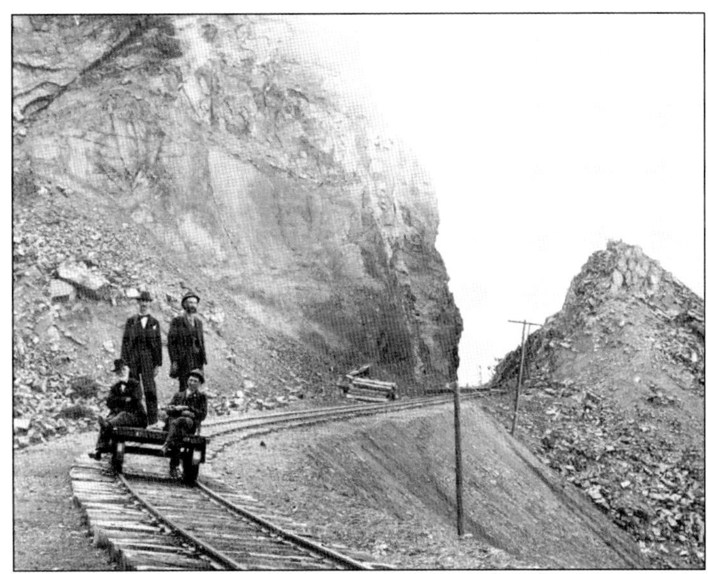

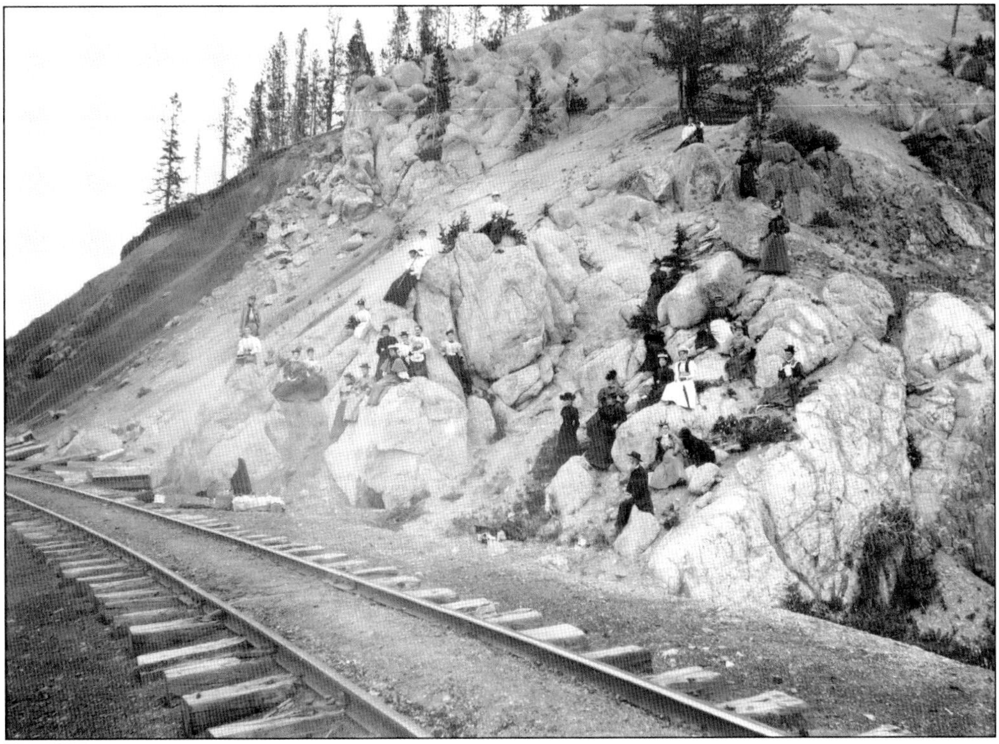

Enjoying a Picnic Lunch. Accompanied by a dog, these adventuresome men and women climbed the crumbling slopes beside the tracks at Rocky Point for this photograph. Their picnic baskets sit beside the tracks. They will probably board a train that will take them to Breckenridge as part of their afternoon excursion. The railroad also offered excursions on a regular basis to points in the Ten Mile Canyon. (Courtesy of the Maureen Nicholls collection.)

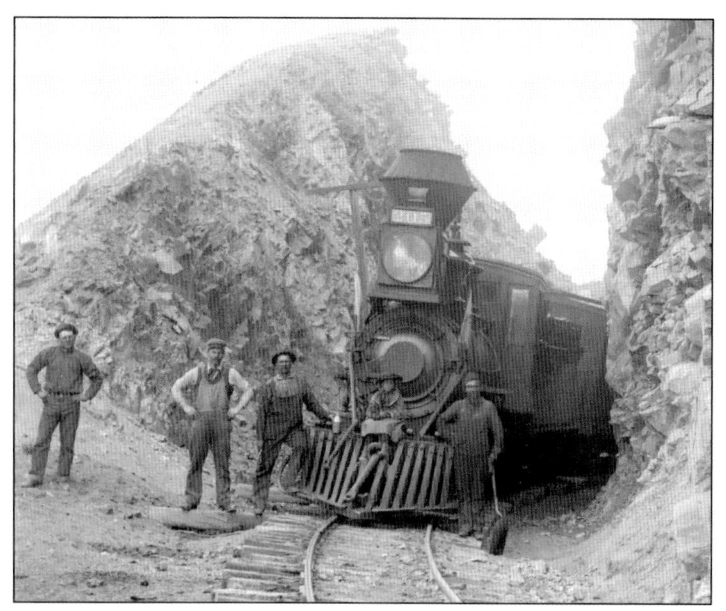

A Special Young Lady. A passenger train pauses at Rocky Point on its way to Boreas Pass. While the crew poses for Clinton H Scott, a local photographer, the young lady occupies a place of honor on the pilot of engine 205. Because of the view overlooking Breckenridge and the Ten Mile Range, trains often stopped for photographs at Rocky Point. (Photograph by Dr. Clinton H Scott, courtesy of the Ed and Nancy Bathke collection.)

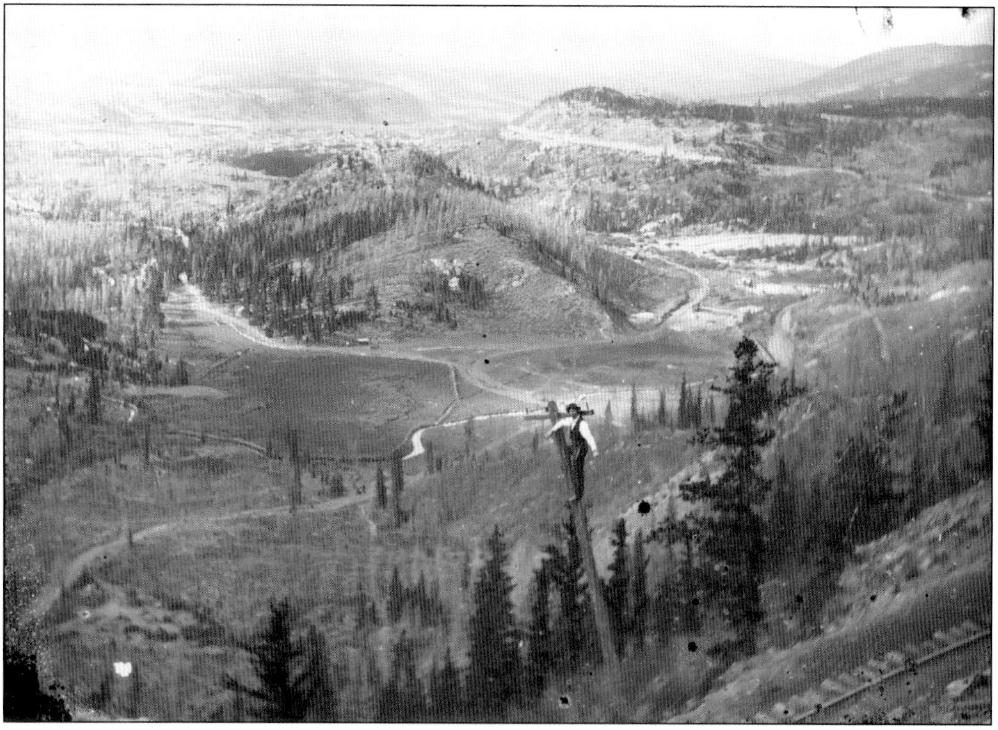

Charlie Squires. Charlie Squires, a telegraph lineman, maintained the wires along the railroad right-of-way. He worked for the Denver, South Park & Pacific as well as the Denver & Rio Grande. Clearly comfortable working in precarious locations, Squires posed for photographer, Clinton H Scott, near Rocky Point. In the distance are Hookeye Curve, Little Mountain, Barney Ford Hill, Breckenridge, and the Ten Mile Range. (Courtesy of the Denver, South Park & Pacific Historical Society.)

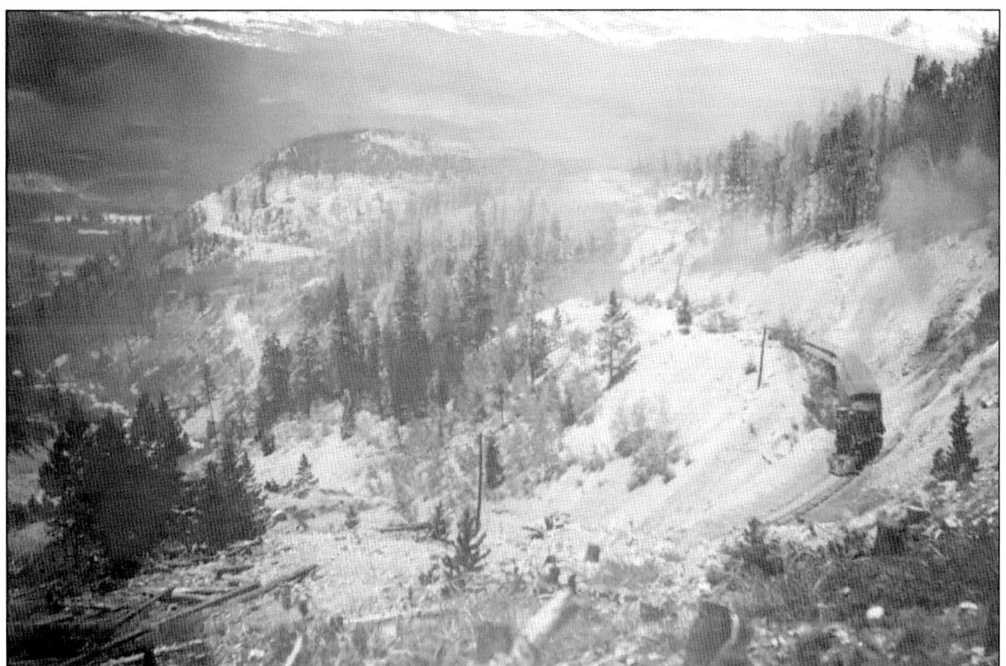

Unstable even in the Summer. The repeated weight of trains, such as this one in 1898 climbing to Boreas Pass, enhanced the downslope movement of rocks made unstable by winter and summer weather conditions. Steep slopes covered with severely weathered bits of rock moved slowly or rapidly depending on their ability to withstand the weight of engine and cars. Even slow movement could eventually displace ties and rails enough to cause derailments. (Courtesy of the Summit Historical Society.)

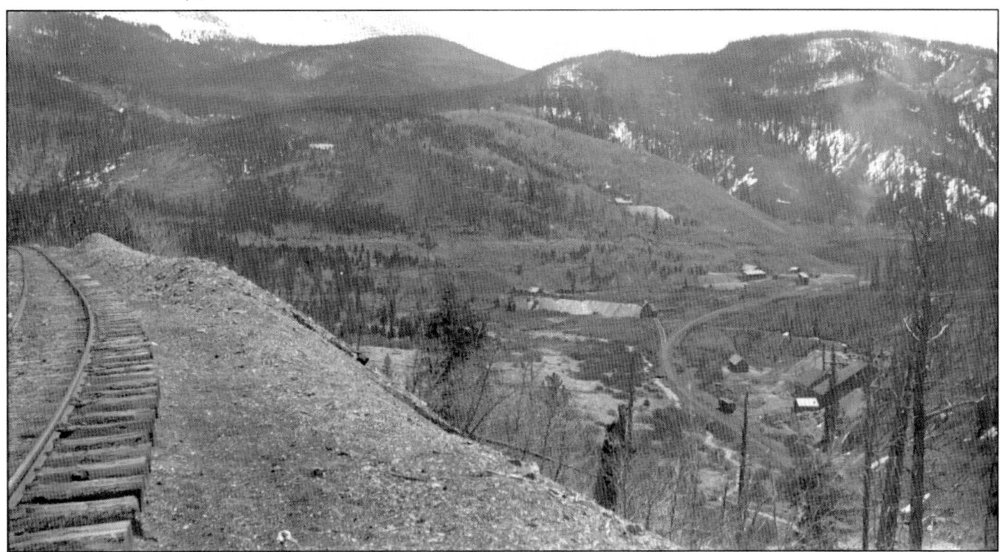

Illinois Gulch, c. 1900. A solitary boxcar sits on the Little Mountain spur in the lower right. Under a plume of smoke, an eastbound train on Hookeye Curve begins its climb to Boreas Pass. Extensive mining operations cover the floor of the gulch. A concentration mill, identified by its sloping roof, sits on a hillside in the lower right corner, while a mine dump can be seen in the center of the photograph. (Courtesy of the Denver, South Park & Pacific Historical Society.)

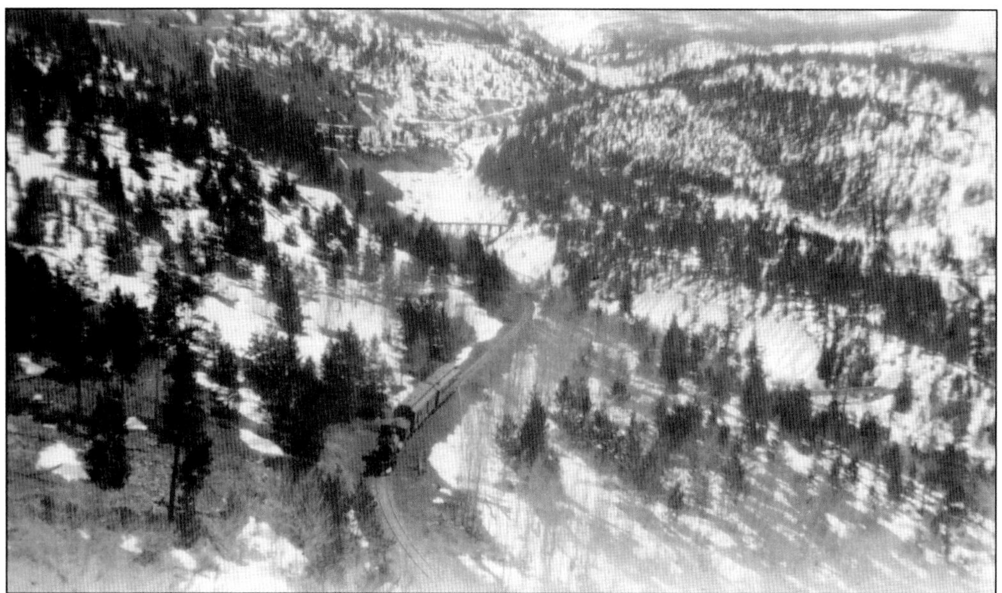

The Climb to Boreas, c. 1930s. An eastbound passenger train climbs from Breckenridge to Boreas Pass in this photograph, taken from the top of Barney Ford Hill. The Gold Pan trestle can be seen in the middle distance. A two-lane road replaced the trestle. Even more of the grade leading to Boreas Pass appears farther in the distance. (Courtesy of the Denver, South Park & Pacific Historical Society.)

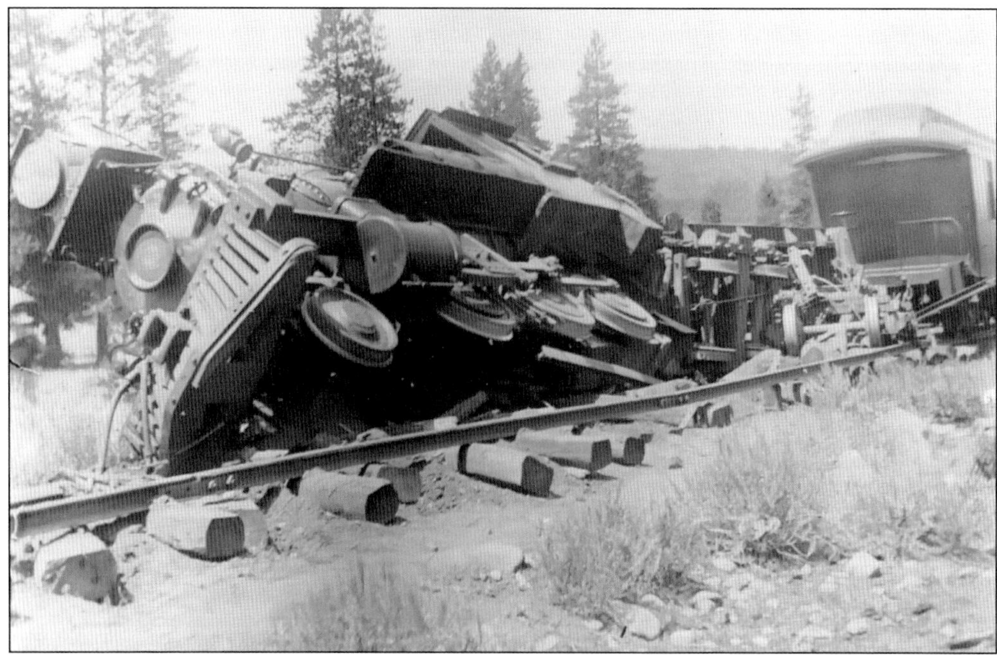

Oops! Before trains began the descent from Boreas Pass, brakemen set the brakes so that the trains would not descend at more than five miles per hour. To stop a train moving at that speed, enough braking power to actually lift the train from the tracks would be needed. A train descending a 4.5-percent grade doubled its speed every 15 seconds unless checked by strong brakes. (Courtesy of the Summit Historical Society.)

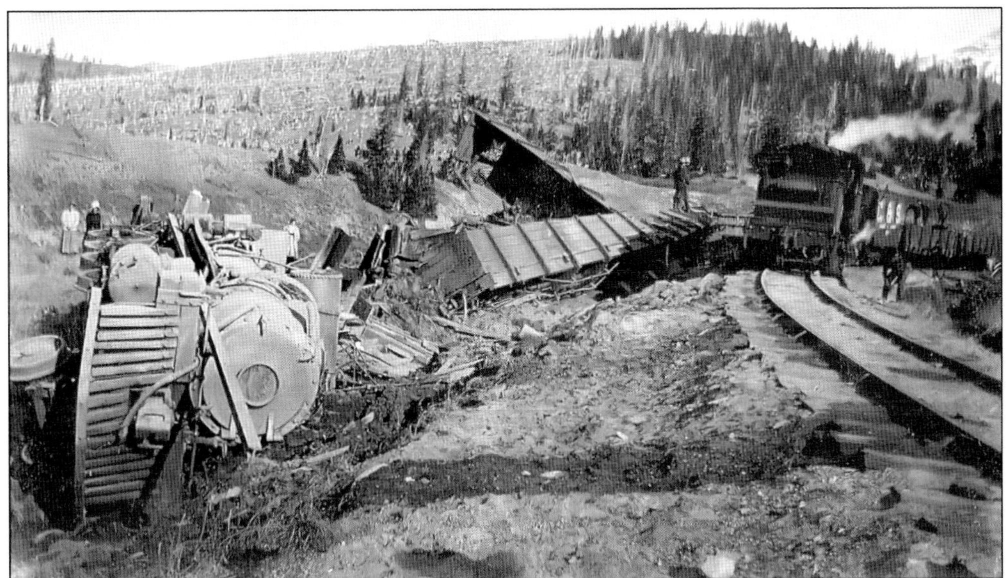

ACCIDENTS HAPPENED. Before railroad companies installed more-reliable Westinghouse brakes on rolling stock, brakemen had to depend on Eames vacuum brakes that often failed on the steep slopes, resulting in runaway trains. If the train crew felt it could no longer control the train and it was unsafe to stay on board, they made the dangerous decision to jump. They called it "joining the birds." (Courtesy of the Clair Dungan collection.)

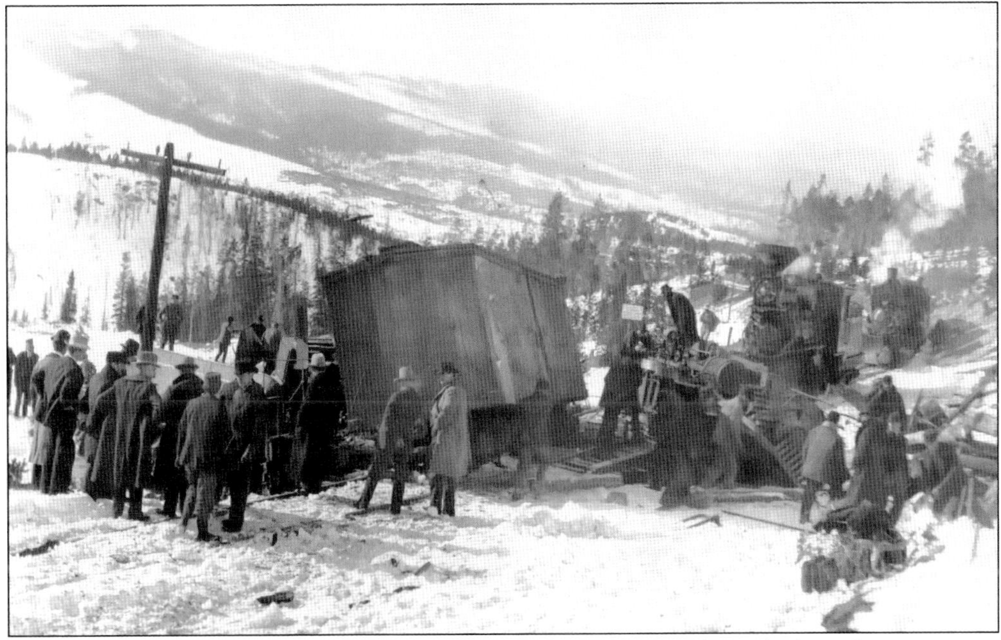

DERAILING AT WASHINGTON SPUR. Wrecks happened too often in the early days of narrow-gauge railroading. On February 6, 1901, a westbound Colorado & Southern freight train descending into Breckenridge derailed at the Washington spur because of ice on the track. Engine 60 lies on its side. To the left of refrigerator car 24011, just out of site in this view, engine 70 and flanger plow 08 have also derailed. (Photograph by Dr. Clinton H Scott, courtesy of the Todd Hackett collection.)

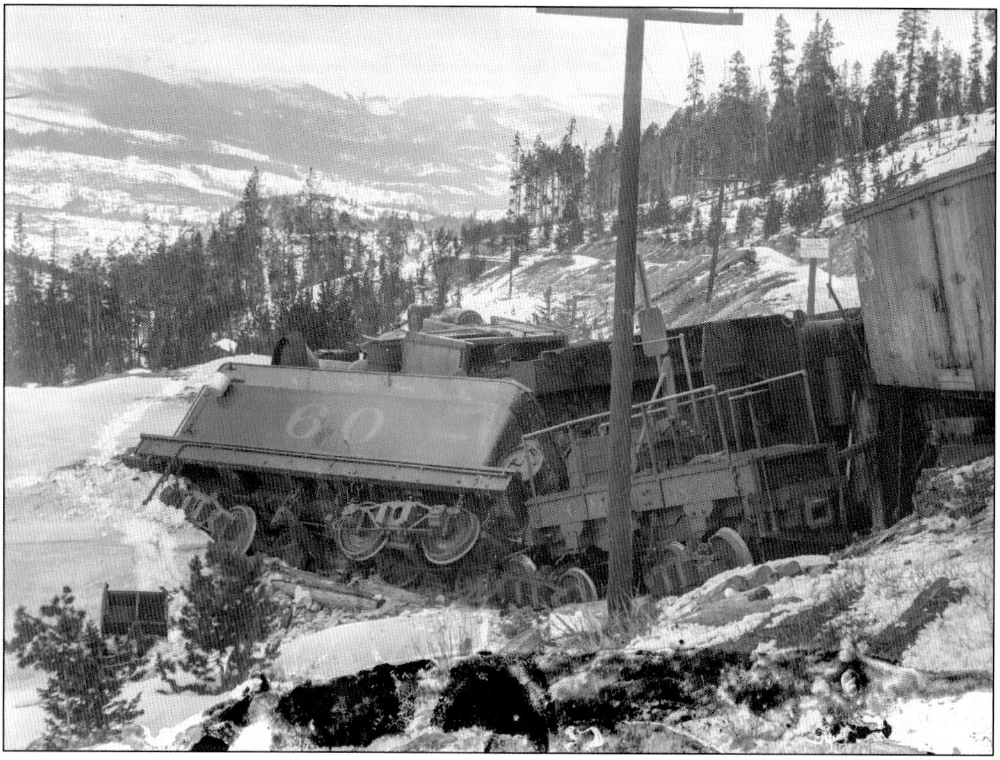

Wreck Aftermath. From the other side of the wreck, refrigerator car 24011, originally a Tiffany patent refrigerator car, now stands on the right. Engines 60 and 70, along with flanger plow 08, used to clear the snow from the tracks, headed the train. The engineer on engine 70, Curley Colligan, spent 14 months in the hospital recovering from his injuries before returning to work. (Courtesy of the Denver, South Park & Pacific Historical Society.)

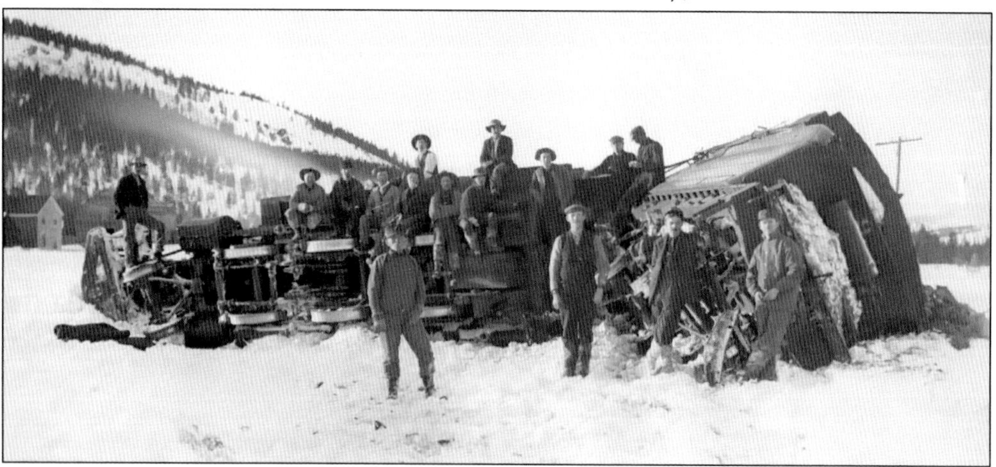

Accident Clean-Up. When accidents happened, the railroad brought heavy equipment to lift the engine and cars back onto the tracks. Workers replaced damaged tracks. Sometimes an engine derailed when ice from a leaking water tank covered the tracks. Priest flangers, mounted on the engine just ahead of the pony truck wheels, scraped ice from the inside and top of the rails. In winter, engines carried sand to dump on tracks for added traction. (Courtesy of the Summit Historical Society.)

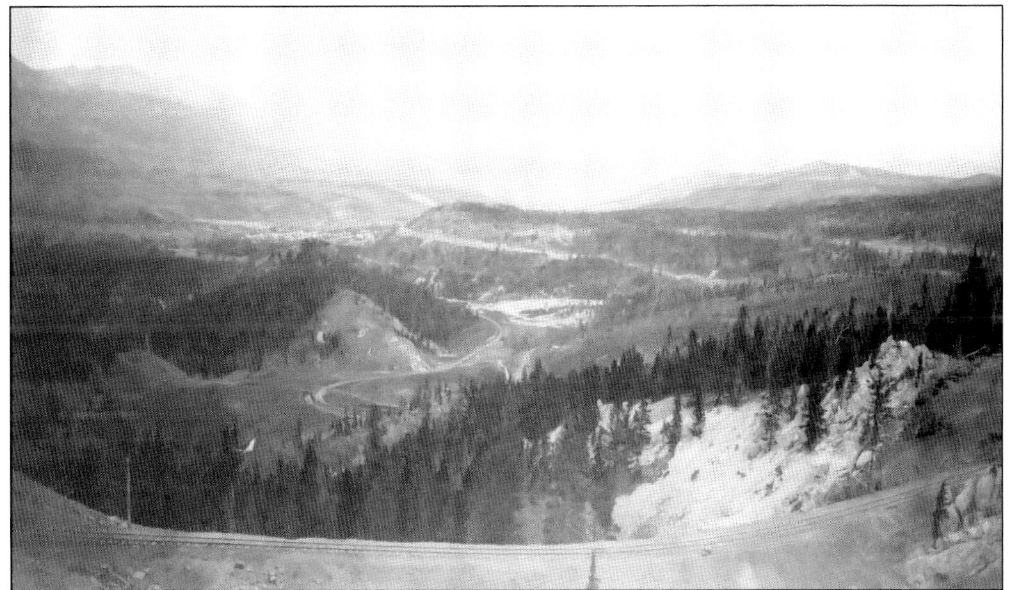

Hookeye Curve from Rocky Point. Trains descending from Rocky Point went around Barney Ford Hill before reaching Hookeye Curve, in the foreground, passed Little Mountain, and then headed to Breckenridge. It is possible on the photograph to see the cut on Barney Ford Hill that the train followed before reaching Hookeye Curve in Illinois Gulch. Breckenridge is in the distance. (Courtesy of the Denver, South Park & Pacific Historical Society.)

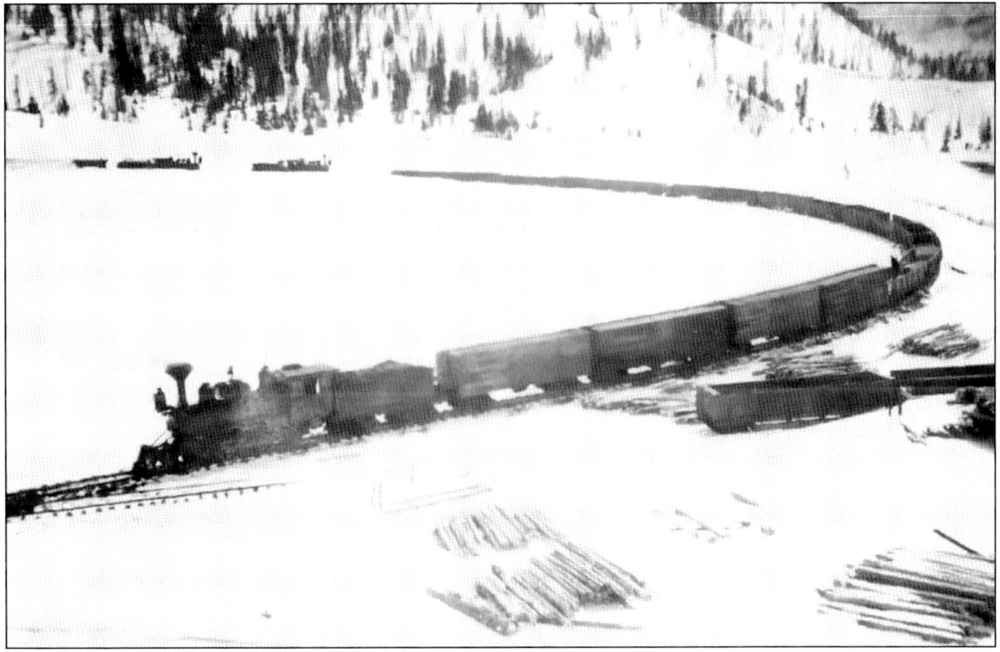

Hookeye Curve. On its final approach to Breckenridge, this 20-car freight train rounds Hookeye Curve. Two helper engines, one with a caboose, follow the train. Because the small engines could not negotiate much more than a four percent grade, many curves such as this were required to smooth out the steep increases in elevation between Breckenridge and Boreas Pass. (Courtesy of the Bill Fountain collection.)

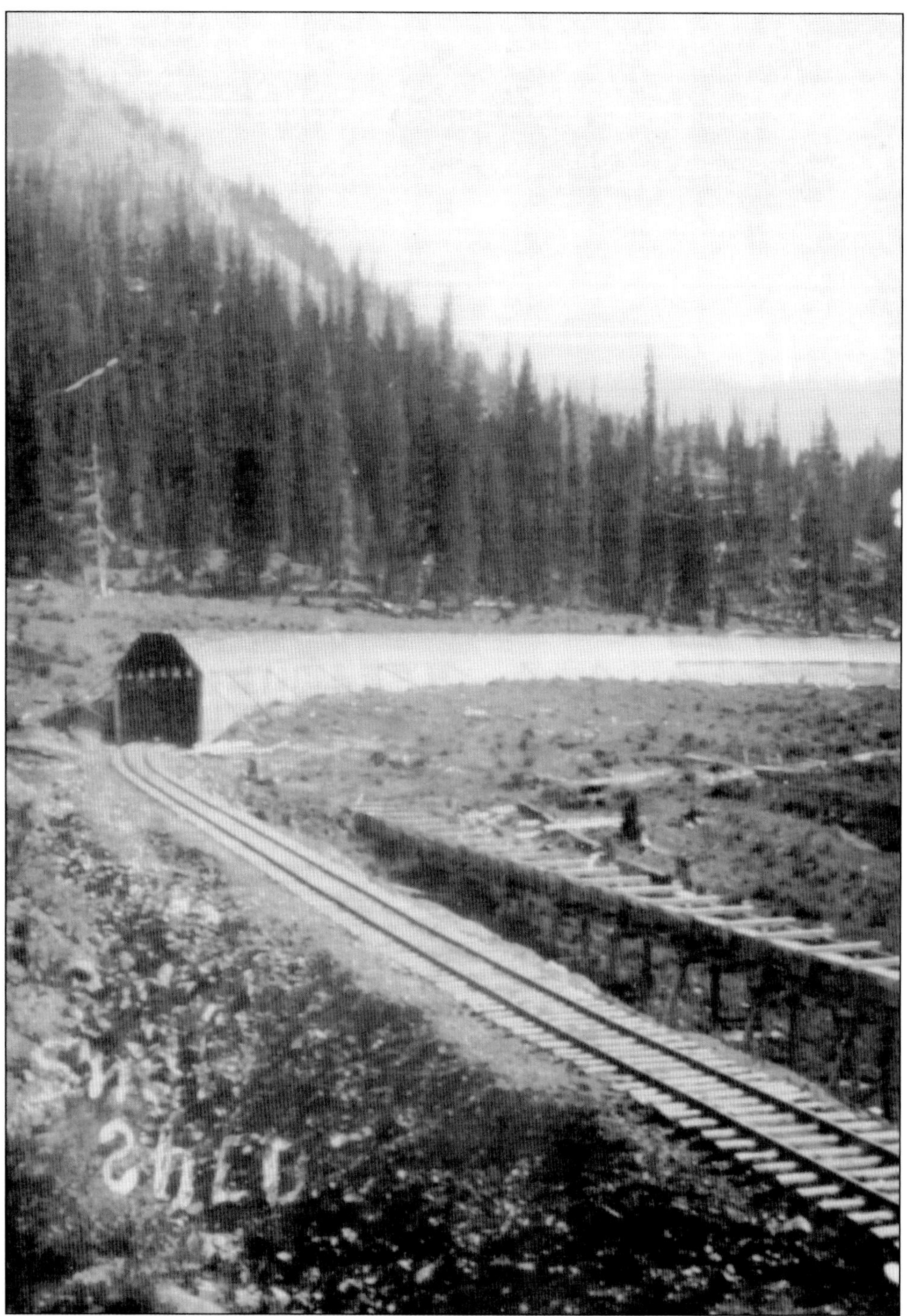

Snow Shed on Hookeye Curve. Railroad employees built wooden snow sheds in areas prone to avalanches or deep snow drifts. This snow shed covered part of Hookeye Curve in Illinois Gulch in the 1880s. Reaching well over 500 feet in length, the shed stood more than 16 feet tall and over 13 feet wide. In the distance beyond the snow shed, Rocky Point can be seen. (Courtesy of the Denver, South Park & Pacific Historical Society.)

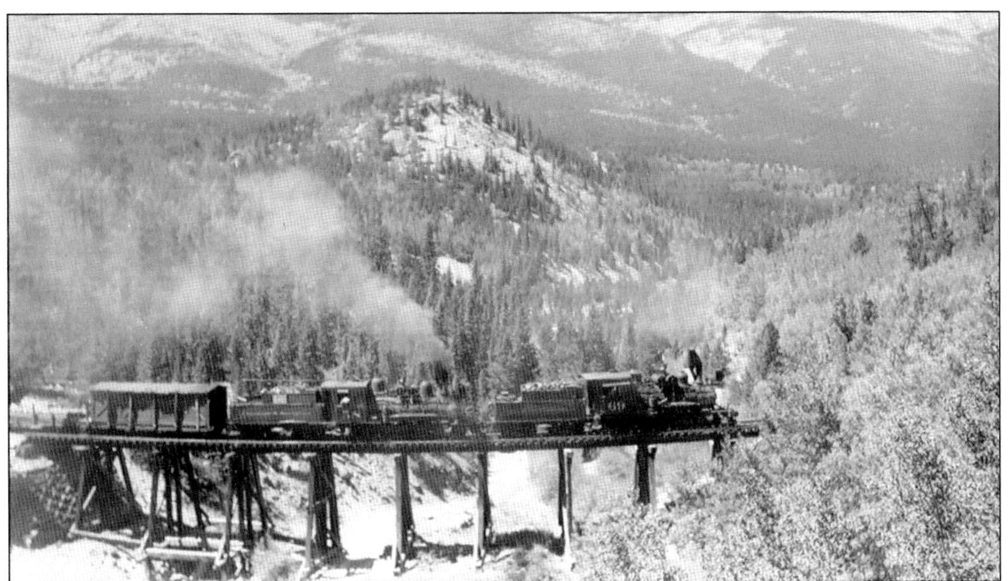

Gold Pan Trestle. The Gold Pan trestle bridged Illinois Gulch east of Breckenridge. The 10-span wood-frame structure, 19 feet tall, extended 158 feet across the gulch. Engine 69, built by Cooke and weighing 58,300 pounds, hauled passengers and freight from February 1884 until scrapped in the late summer of 1938. Engine 58, also built by Cooke and weighing 62,900 pounds, worked from July 1883 until July 1916. (Courtesy of the Denver, South Park & Pacific Historical Society.)

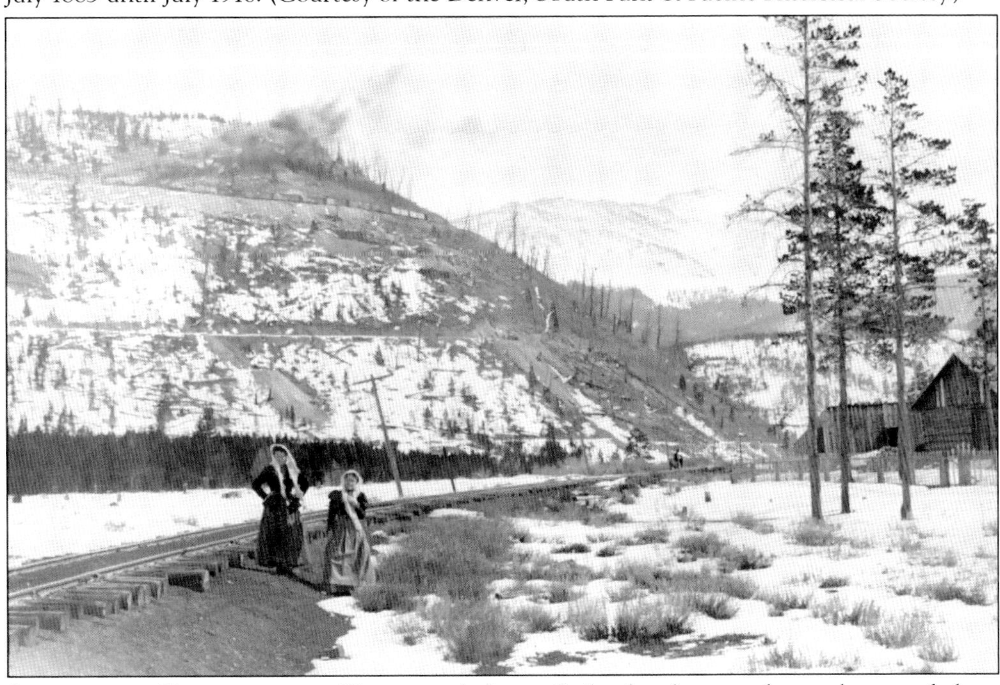

Smile for the Photographer. Two young ladies smile for the photographer as they stand along the Denver, South Park & Pacific tracks leading into Breckenridge. Behind them, an eastbound train climbs Barney Ford Hill on its way to Boreas Pass. Today, the Breckenridge High Line Railroad Park with children's playground sits along the former High Line tracks near where the women stand. (Courtesy of the Denver, South Park & Pacific Historical Society.)

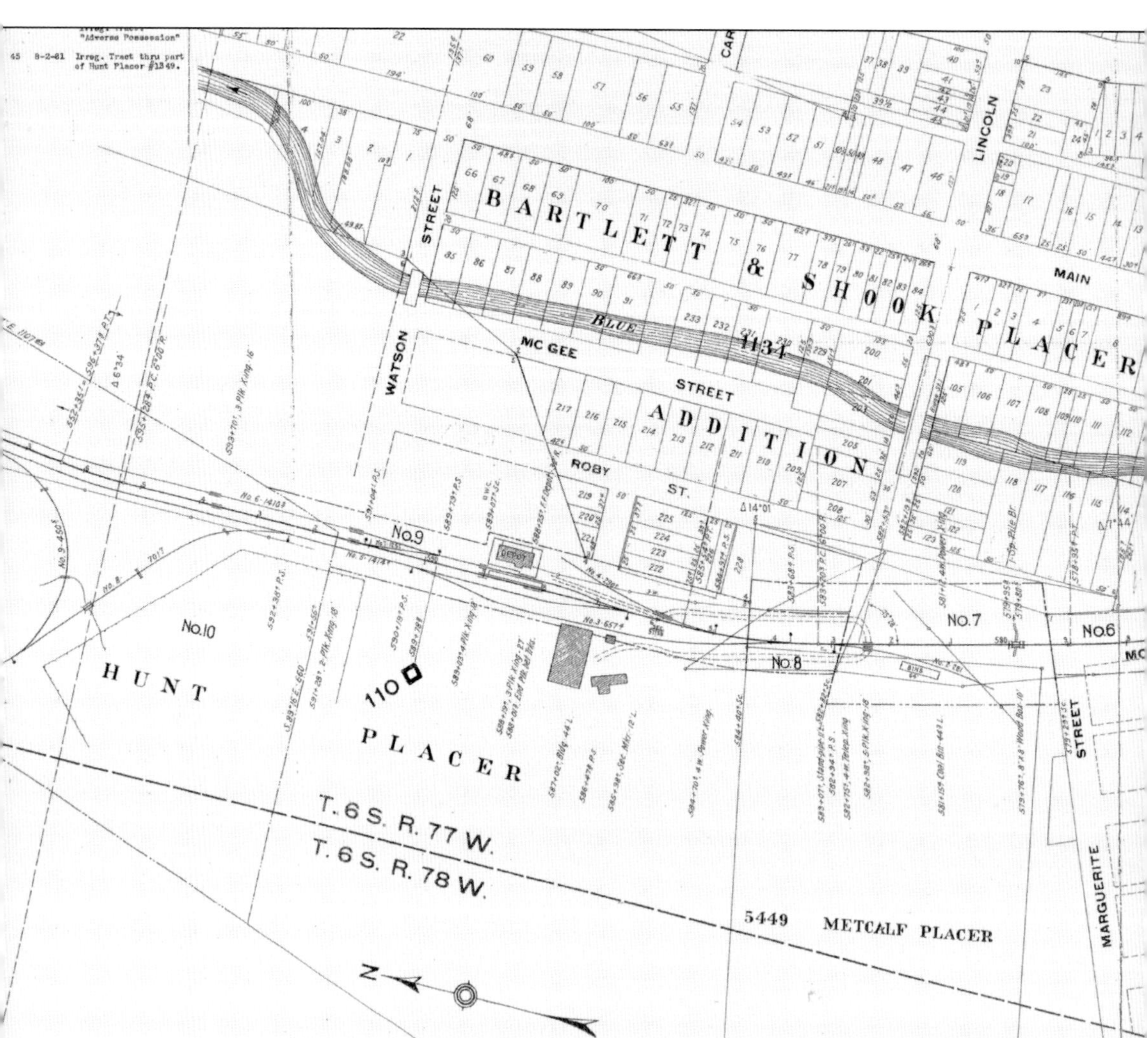

COLORADO & SOUTHERN 1918 INTERSTATE COMMERCE COMMISSION MAP. In Breckenridge, the tracks and all facilities were found west of the Blue River. The rails crossed the Blue River on the Maggie placer and proceeded north following Montgomery Street (now Park Street). The map shows the passenger depot. A separate freight depot sat just north of the passenger depot on the same side of the tracks. (Courtesy of the Denver, South Park & Pacific Historical Society.)

Three

Breckenridge, North to Dickey

The original survey called for the line from Breckenridge to meet a line from the east at Dillon. By revising the plans so that the lines met at Dickey (also called Placer Junction), two miles south of Dillon, the Denver, South Park & Pacific saved four miles of track and shortened the distance to Leadville. From Dickey, the line joined the original Ten Mile survey near Frisco. Dickey functioned as the junction between the Montezuma and Ten Mile mining districts, becoming the switching point leading to Dillon and Keystone. The railroad constructed a coaling station, depot, 47,500-gallon water tank, 12-pocket coal chute (1902), and side tracks for 188 cars. There was a wye as well as a roundhouse (1902) with two stalls to hold four helper engines needed for the trip over Boreas and Fremont Passes.

Accidents happened. The *Summit County Journal* reported on September 15, 1883, that a dog named Rover was "thoughtless enough to get in the way of a Denver, South Park locomotive" and the result was "too many pieces of dog to be of service." In December 1887, six fully loaded ore cars broke loose in Breckenridge when their brakes failed on ice-covered track, and they rolled toward Dickey. Because there was a 60-foot drop in elevation per mile between Breckenridge and Dickey, six miles away, the cars jumped the track when they could not negotiate the turn at the switch that was set for Frisco, destroying much of the depot.

Some near-tragedies had happy endings. As a coal train descended Barney Ford Hill near Breckenridge, the engineer and fireman, thinking the train was a runaway, jumped off after reversing the engine. Not knowing the others had jumped, the conductor and brakeman walked along the roofs of the cars and set the brakes on each car by hand, finally stopping the train at the Adams Avenue crossing in Breckenridge. Fifteen minutes later, the engineer and fireman came running along the tracks, surprised to see their train in one piece.

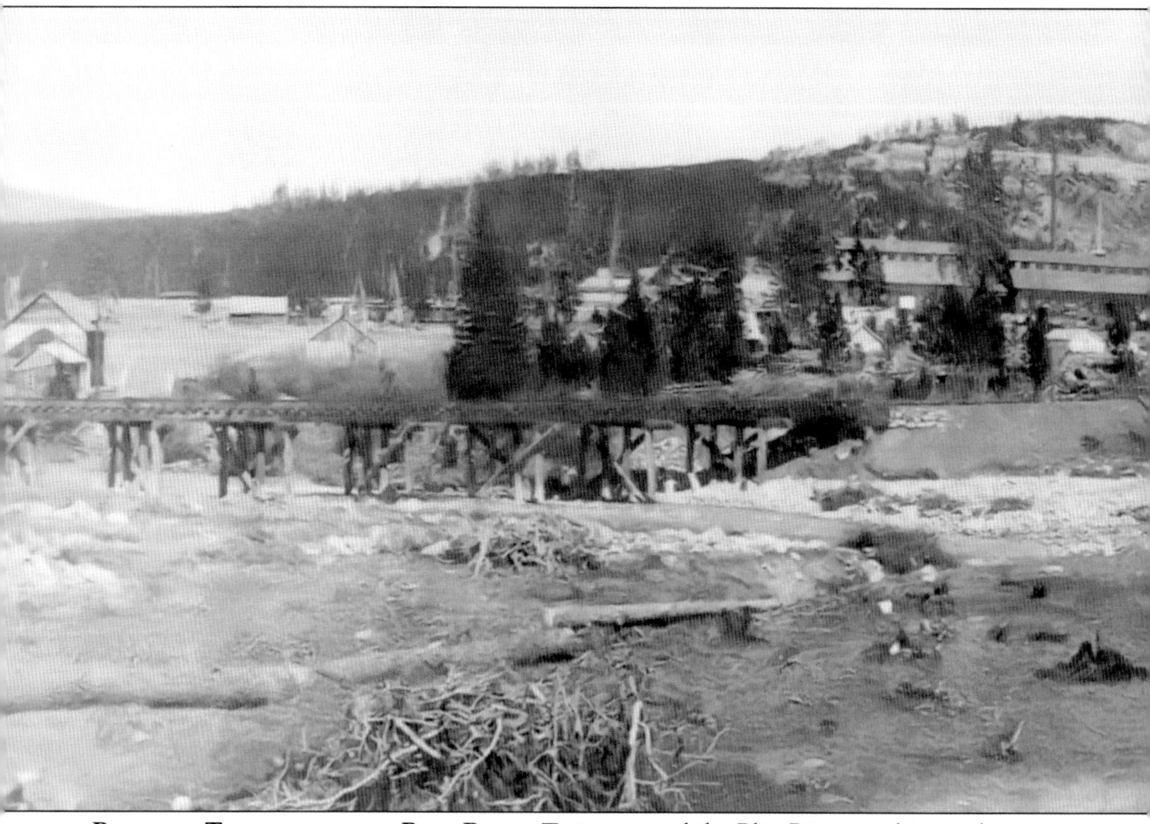

Railroad Trestle over the Blue River. Trains crossed the Blue River on this trestle, passing near the Gold Pan mining facilities at the southern end of town. Eventually, rocks from the pit operation inundated the supports on the eastern end of the trestle. The Blue River continued to flow under the western side of the trestle. A portion of the trestle remains in the Blue River today. (Courtesy of the Maureen Nicholls collection.)

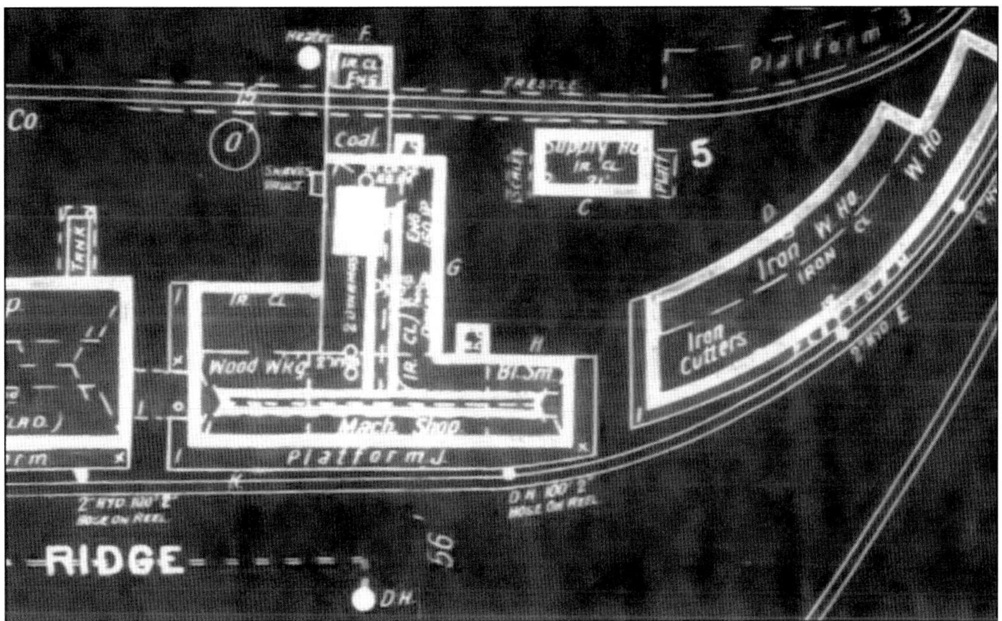

Gold Pan Shops in Breckenridge. The three large buildings comprising the Gold Pan Shops were located on Ridge Street. The curved building housed the iron-cutting operation. A 31-car spur, named the Gold Pan spur, carried coal to the shops and continued beyond the buildings for about 1,000 feet. Flatbed cars on the spur carried hydraulic pipes from the pipe shop in the northernmost building to dipping tanks north of the buildings. (Courtesy of the Maureen Nicholls collection.)

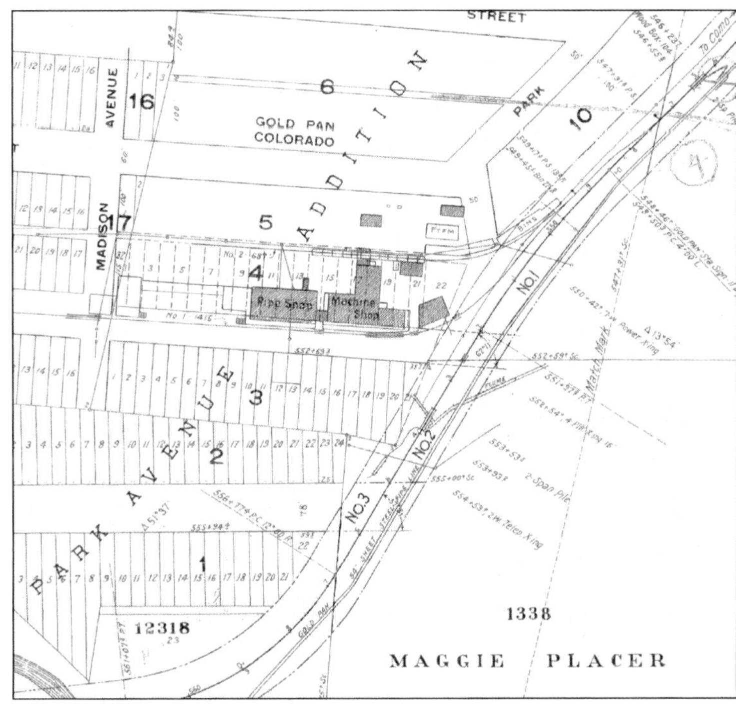

Map Showing Gold Pan Shops in Breckenridge. The Gold Pan Company constructed its facilities on Ridge Street next to the main line at the southern end of town. Touted as the "finest machinery plant in the world," the company, which began operating in October 1900, produced water pipes for placer mining operations with boiler plate brought by the railroad. (Courtesy of the Denver, South Park & Pacific Historical Society.)

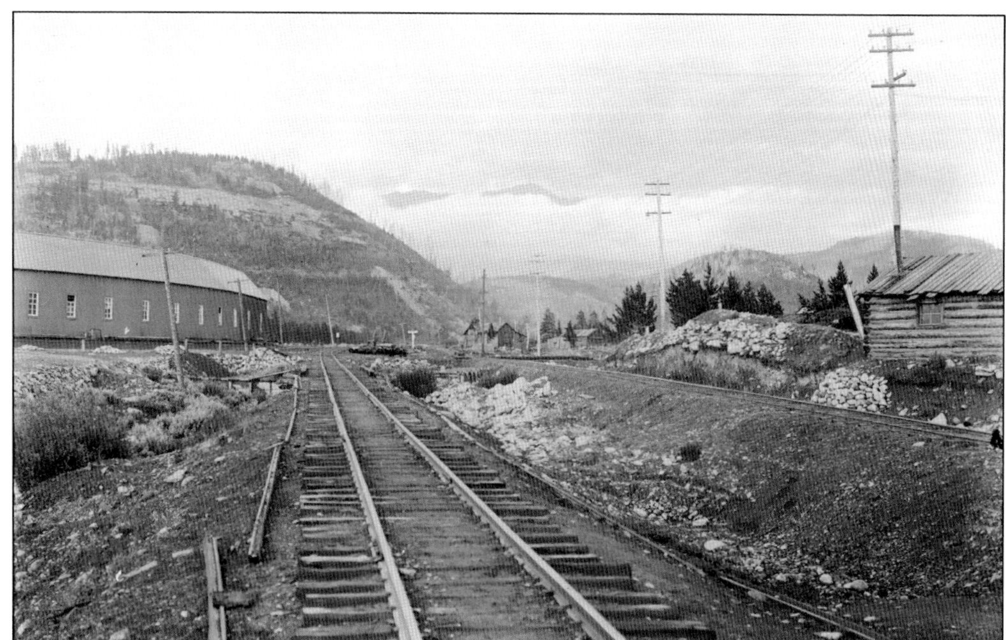

Gold Pan Iron Warehouse and Cutters Shop looking South to Rocky Point. The company used the 20-foot-by-40-foot two-story building to store boiler plate for making pipes. The shape of the building, nicknamed the "roundhouse" by some, fit the curve of the spur as it branched off the main line into Breckenridge. (Photograph by Dr. Clinton H Scott, courtesy of the Denver, South Park & Pacific Historical Society.)

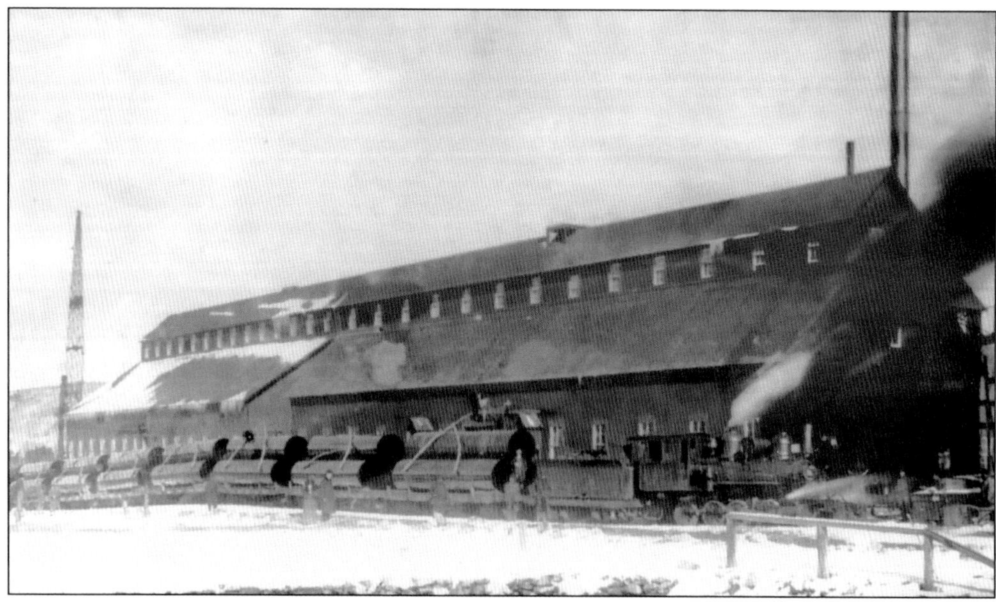

Loading Pipes at the Gold Pan Shops. The Gold Pan Shops fabricated pipes for hydraulic mining operations and water companies operating in the county. Some with a diameter of five feet weighed as much as seven tons. After a system of pulleys dipped the heavy pipes in a vat filled with heated asphaltum, railroad cars transported them to a variety of sites. (Courtesy of the Denver, South Park & Pacific Historical Society.)

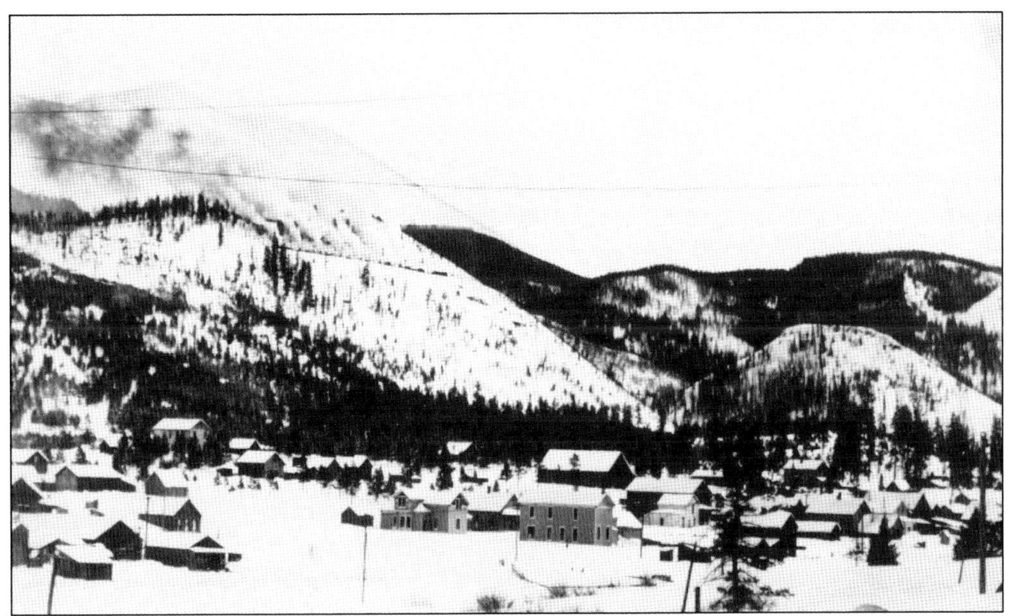

Blockade of 1898–1899. The winter of 1899 proved particularly difficult for the railroad. The rotary snow plow could not keep up with the snow, and the line remained closed for 78 days, from February 6 until April 24. By the time men from town shoveled open a road to Como, food supplies had dwindled in Breckenridge. Prices almost doubled at a time when many had no jobs. (Courtesy of the Summit Historical Society.)

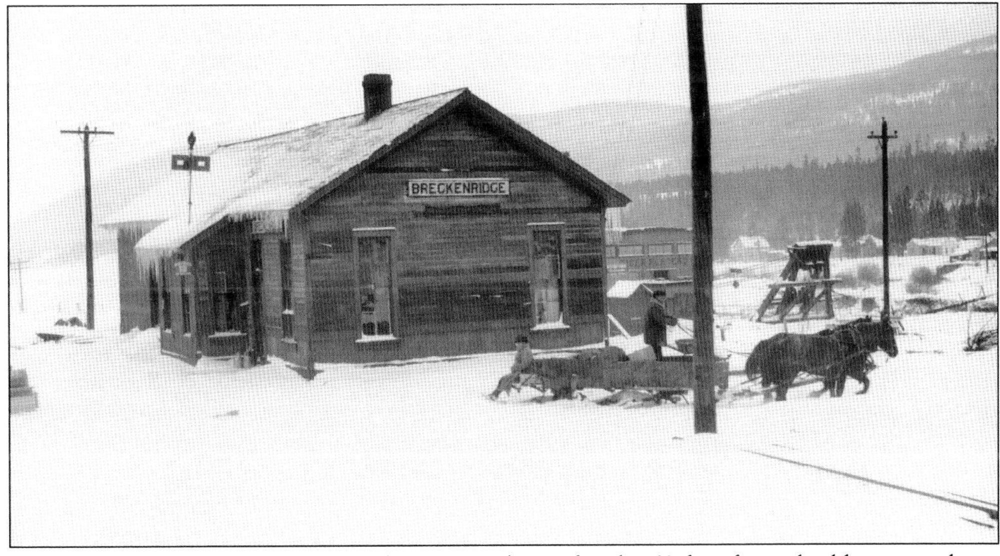

Breckenridge Train Station. Built in 1882, the 24-foot-by-60-foot frame building served as a depot, living quarters, and freight house. Typical of Western mining towns, mining-related buildings in Breckenridge such as mills, smelters, sawmills, storage sheds, coal bins, and warehouses, as well as the depot, lined the tracks. They would be on the opposite side of the river from the main businesses of town. (Courtesy of the Summit Historical Society.)

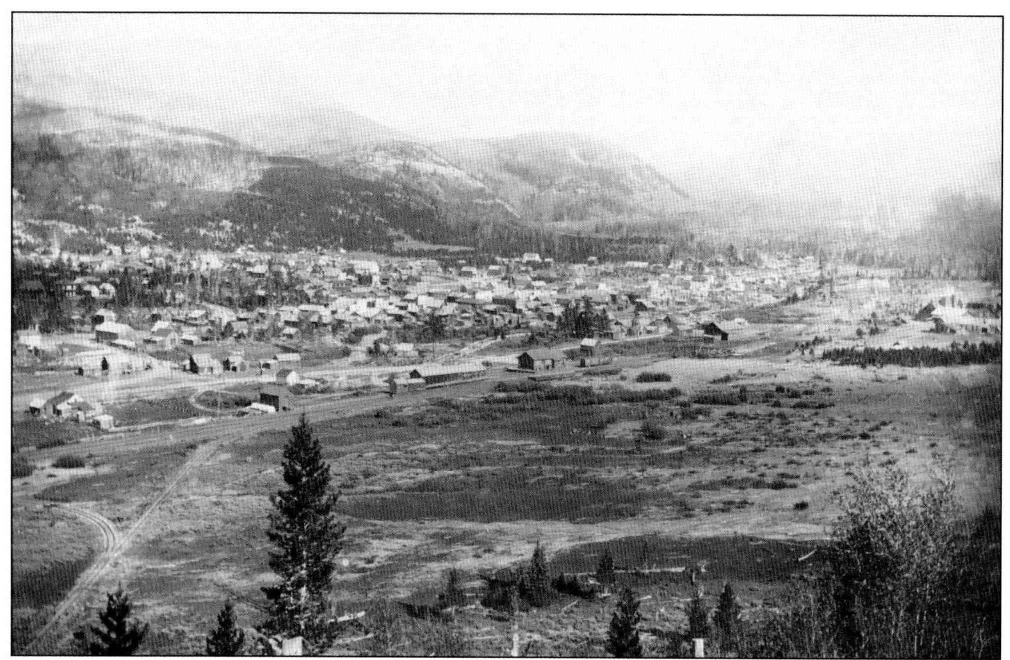

Breckenridge Railroad Buildings and Wye. In this c. 1898 Scott photograph, the railroad facilities stretch from right to left: the depot and yard with two boxcars in front; the coal bins directly across the tracks from the depot; the freight house to the left of the depot; and the wye for turning engines at the lower left. Today, the Breckenridge gondola rises above the last traces of the wye. (Photograph by Dr. Clinton H Scott, courtesy of the Ed and Nancy Bathke collection.)

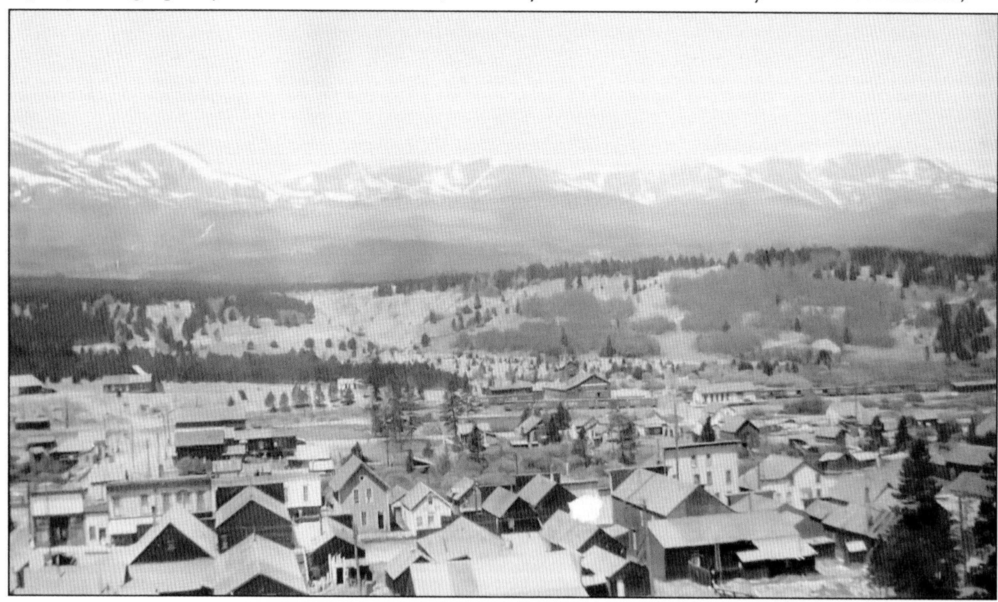

Colorado & Southern Depot. An unknown photographer took this photograph a few years later than the previous photograph, looking west instead of east. The Kilton ore sampler is in the center of the photograph, with the light-colored Colorado & Southern (C&S) depot to the right. C&S boxcars sit on the tracks near the depot. The Ten Mile Range rises in the distance. (Courtesy of the Denver, South Park & Pacific Historical Society.)

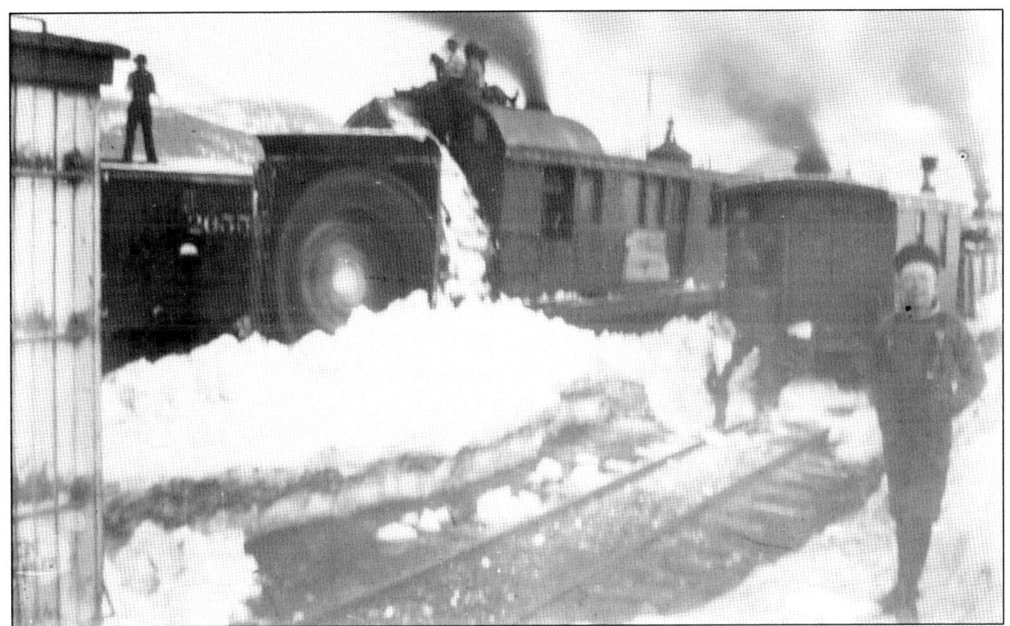

Testing the Rotary. Deep snow challenged the rotary snow plow and crews that kept the tracks clear. Before tackling the deep drifts over the passes, the rotary crew tested the plow and its machinery to be sure the plow did not experience a breakdown far from repair facilities. The rapidly spinning blades of the plow indicate that the crew conducted such a test in the Breckenridge railroad yard before heading out. (Courtesy of the Denver, South Park & Pacific Historical Society.)

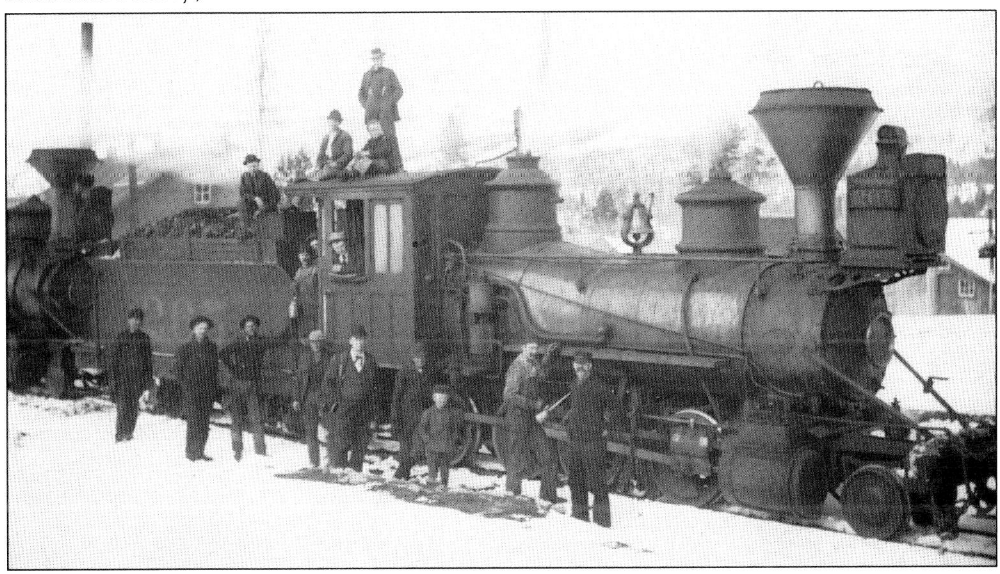

Engine 265. Well-oiled and carrying a full load of coal and water, Denver, Leadville & Gunnison engine 265, built in 1886 by the Rhode Island Locomotive Works, pauses with another helper engine just south of the Breckenridge depot before beginning its climb over Boreas Pass. In this 1898 Clinton H Scott photograph, the train crew and several guests pose for the photographer before tackling the heavy snow awaiting them along the High Line. (Photograph by Dr. Clinton H Scott, courtesy of the Ed and Nancy Bathke collection.)

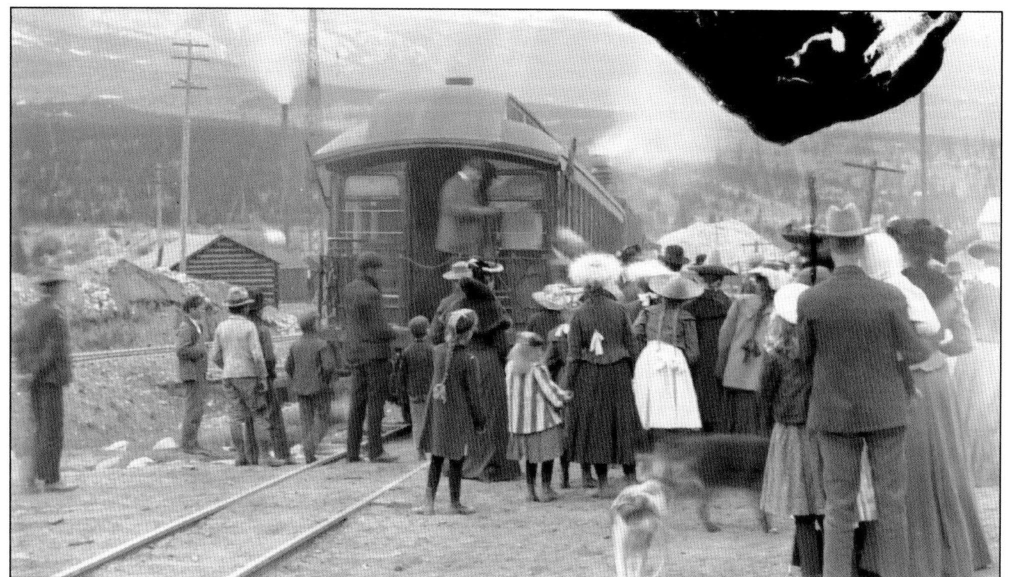

Very Important Passenger in Breckenridge. On May 24, 1904, a train consisting of two business cars arrived with German prince Phillip Ernst, the eighth prince of Hohenlohe-Schillingsfurst, and his party. While there, they toured a gold mine and visited the Gold Pan Shops. In this Clinton H Scott photograph, the prince has already stepped from the train while another of his party leaves the rear platform. (Courtesy of the Denver, South Park & Pacific Historical Society.)

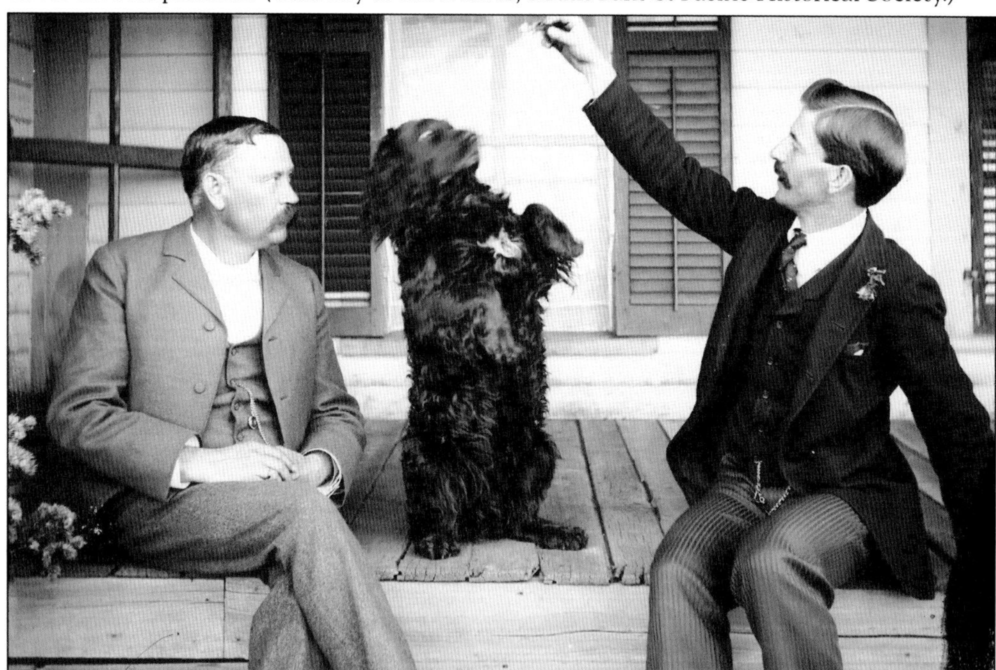

Dr. Clinton H Scott. Dr. Scott, on the right, offers a treat to a furry friend. A railroad surgeon for the Denver, South Park & Pacific, he lived in Como in the 1880s before moving to Breckenridge, where he stayed until 1905 before returning to his native Pennsylvania. An avid photographer, he recorded mining and railroad scenes throughout the county for many years. (Courtesy of the Denver, South Park & Pacific Historical Society.)

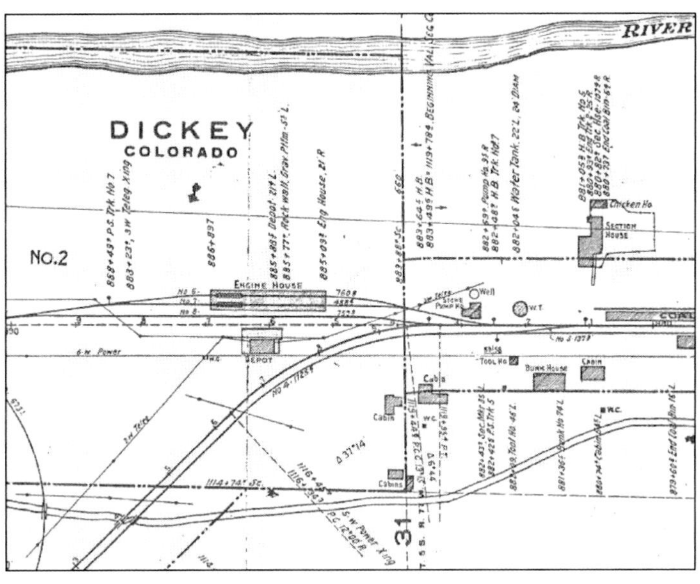

MAP OF RAILROAD FACILITIES IN DICKEY. This close-up of a 1918 Interstate Commerce Commission map shows the railroad facilities at Dickey. The engine house, depot, section house, water tank, pump house and well, bunk house, and various other outbuildings are highlighted. Even the chicken house, located behind the section house, is included. (Courtesy of the Denver, South Park & Pacific Historical Society.)

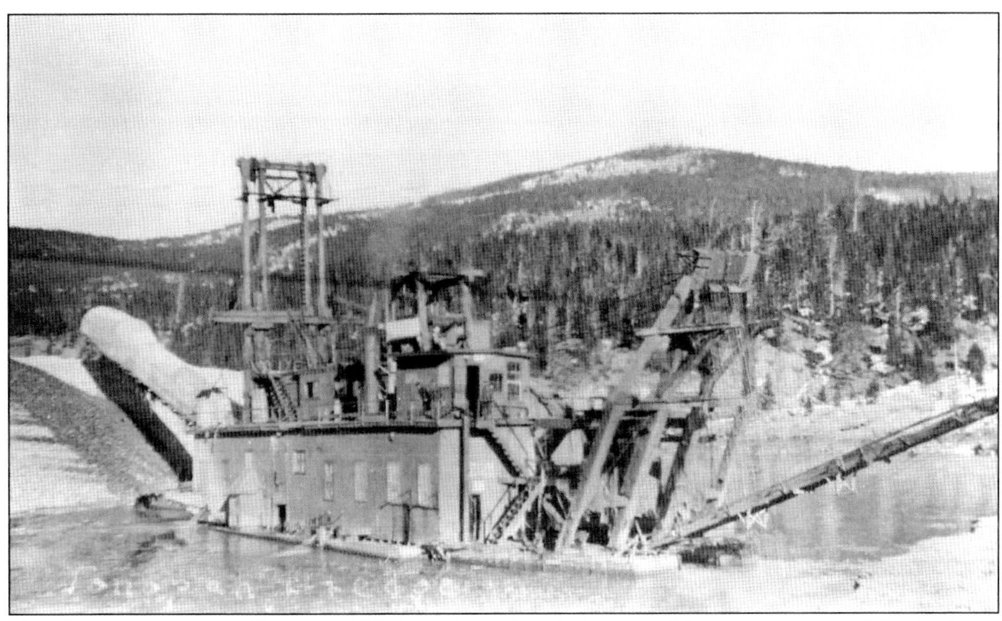

THE RAILROAD AND THE DREDGES. Without the railroad, there would have been no gold dredge boats in Summit County. Between 1898 and 1942, nine dredges dug deep into the Swan River, French Gulch, and the Blue River looking for gold. The railroads carried lumber from the West Coast and dredging machinery from San Francisco and Milwaukee, Wisconsin. Coal arrived by rail from nearby mines to power some of the dredge boats. (Courtesy of the Bill Fountain collection.)

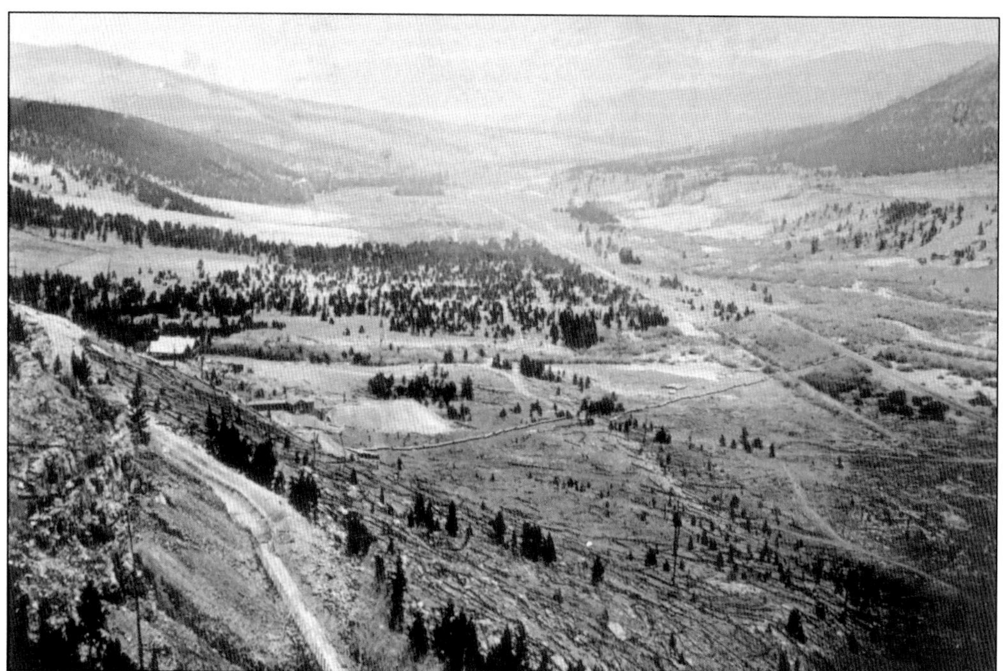

Railroad Grade Leading to Dillon. The railroad grade from Breckenridge to Dillon cut a straight path through hydraulic mining operations lining both sides of the Blue River. When the Tonopah Company's dredge began working in the Blue River, moving south into Breckenridge, it came perilously close to the railroad right-of-way and the adjacent road to Dillon. Dynamiting the river bank to aid dredging threatened to destabilize the ground under the railroad. (Courtesy of the Denver, South Park & Pacific Historical Society.)

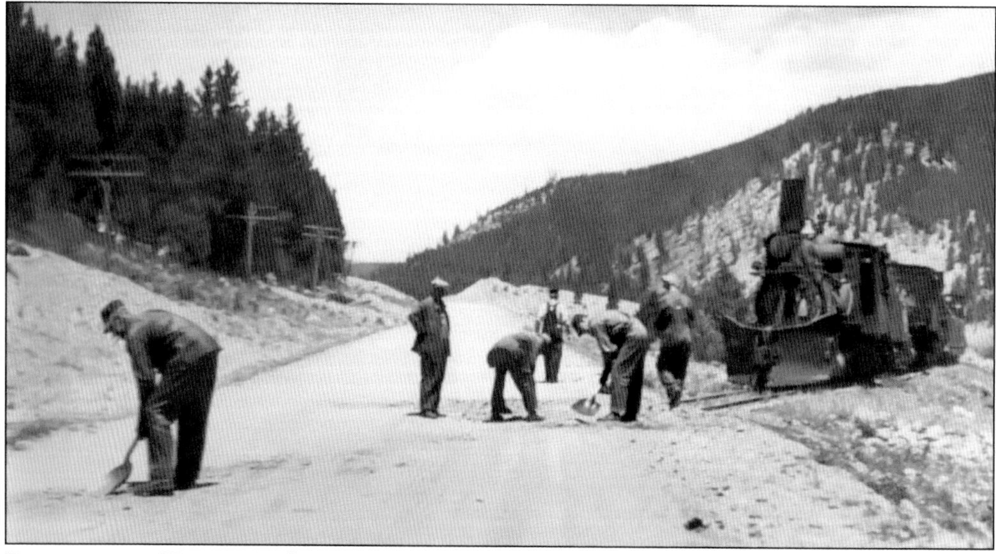

Removing the Tracks. In the summer of 1938, a year after ending service in Summit County, the railroad began removing its tracks. The crews started at Fremont Pass, worked their way through the Ten Mile Canyon to Frisco, and turned south toward Breckenridge. Before the train could cross this road a few miles north of Breckenridge, workers had to remove dirt by hand that had accumulated around the rails. (Courtesy of the Denver, South Park & Pacific Historical Society.)

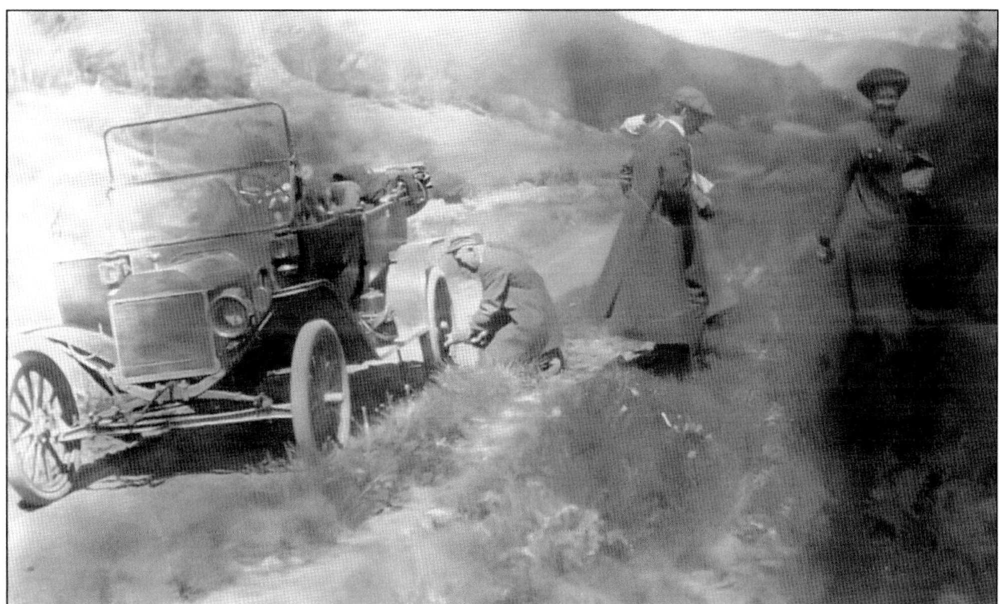

The Beginning of the End. Although the gradual decline of mining activity contributed to the demise of the railroads, the biggest factor was the emergence of cars, trucks, and the road system to support them. Rough roads and flat tires did not deter the motorists. While the emergence of tourist railroads saved a few declining rail lines, this phenomenon came too late for the railroads in Summit County. (Courtesy of the Denver, South Park & Pacific Historical Society.)

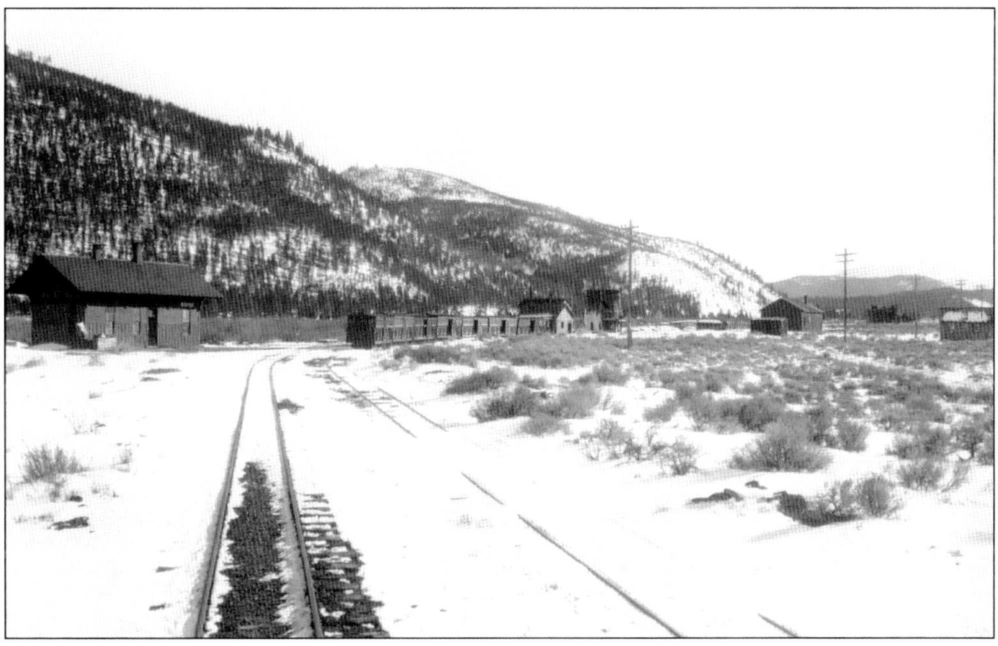

Railroad Facilities in Dickey. Because of Dickey's importance, the railroad constructed extensive facilities west of the Blue River. The two-stall engine house, well to supply the water tank, stone pump house, tool house, and coal chutes lined the track to the south. Cabins and a bunkhouse provided sleeping quarters for workers. Lake Dillon now covers the entire site. (Courtesy of the Denver, South Park & Pacific Historical Society.)

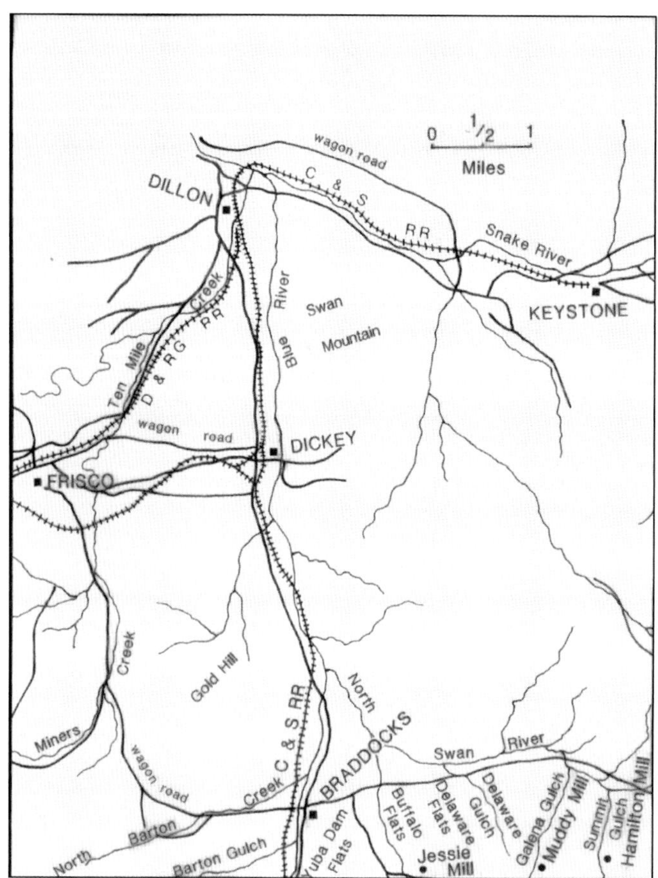

Saving Time and Track. Originally, the Denver, South Park & Pacific plans called for routing the line to Leadville through Dillon. By revising the plans so that the main and branch lines met at Dickey, two miles south of Dillon, the railroad saved four miles of track and shortened the distance to Leadville. The main line returned to the original survey through the Ten Mile Canyon near Frisco. (Reproduction by Sandra F. Pritchard Mather.)

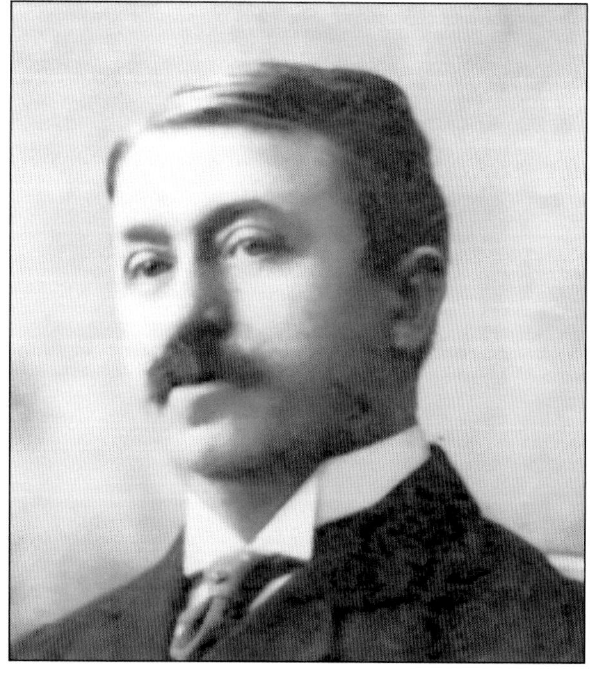

Frank Trumbull. Frank Trumbull, a savvy businessman, began his career with the railroad as a bookkeeper and auditor. Appointed as receiver for the Denver, Leadville & Gunnison during its bankruptcy proceedings, he improved the railroad's finances to the point that the company attracted investors. He oversaw the formation of the Colorado & Southern Railway and served as its first president. (Courtesy of the Denver, South Park & Pacific Historical Society.)

Dept. No. Form 601—6-95-15M. Treasurer's No. Audit No. 85

The Union Pacific, Denver & Gulf Railway Company.

FRANK TRUMBULL, Receiver.

Charge B. 47 85 To Frank Trumbull

Of Denver Colo

Pay Same

Month of January 1897 29th Address Same

1897 Jany For amount allowed by order of the Court on account as compensation for services as Receiver for the month of January 1897 833 33

833 33

SIGN ORIGINAL AND DUPLICATE VOUCHERS, AND DO NOT DETACH

Deduct 40 cts. for Hospital Fund. ORIGINAL.

CORRECT: CORRECT: CALCULATIONS CORRECT: R. S. Watkins

APPROVED: Frank Trumbull RECEIVER. The above account has been examined, found correct, and is hereby approved for payment. AUDITOR.

Received, Feby 29 1897, from The Union Pacific, Denver & Gulf Railway Company, Frank Trumbull, Receiver, Eight Hundred Thirty three & 33/100 DOLLARS, in full payment of above account.

($ 833 33) Frank Trumbull

NOTE.—The Receipt to this Voucher must be dated and signed by the party in whose favor the Voucher is made, or when signed by another party, the authority for so doing must in all cases accompany it.

UNION PACIFIC, DENVER & GULF RAILWAY COMPANY VOUCHER. The voucher approved Frank Trumbull's compensation for services rendered as the court-appointed receiver of the railroad for the month of January 1897. He received $833.33 monthly, for a yearly salary of $10,000. In January 1899, the investors combined the Denver, Leadville & Gunnison with the Union Pacific, Denver & Gulf Railway Company, forming the Colorado & Southern Railway. (Courtesy of the Denver, South Park & Pacific Historical Society.)

The Denver, Leadville & Gunnison Ry. Co.

FRANK TRUMBULL, Receiver.

TELEGRAPHIC TRAIN ORDER No. 9

Superintendent's Office 1897

31 For ... to C & E Eng 272 31

Eng 272 Two ... Will Run Extra from Dickey to Keystone & Return 12 miles per Hour

SLR

CONDUCTOR AND ENGINEMAN MUST EACH HAVE A COPY OF THIS ORDER.

Time received 1 03 M. Given at 1 04 M.

CONDUCTOR	TRAIN	MADE	AT	RECEIVED BY

TRAIN ORDER. This Denver, Leadville & Gunnison order, executed in 1897, directs engine 272 to travel from Dickey to Keystone and return at 12 miles per hour. Issued from the superintendent's office in Como, it specifies that both the engineer and conductor will receive a copy of the order. They received the order at 1:03 p.m. and issued it to the crew one minute later. (Courtesy of the Andy Anderson collection, Denver, South Park & Pacific Historical Society.)

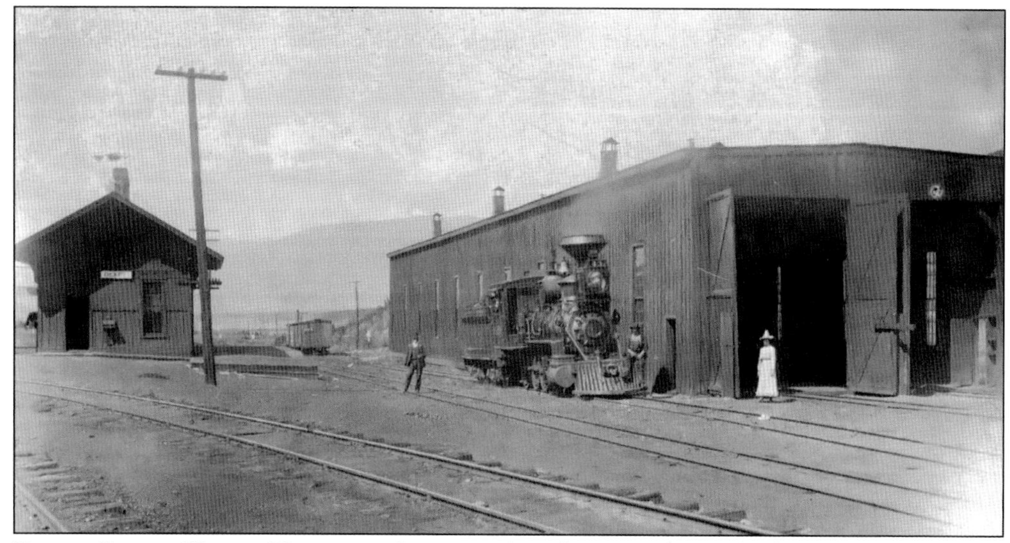

Dickey Engine House. The engine house sat directly across the tracks from the depot. In the engine house, men serviced the locomotives, keeping them ready to help pull trains over Boreas and Fremont Passes. The track in the foreground led to Frisco; the track to Dillon ran between the buildings. The engine next to the engine house has a McConnel smokestack, also called a sunflower or pancake smokestack. (Courtesy of the Summit Historical Society.)

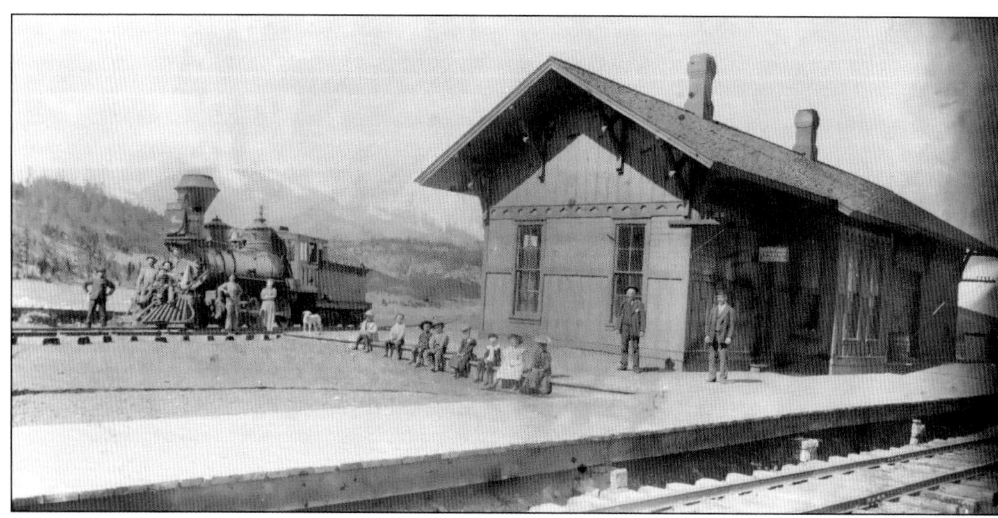

Dickey Depot. According to the *Summit County Journal*, in December 1887, six fully loaded ore cars broke loose in Breckenridge and rolled along the track toward Dickey. Because of the 60-foot drop in elevation per mile between Breckenridge and Dickey, six miles away, the cars, moving too rapidly to negotiate the curve, jumped the track and flew through the air, destroying part of the depot. (Courtesy of the Denver, South Park & Pacific Historical Society.)

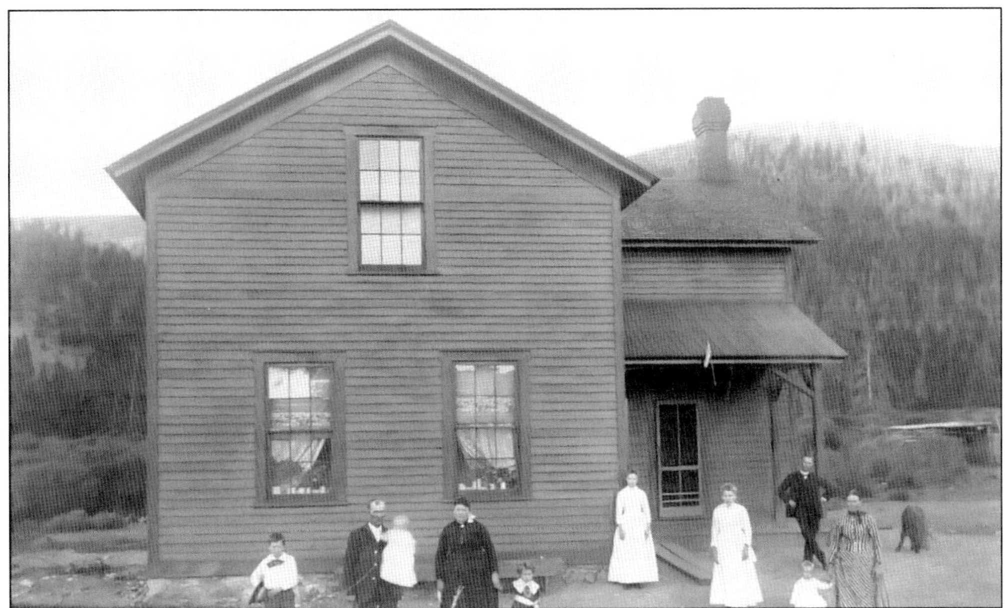

Dickey Section House. At intervals along the line, the railroad built section houses to provide food and lodging for workers who maintained the tracks and other facilities. The two-story frame building sat between the coal bins and the Blue River. In this 1890s view looking east, members of the Hedenskog family pose for the photographer. Potted plants grow on the windowsills of the first floor, and curtains cover the windows. (Courtesy of the Frisco Historic Park & Museum.)

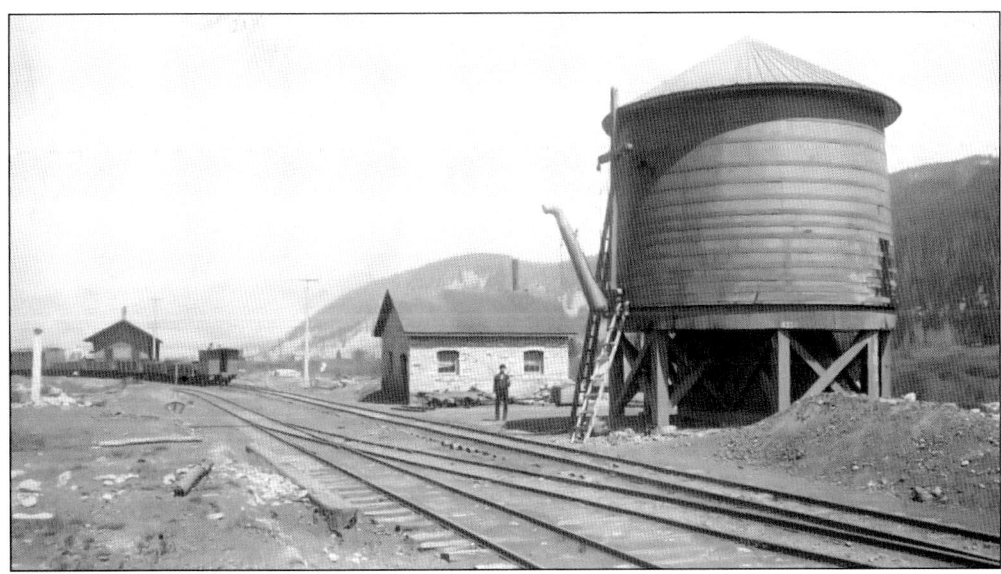

Dickey Pump House, Water Tank, and Depot, c. 1890. A northbound freight train waits in front of the depot on its way to Frisco. A well, whose shingled conical roof can be seen behind the ladders at the water tank, supplied the 47,500-gallon water tank. The track just beyond the caboose leads to Dillon. The siding to the right of the caboose will probably become the track to the yet-to-be-built engine house. (Courtesy of the Frisco Historic Park & Museum.)

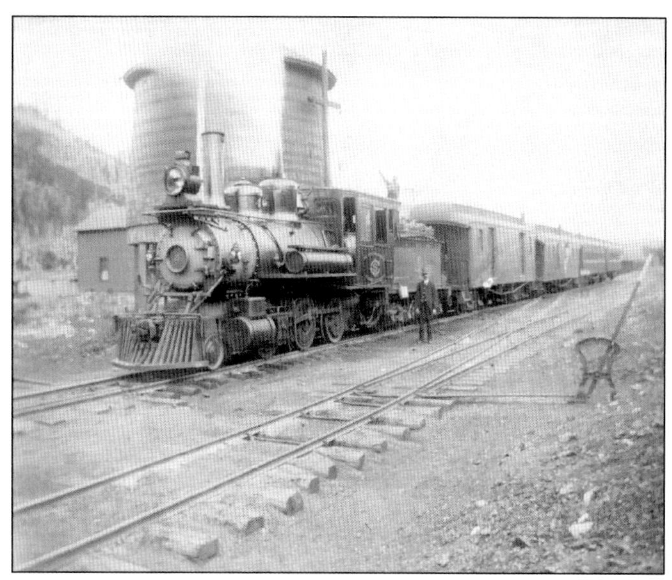

Refilling the Tender at Dickey Water Tank in 1903. After westbound engines took on water at Dickey, they refilled at Solitude Station, near Wheeler (Copper Mountain), before starting the climb to Kokomo, six miles away and 800 feet higher. After another refill at Kokomo, the engine arrived at Robinson, two miles farther and 94 feet higher. The elevation at Dickey was 9,004 feet (2,744 meters); the elevation at Robinson 10,860 feet (3,310 meters). (Courtesy of Ed and Nancy Bathke collection.)

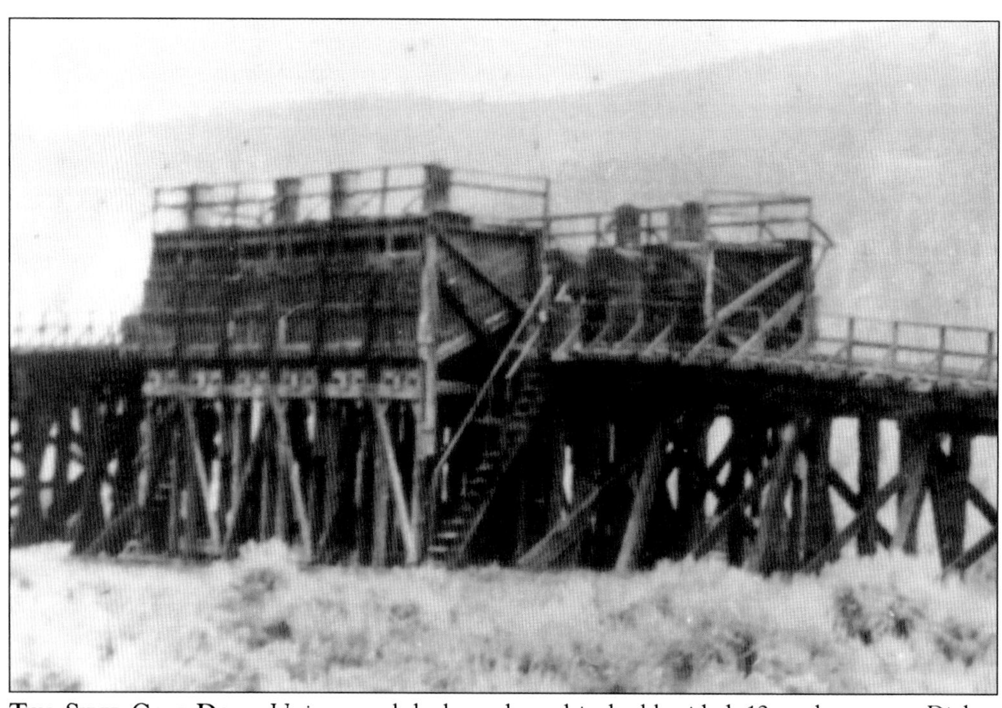

Two-Sided Coal Dock. Unique coal docks such as this double-sided, 12-pocket one at Dickey replaced the older style that required shoveling the coal twice, from the gondola cars into the coal bins and again into the engine's tender. With the newer style, men shoveled only once—from the gondola cars into the bins. The coal dropped by gravity into the tender. (Courtesy of the Denver, South Park & Pacific Historical Society.)

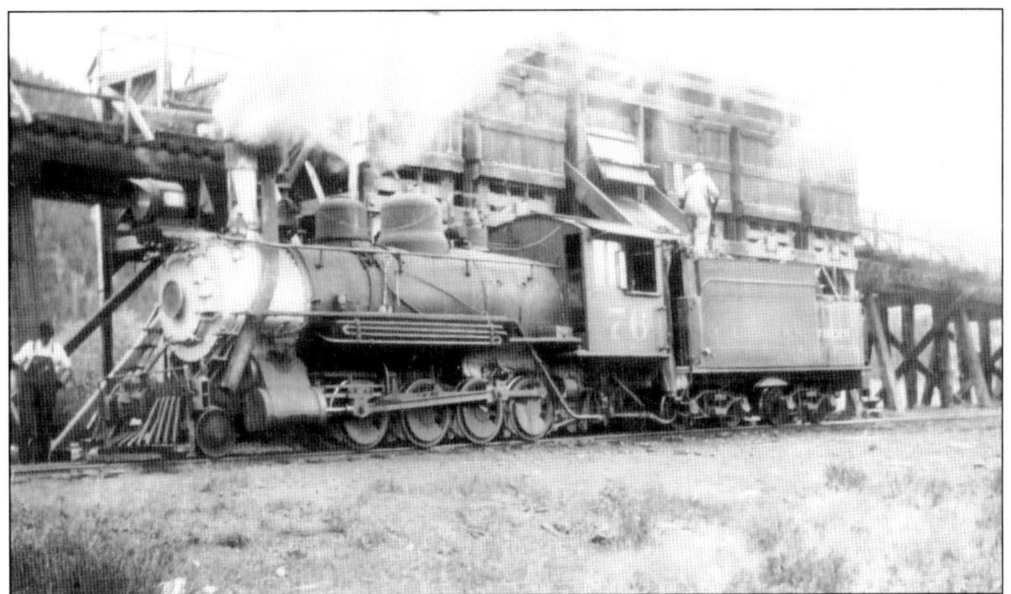

Coaling at Dickey. Engine 76 takes on coal at the two-sided coal dock at Dickey. When the chute opens, coal will flow by gravity into the tender. Locomotives pushed gondola cars filled with coal up the center ramp, where workers shoveled the coal into the bins. Engineers pushing the gondola cars up the ramp had to be sure to stop in time so that the cars did not go off the other end of the ramp. (Courtesy of the Denver, South Park & Pacific Historical Society.)

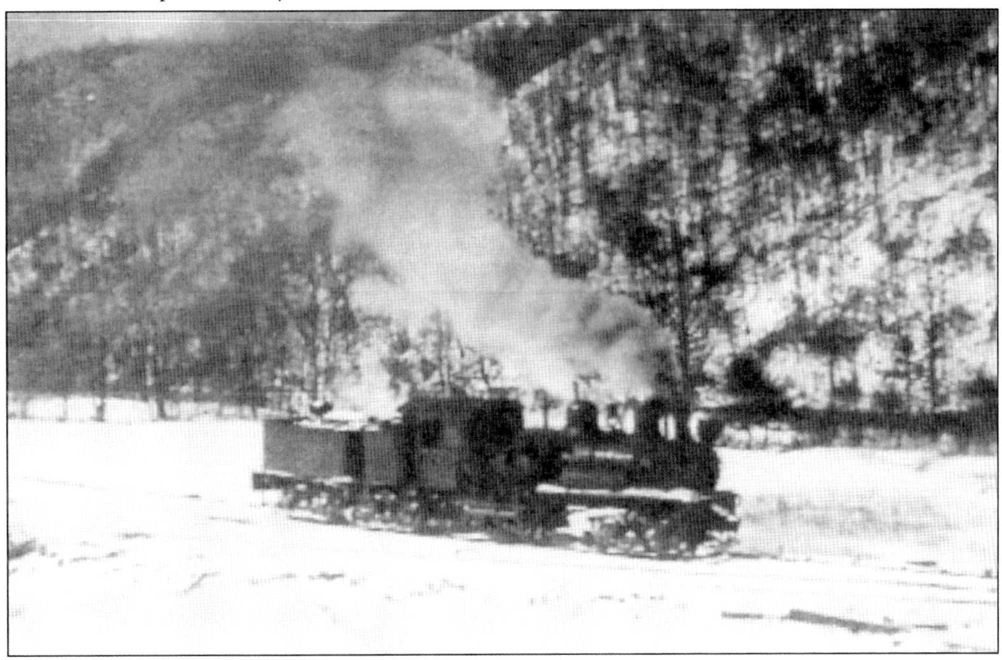

Burning Coal. Smoke and cinders announced the arrival of the train. Coal, a large part of the tonnage carried by the railroads, came from the King mines at Como and Baldwin mines in Gunnison. Owned by Union Pacific, the mines provided coal for Denver, South Park engines. The railroads preferred Baldwin coal despite its higher cost because it burned at a high temperature, producing less ash and fewer clinkers. (Courtesy of the Bill Fountain collection.)

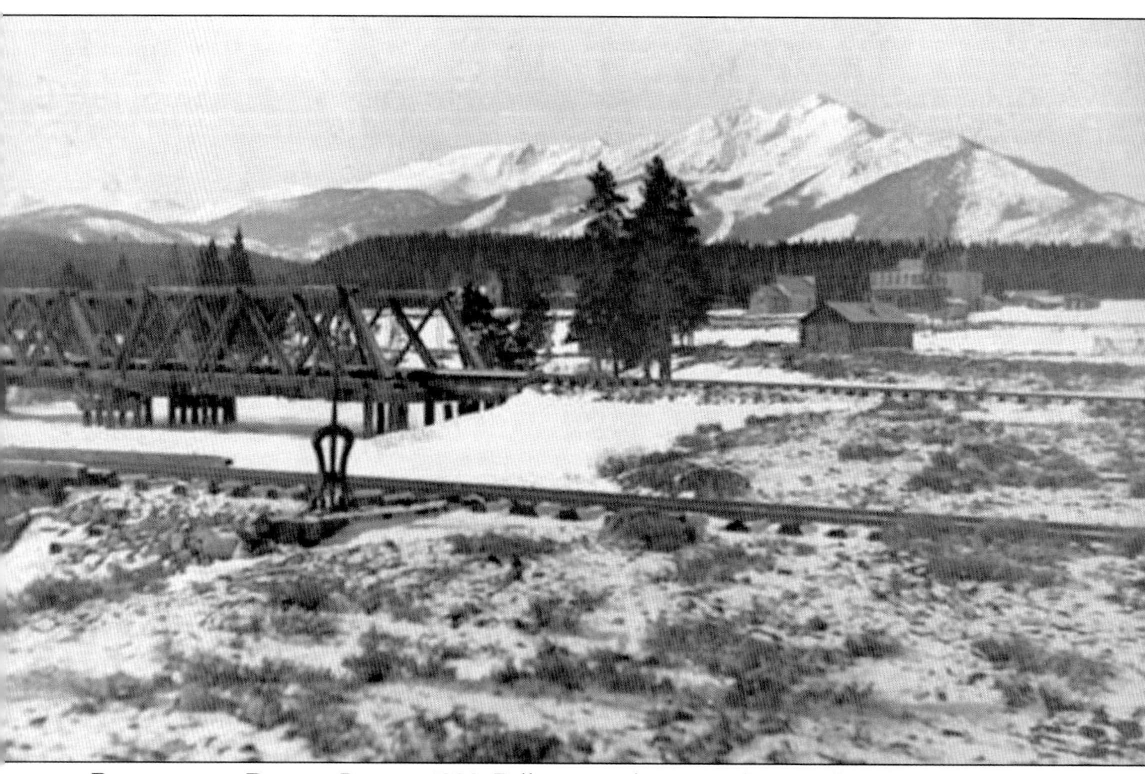

Railroads in Dillon. Prior to 1900, Dillon moved twice to be sure that the town embraced both railroads. In this photograph, looking west around 1912, the Colorado & Southern (C&S), formerly the Denver, South Park, tracks lie in the foreground, with those of the Denver & Rio Grande (D&RG) in the distance. The two railroads built differing styles of bridges to cross the stream. C&S used trestles with under-track support, while the D&RG used over-track support bridges mounted on trestle bents. (Courtesy of the Summit Historical Society.)

Four

Dillon and Keystone

Dillon's name and location are intimately tied to the railroad. On July 26, 1881, the Dillon Mining Company, led by Harper M. Orahood, Peter Halbert "Hal" Sayre, and others of Denver, patented a 320-acre townsite stretching mainly northeast of the Snake River. Savvy businessmen, they expected the railroad to run its tracks over one of the mountain passes, along the Snake River, and on to Leadville. Sayre, a trustee of the Denver, Georgetown, Utah Railway Company in 1872, knew the plans proposed by various companies for building into the mountains.

Hoping to make sure that the railroad would cross their townsite, the leaders of the company named their town for Sidney Dillon, an entrepreneur and incorporator for the Union Pacific Railroad. In March 1881, he became president of the Union Pacific. Four months later, the Dillon Mining Company appeared. The town's moves reinforce the importance of the railroad to the town. The first move, to a spot between the Blue River and Ten Mile Creek, incorporated the tracks of the Denver & Rio Grande, which arrived in November 1882. The second move, a month later to a site west of the Ten Mile Creek, assured that the town now included the newly arrived tracks of the Denver, South Park & Pacific as well as those of the Denver & Rio Grande.

The Denver, South Park proposed an extension that would tap the mines of the Montezuma and Chihuahua mining districts, cross Loveland Pass, and connect with the Georgetown line. The company's tracks arrived in Keystone, seven miles east, in January 1883. The people of Montezuma and Chihuahua began an active campaign to get the attention of the railroad. Newspapers were filled with anticipation; mining companies and individuals cajoled, petitioned, and threatened; and officials of the lines visited the mines to see the potential for themselves. But despite vociferous urging by many, the company did not build the extension. In 1884, while residents again tried desperately to obtain service, the South Park discontinued its trains to Keystone, saying the line was not profitable.

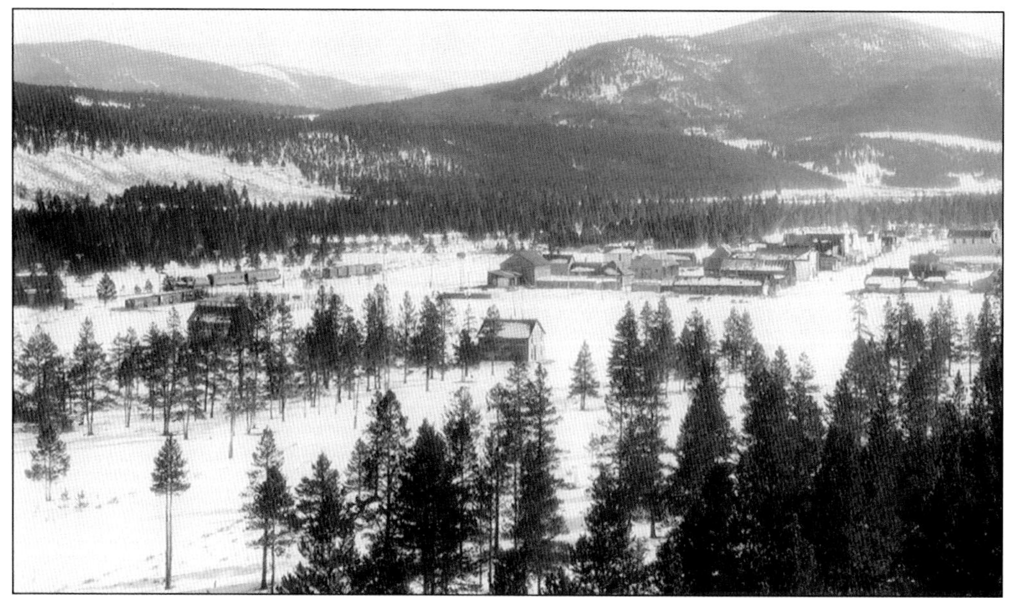

Dillon Railroads. Both narrow-gauge railroads served Dillon. The lifeblood of the county before the automobile, the railroads carried freight, coal, lumber, cattle, sheep, ore, and passengers. However, they were not the panacea people expected. High rates, irregular schedules, unclean cars, and inefficient engines plagued the railroads and reduced profits. (Courtesy of the Frisco Historic Park & Museum.)

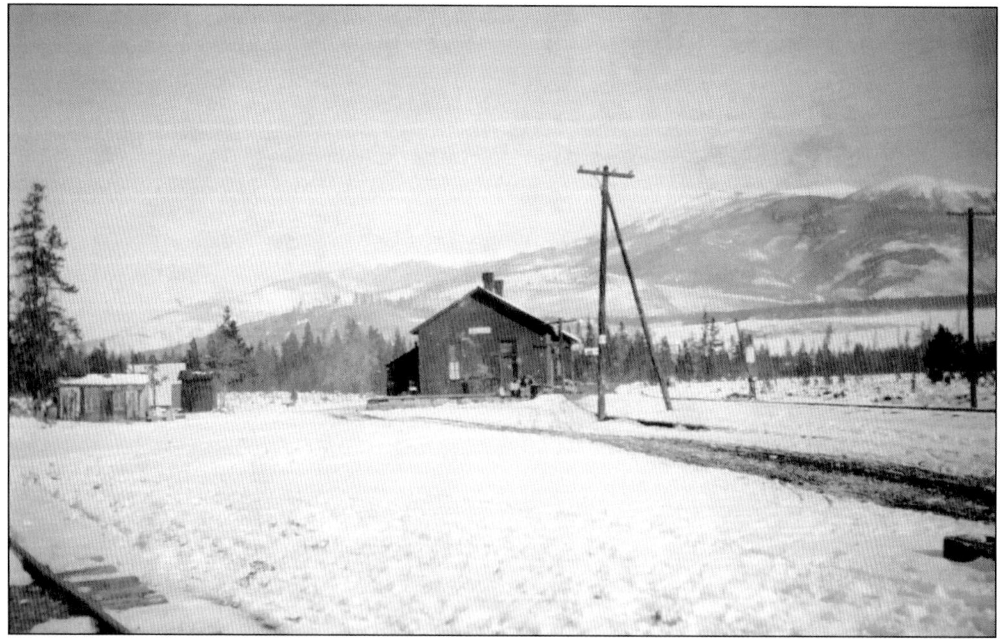

Railroad Facilities in Dillon. The Denver, South Park and the Denver & Rio Grande shared a depot in Dillon. Located on the southwest corner of Ninth Street and Ryan Avenue, the depot had a 232-foot-long boardwalk extending to the south. Although the town plat map shows room for thousands of residents and an extensive grid of streets and avenues, the town had only two major north-south streets. (Courtesy of the Summit Historical Society.)

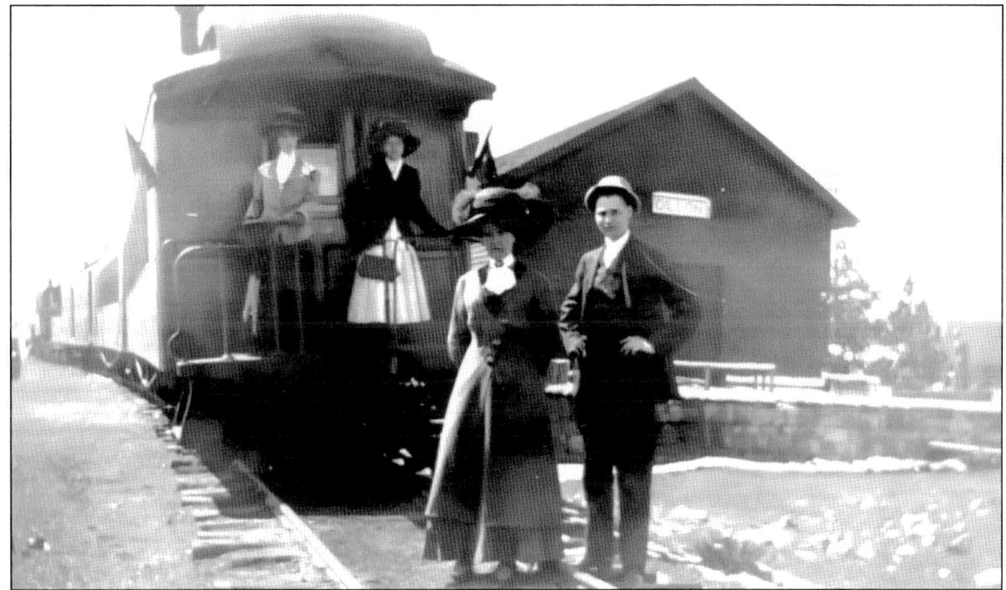

Ready to Travel. This nattily attired couple and their friends pose at the rear of the train next to the Dillon depot. Both the Denver, South Park & Pacific and the Denver & Rio Grande arrived in Dillon in late 1882. They shared the depot. Despite plans to do so, the Denver & Rio Grande never built beyond Dillon. The South Park line extended its tracks to Keystone. (Courtesy of the Denver, South Park & Pacific Historical Society.)

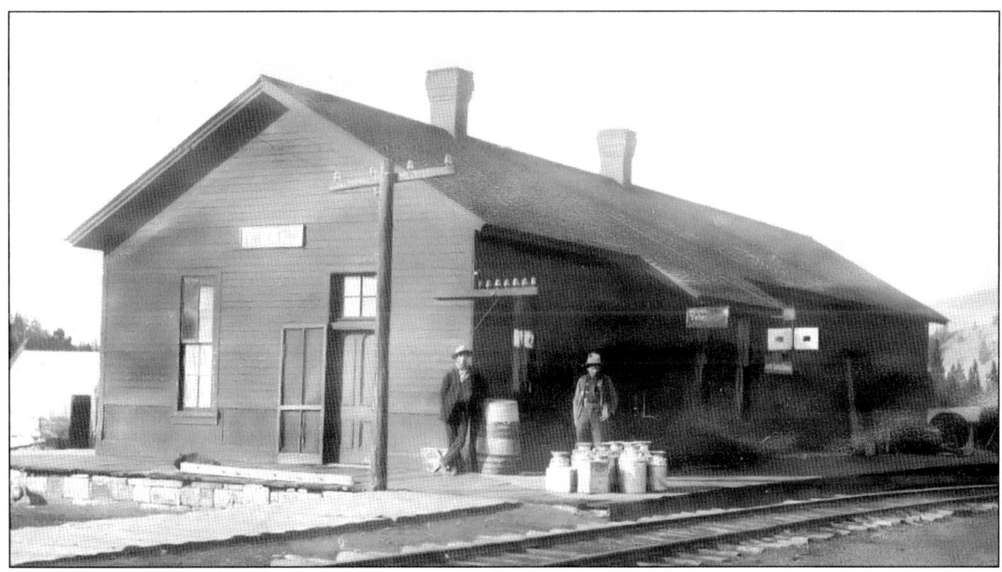

Cream Heading to Market. The town of Dillon moved twice so that the facilities of both railroads would be located within town limits. A two-passenger-car train moves through town on the Denver, South Park & Pacific right-of-way. Ranchers from the lower Blue River brought their cattle, sheep, hay, and cream to Dillon to await transport to markets in Denver and farther east. (Courtesy of the Denver, South Park & Pacific Historical Society.)

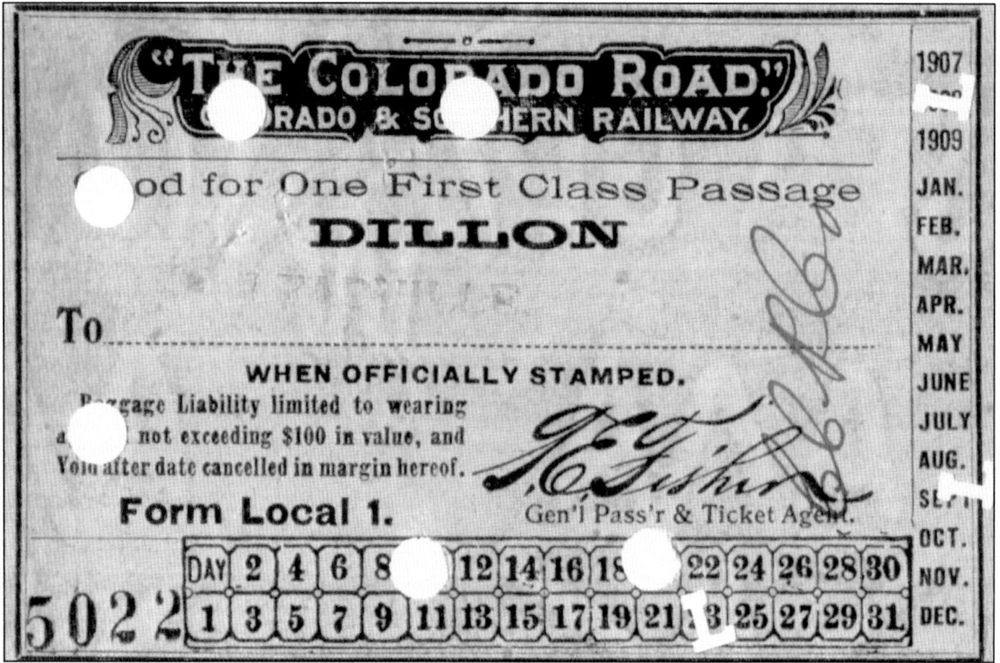

Ticket from Dillon to Leadville. This Colorado & Southern Railway ticket for passage from Dillon to Leadville from September 1908 carried the new slogan "The Colorado Road." The ticket noted that the company's baggage liability did not exceed $100, a princely sum in the early 20th century. T.E. Fisher served as passenger and ticket agent for many years. (Courtesy of the Denver, South Park & Pacific Historical Society.)

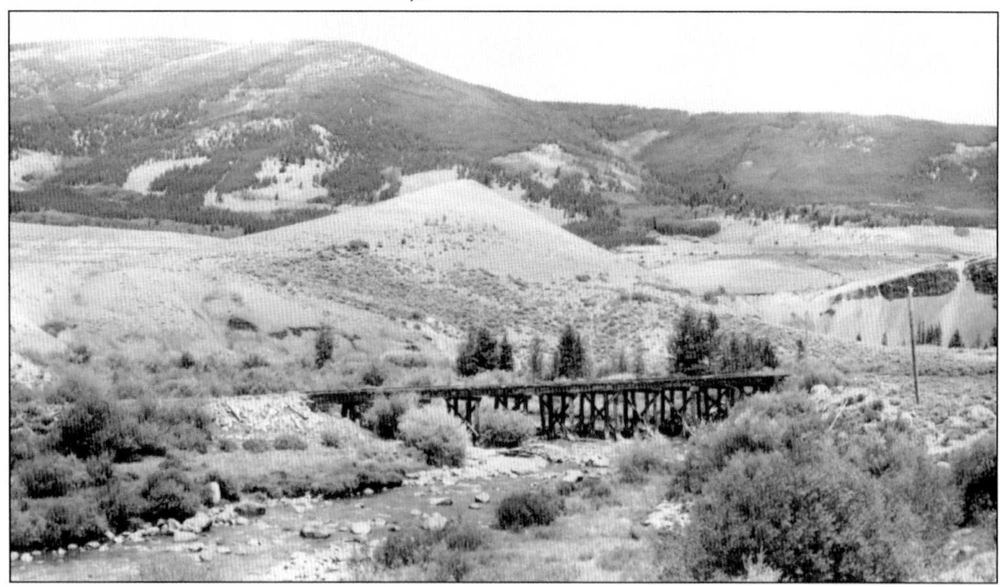

Snake River Trestle. About a mile east of the Dillon depot, trains crossed the Snake River on the way to Keystone. Today, Lake Dillon covers the site. Just to the right of the trestle is the old right-of-way. The area where Swan Mountain Road connects to Colorado Highway 6 was known as Colligan. By July 14, 1939, the date of this photograph, the rails had been removed for about a year. (Courtesy of the Denver, South Park & Pacific Historical Society.)

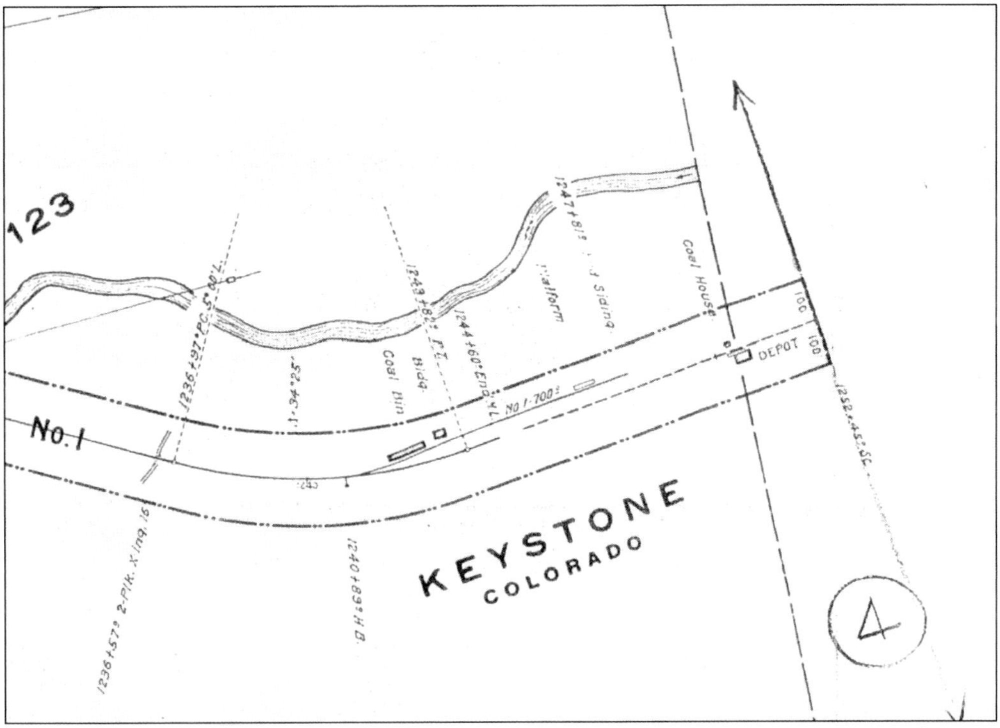

Colorado & Southern Map of Railroad Facilities in Keystone. By January 1883, the rails extended to Keystone from Dillon, a distance of 6.8 miles. The map shows a coal house facing the depot from the opposite side of the tracks and a coal bin next to the tracks west of the platform. From there, stages carried freight and passengers six miles to Montezuma and seven miles to Chihuahua on Peru Creek. (Courtesy of the Denver, South Park & Pacific Historical Society.)

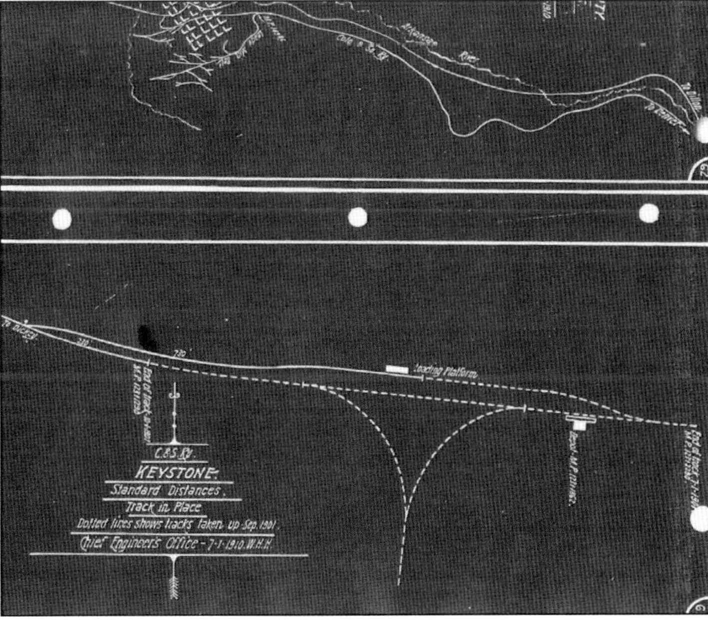

Map of Railroad Facilities in Keystone. By 1883, the Denver, South Park & Pacific line ended at Keystone. Facilities included a wye, depot, and loading platform. After the railroad removed some of the rails in September 1901, the depot no longer sat along the track. Prior to the 1890s, a daily (except Sunday) mixed train provided service from Breckenridge and Dillon. (Courtesy of the Denver, South Park & Pacific Historical Society.)

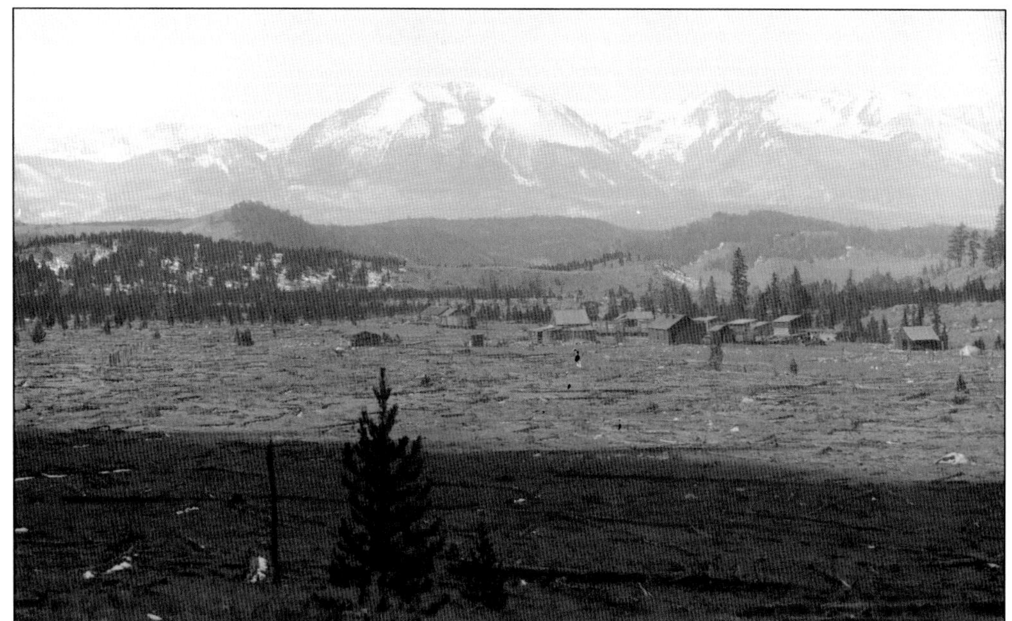

End of the Line. The Denver, South Park intended to extend the line along the Snake River to serve the Montezuma and Chihuahua mining districts and then join the Georgetown, Breckenridge & Leadville line that had been surveyed over Loveland Pass to the confluence of the Snake River and Peru Creek. When the railroad realized that the amount of ore coming from Montezuma would not generate handsome profits, it cancelled the plans. (Photograph by Dr. Clinton H Scott, courtesy of the Denver, South Park & Pacific Historical Society.)

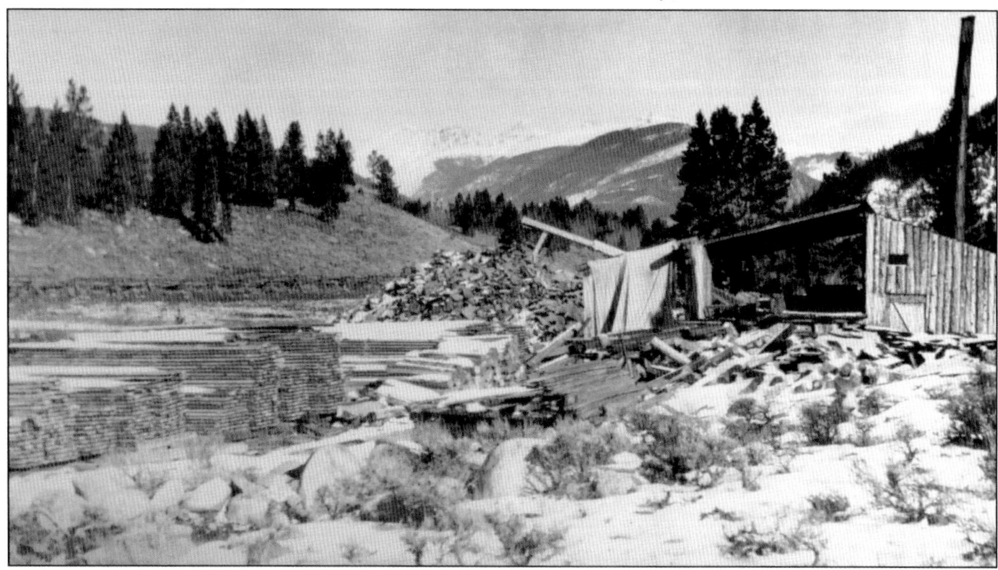

Sawmill in Keystone. Keystone and the surrounding area provided lumber for mills, mining operations, buildings, and railroad ties. Sawmills worked constantly to provide the sawn lumber. Waste lumber piled next to this sawmill became fuel for heating homes and other structures. Crews cleared many of the surrounding hillsides of trees to keep the sawmills running. Flatcars carried the sawn lumber to markets in the county and beyond. (Courtesy of the Denver, South Park & Pacific Historical Society.)

Five

Frisco and the Ten Mile Canyon

Knowing that its economic future rested with the railroad and wanting to be near the rights-of-way, Frisco donated land to both the D&RG and the DSP&P to insure their presence in town. The town granted the Denver & Rio Grande a 40-foot right-of-way in the alley between Main and Galena Streets with the condition that the railroad build a "good and sufficient depot" to accommodate business. The town donated 12 lots to the Denver, South Park, & Pacific as well as one block intended to be the town square. The right-of-way ran along the base of Mount Royal. Hoping to entice the Denver, South Park to move its headquarters to Frisco, the town discussed inducements that could be offered. Despite the concerted efforts, the dream of transforming Frisco into a major transportation hub never materialized.

Because both railroads planned to link the mines of the Ten Mile Canyon with smelters in Denver and Leadville, a way to fit two rights-of-way into the poorly drained, narrow canyon had to be found. Since it was there first, the Denver & Rio Grande chose the best route—the west side of the canyon. The railroad tried a variety of legal measures to prevent the South Park from entering the canyon and taking away business. A court decision in favor of the South Park allowed the railroad to build in the canyon as long as its facilities, including snow sheds, fences, and depot grounds, remained more than 50 feet from the center line of the Denver & Rio Grande right-of-way.

South of Kokomo, the width of the canyon became too narrow to maintain the 50-foot separation, requiring a judge to rule that the South Park could make two crossings over the Denver & Rio Grande tracks on trestles. To slow construction, the Rio Grande stationed engines on the tracks at the construction sites. Despite all of the problems, the South Park line to Leadville opened on December 21, 1884. The miners and merchants welcomed both railroads. The *Breckenridge Daily Journal* editor remarked that competition between the two would increase trade, cut travel time to Denver, open markets for ores at reasonable rates, stimulate prosperity, and hasten development.

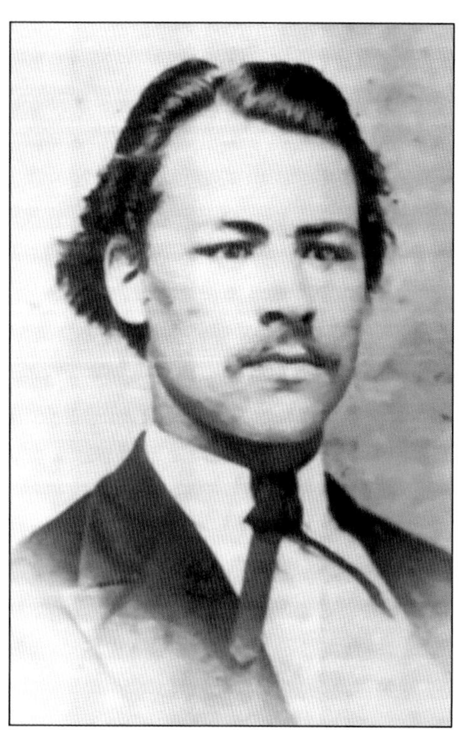

Henry Recen. Henry Learned, an agent for the St. Louis–San Francisco Railway Company, posted a sign on Henry Recen's cabin along the Ten Mile Creek that read "Frisco City." The word "Frisco" is derived from the "fr" in Francisco, the "is" in St. Louis, and "co" in company. People in the American West added the word "city" to the name of a town to indicate permanence and future growth. When Frisco incorporated, the town dropped "City" from the name. (Courtesy of the Denver, South Park & Pacific Historical Society.)

Map of Railroad Facilities in Frisco. The Denver & Rio Grande tracks followed the alley between Main and Galena Streets in Frisco. The right-of-way proceeded to the end of town before turning south and entering the Ten Mile Canyon. The depot sat beside the tracks at the west end of town. The company bought land for its station grounds on the west side of the Ten Mile Creek. (Courtesy of the Denver, South Park & Pacific Historical Society.)

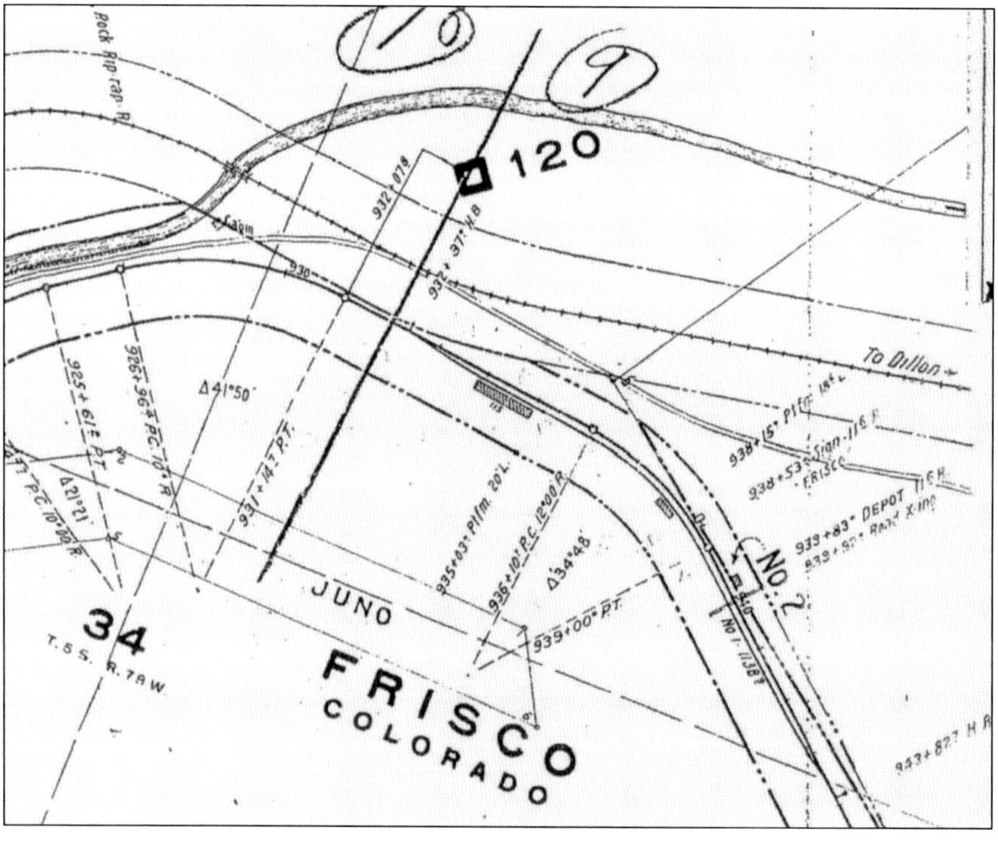

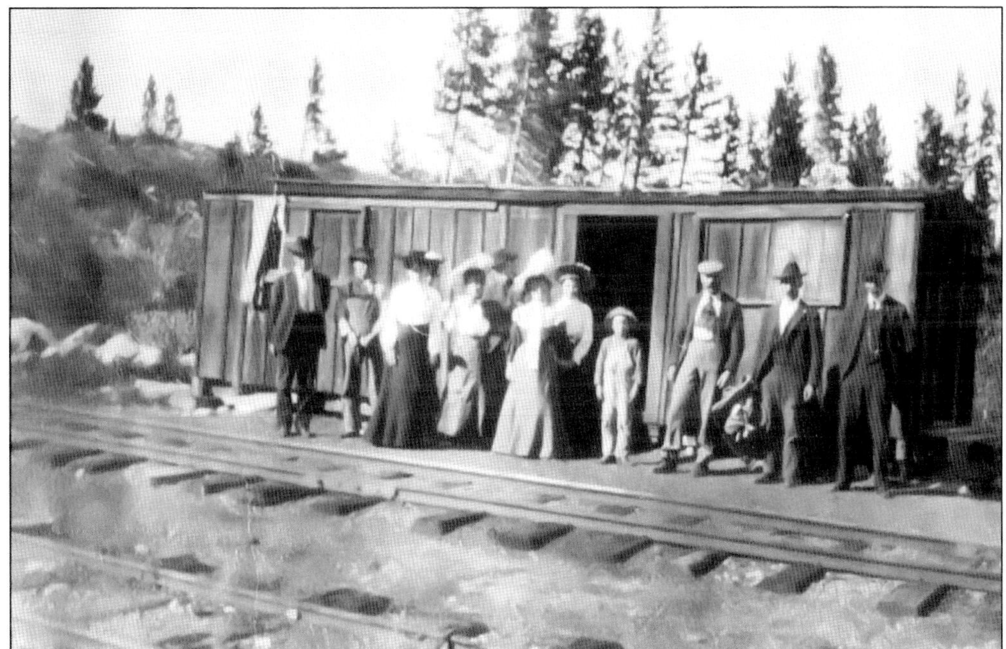

The 1882 DSP&P Passenger Depot in Frisco. Passengers waited beside the "carbody"-style depot for the often-delayed trains. Washed-out bridges, accidents, mud slides, icy tracks, flooding, and avalanches all impacted the schedule. Merchants complained about tardy deliveries. Joe Reeder, a saloon keeper in Breckenridge, planned to lay in a full winter's supply of beer before the "retarded" railroads allowed the beer to freeze in transit. (Courtesy of the Summit Historical Society.)

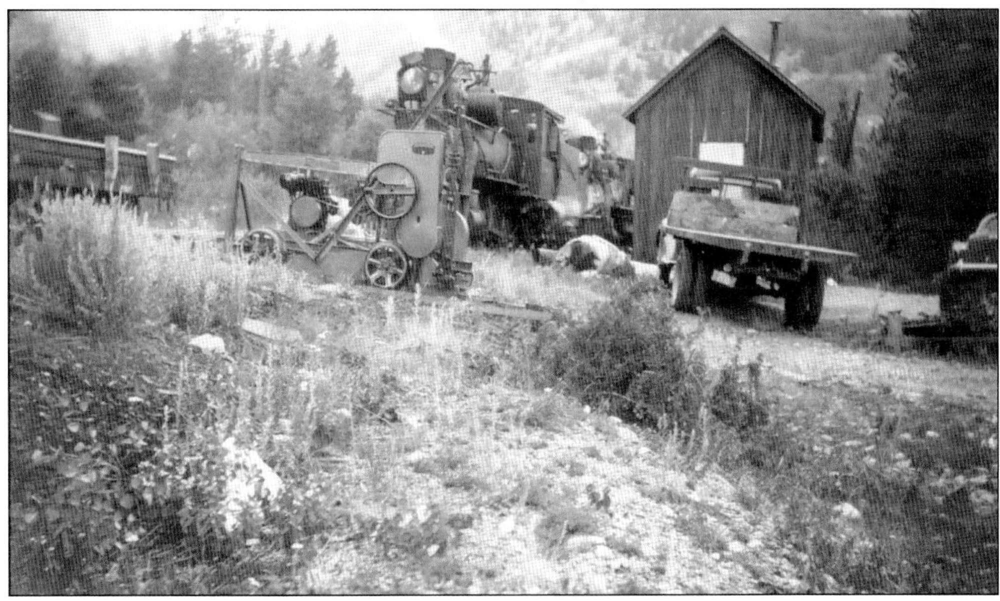

Second Colorado & Southern Railroad Depot, c. 1935–1937. This, the second depot in Frisco, stood at the same location as the earlier carbody depot and served the town until the railroad pulled up its tracks in 1938. Engine 71, leading an eastbound double-headed train, pauses at the depot. A piece of maintenance-of-way equipment sits by the tracks. (Courtesy of the Denver, South Park & Pacific Historical Society.)

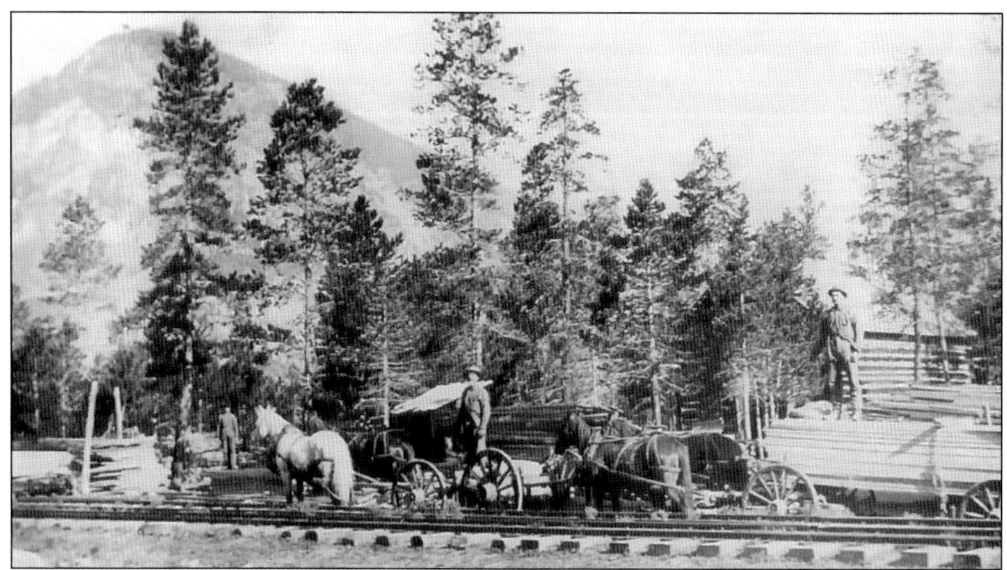

HAULING LUMBER TO THE DENVER & RIO GRANDE. Numerous sawmills near Frisco and throughout the Ten Mile Canyon provided the tremendous amount of sawn lumber required for mines, railroads, and buildings. Freighters hauled the lumber to the railroad for shipment to markets near and far. Here, men with a wagonload of finished lumber wait for the next Denver & Rio Grande train in Frisco. (Courtesy of the Denver, South Park & Pacific Historical Society.)

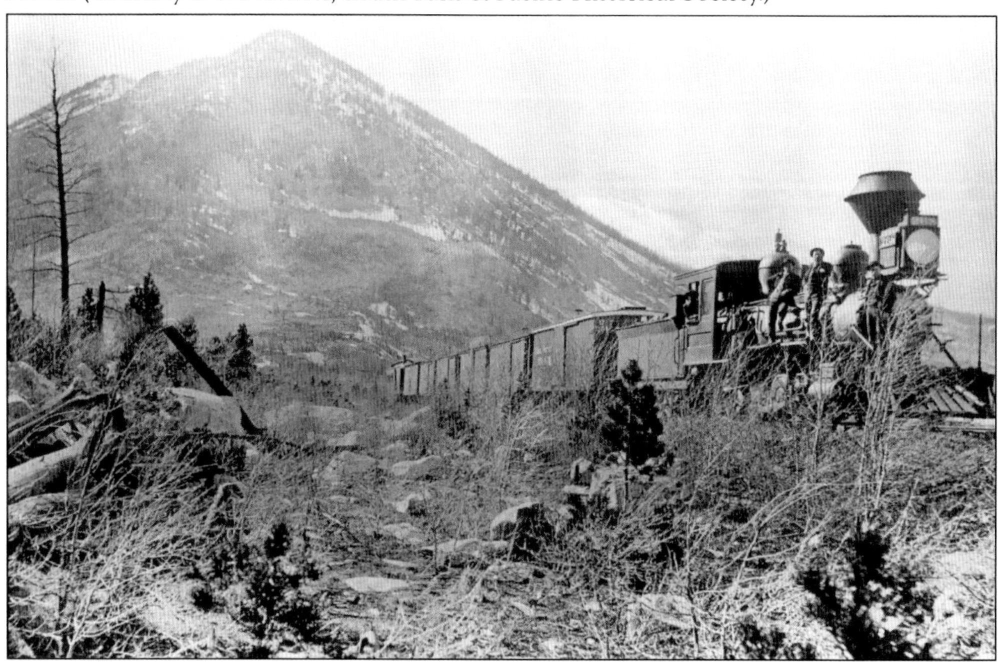

DENVER, LEADVILLE & GUNNISON ENGINE 268. Although county residents as well as newspaper editors complained about the inability of the railroads to meet posted schedules, trains often stopped to allow photographers and passengers to record their trip. In this c. 1895 photograph, the crew of this mixed freight and passenger train poses just south of Frisco for a photographer. The Denver, Leadville & Gunnison tracks hugged Ophir Mountain, passing to the south of Frisco. (Courtesy of the Denver, South Park & Pacific Historical Society.)

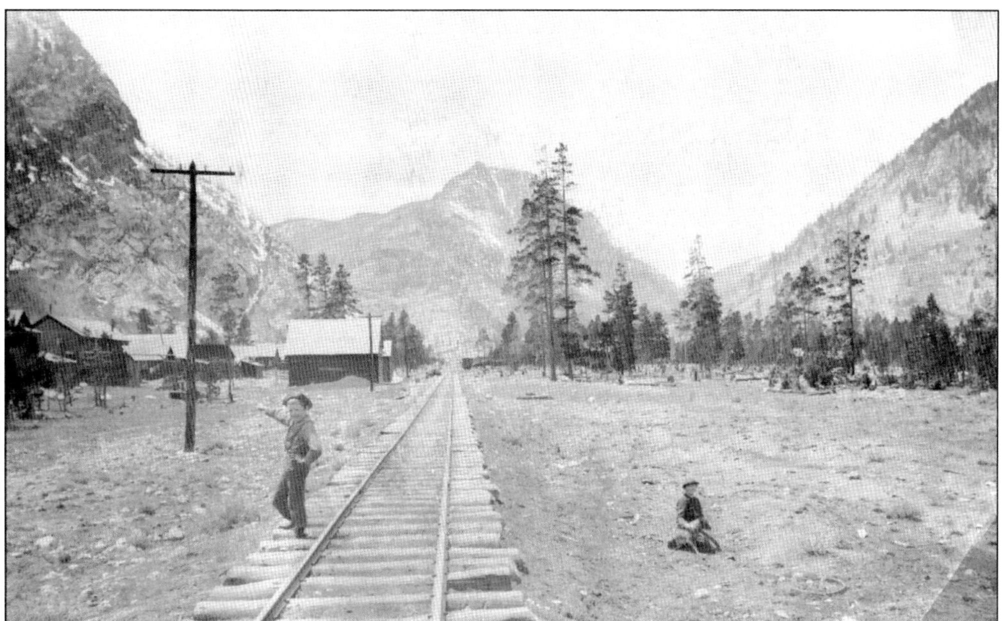

Right-of-Way in Frisco. Both the Colorado & Southern and the Denver & Rio Grande issued postcards to attract customers. This card, originally colorized and published by the Colorado & Southern Railroad, features the Denver & Rio Grande track entering Frisco. The Denver, South Park & Pacific track ran along the base of the mountain to the south. (Courtesy of the Frisco Historic Park & Museum.)

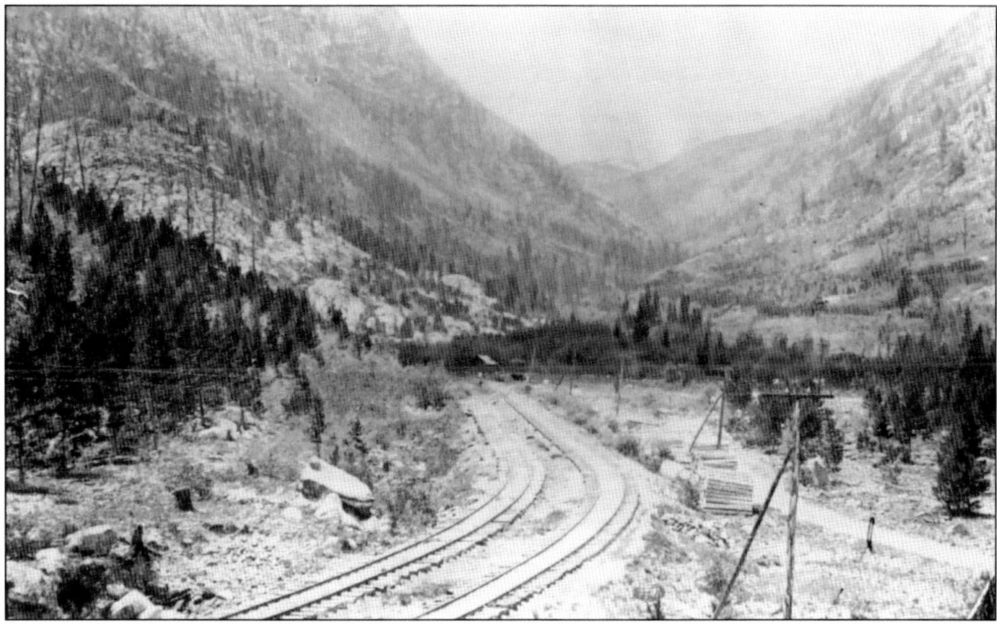

Denver, South Park Track and Siding. The Denver, South Park's tracks were laid along the eastern side of the Ten Mile Canyon. Because none of the facilities of the railroad could be closer than 50 feet to the center of the Denver & Rio Grande right-of-way, one of these tracks is a Denver, South Park & Pacific Track and Siding serving the mines found on the east side of the canyon. (Courtesy of the Summit Historical Society.)

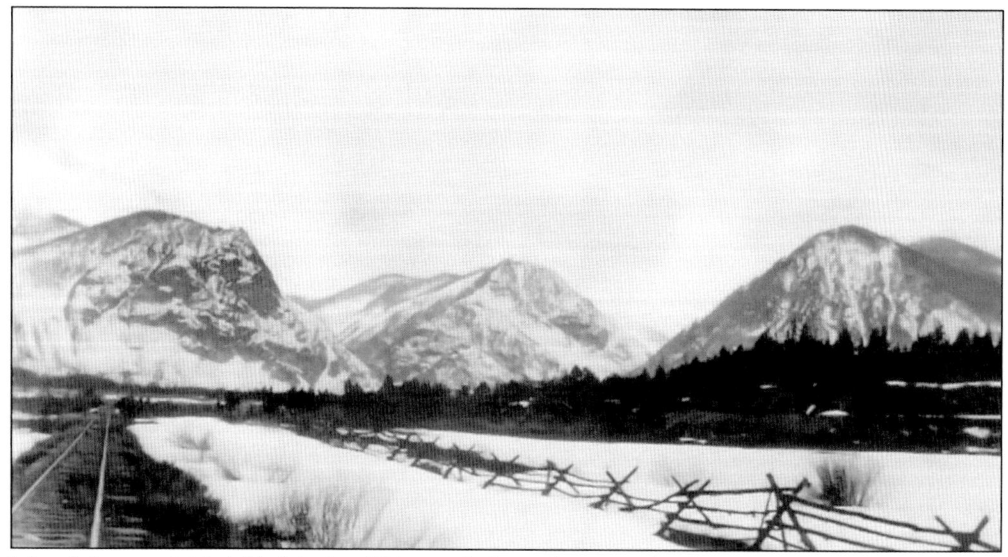

Mile Marker 309. Mile Marker 309 stood along this stretch of Denver & Rio Grande track leading to Frisco and the Ten Mile Canyon. The number "309" indicated the distance in track miles to Denver. Although the town was not that far away as the crow flies, the Denver & Rio Grande route led west to Leadville, south through the Arkansas Valley to Cañon City and Pueblo, and then north to Denver. Dillon Reservoir now covers this ranch land. (Courtesy of the Denver, South Park & Pacific Historical Society.)

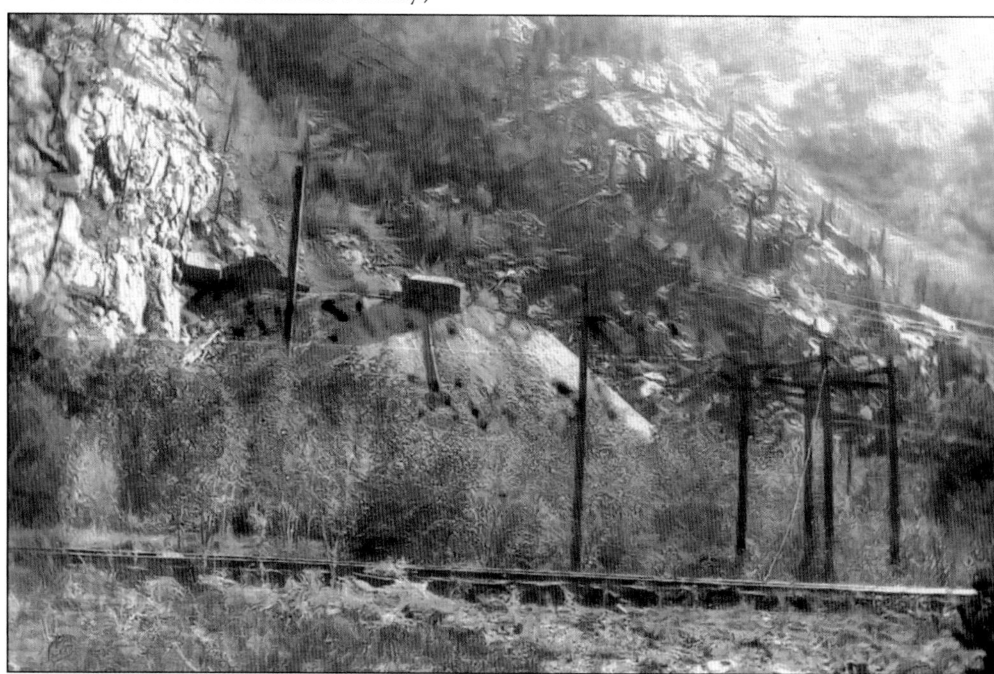

King Solomon Mine. The buildings of the King Solomon mine, west of Frisco, overlook both the Denver, South Park & Pacific tracks on the east side of the Ten Mile Canyon and the Denver & Rio Grande tracks (foreground) on the west side of the canyon. The Ten Mile Creek flows in the willows between the two rights-of-way, and the powerhouse smokestack towers over the trees. (Courtesy of the Denver, South Park & Pacific Historical Society.)

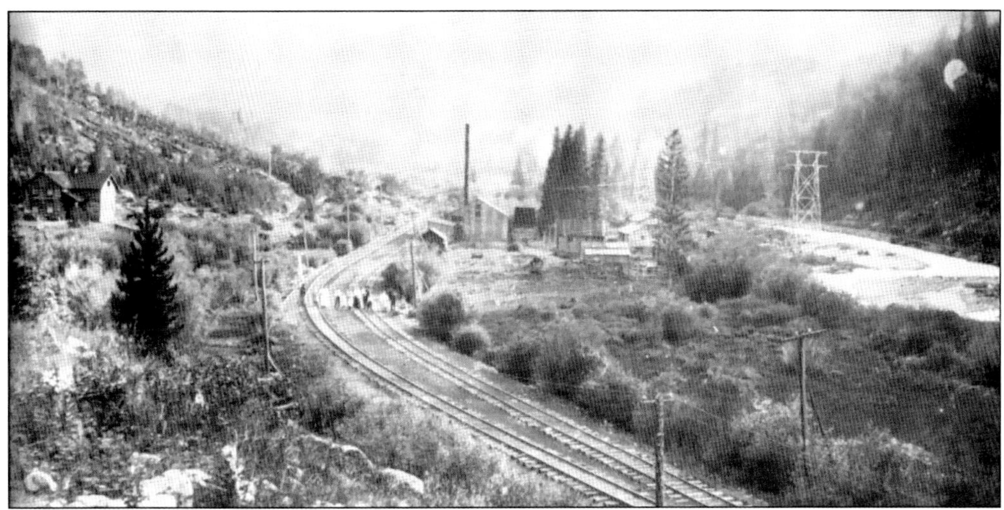

Panorama of Curtin. Sometimes wide and sometimes narrow, the Ten Mile Canyon became a major thoroughfare for goods and people. The Denver, South Park main line and siding hugged the eastern side of the canyon. The section house stood on a rise overlooking the tracks. The power plant, with its towering smokestack, provided power for nearby mines. The Ten Mile Creek flowed west of the settlement. The Denver & Rio Grande laid its tracks on the western side of the canyon. (Courtesy of the Denver, South Park & Pacific Historical Society.)

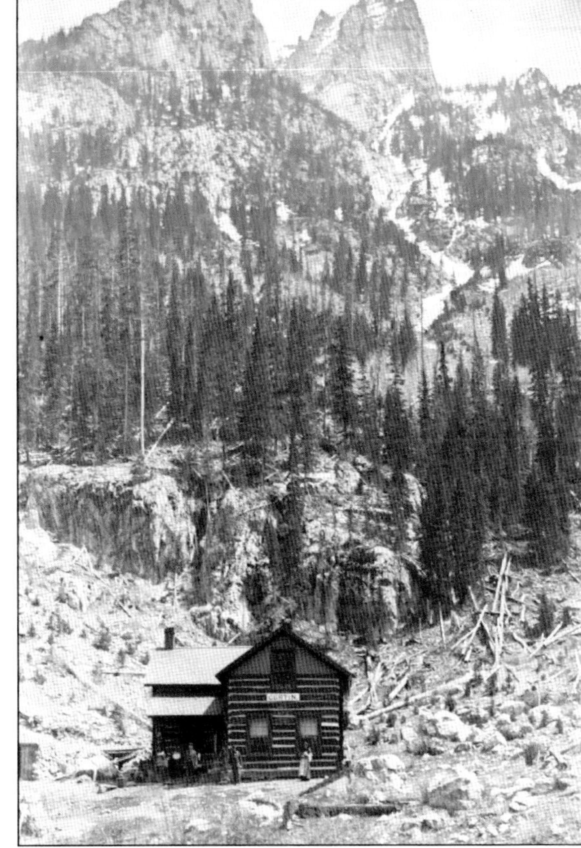

Section House at Curtin. The one-and-one-half-story log section house at Curtin sat on the eastern side of the canyon along the Denver, South Park tracks at an elevation of 9,259 feet (2,822 meters). A spur, named for nearby Uneva Lake, ran 728 feet beside the main track. The stop carried the name of Daniel Curtin, who supervised 160 men laying track in the canyon. (Courtesy of the Ed and Nancy Bathke collection.)

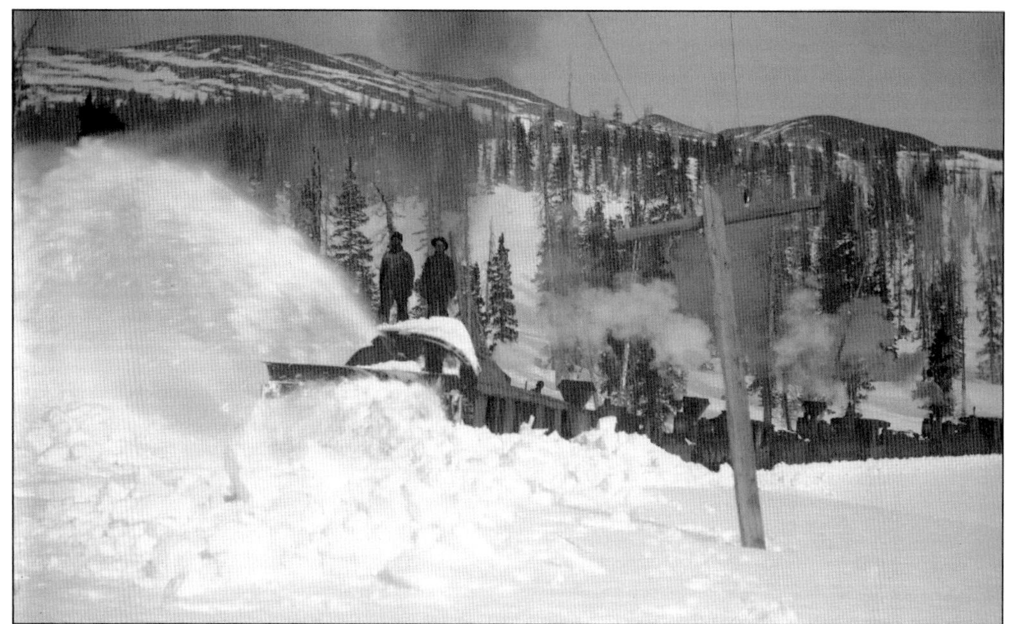

Nearly Buried by Snow. With only one rotary snow plow to serve the county, the train and its crew moved from spot to spot as needed. The Denver, Leadville & Gunnison, successor to the Denver, South Park & Pacific, was one of the first railroads to own a rotary snow plow. (Courtesy of the Bill Fountain collection.)

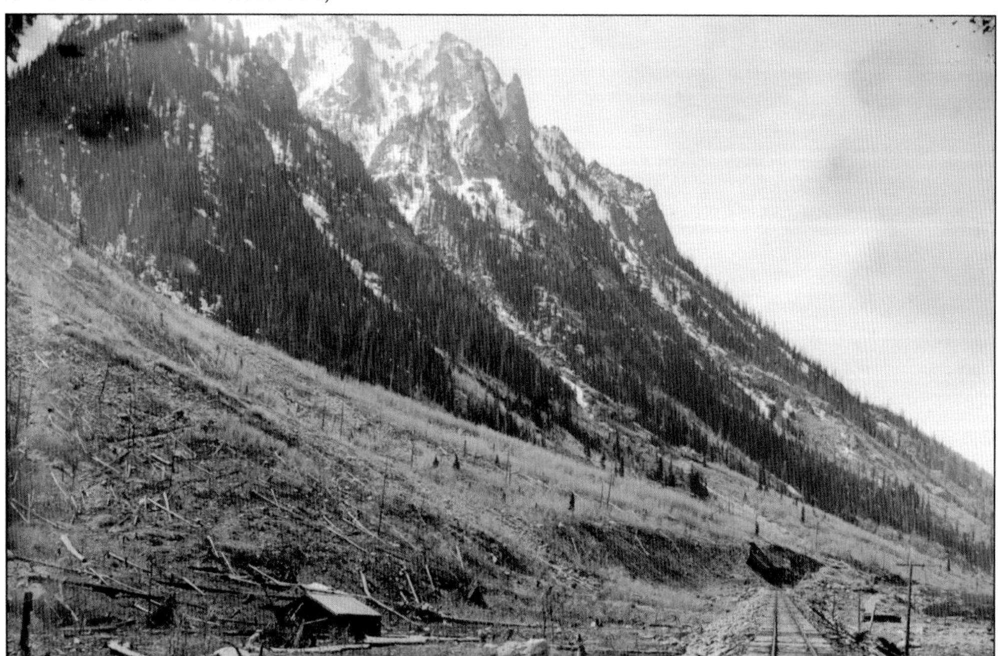

Difficult Construction. Construction in the canyon presented many difficulties. Benches wide enough to hold the tracks had to be blasted into steep mountainsides or through unstable land and rock slides. Gullies were bridged with intricate trestles or filled with tons of rock. Because of the rush to complete the line, crews did little grading. Each year, spring meltwater and crumbling hillsides created further challenges. (Courtesy of the Ed and Nancy Bathke collection.)

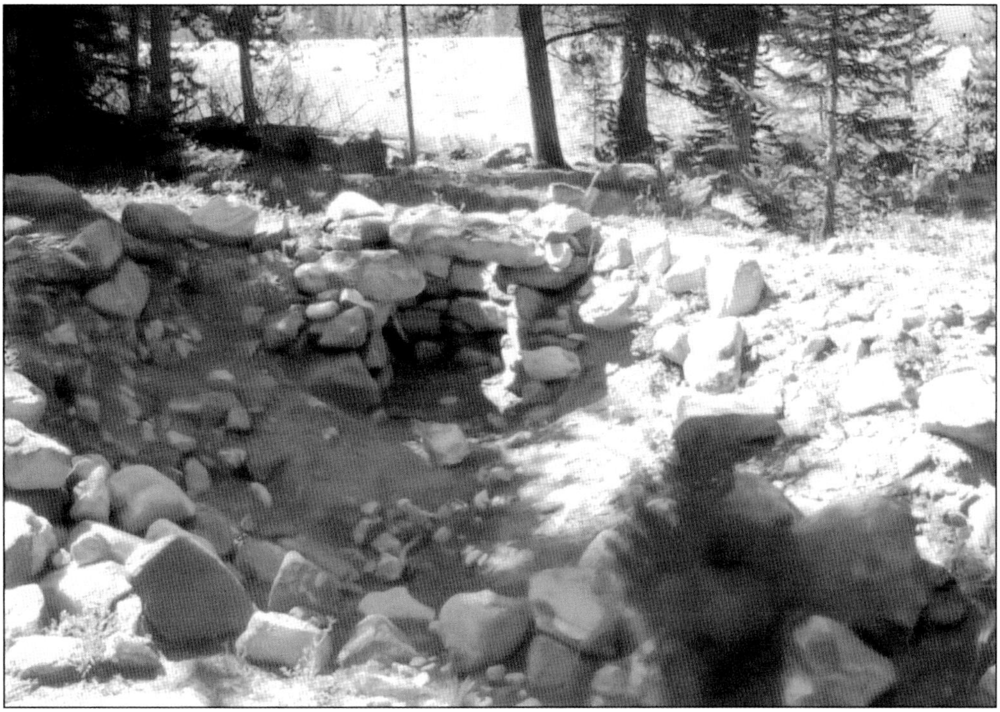

CONSTRUCTION CAMP. The railroad hired hundreds of men to construct the South Park's extension to Leadville. A large portion of them came from Midwestern cities such as Omaha, Chicago, and Kansas City. Not used to heavy labor at high altitude and lacking adequate clothing and blankets, many developed pneumonia. They lived in camps such as the one at Officer's Gulch. Stone foundations for the temporary structures that housed the workers can still be seen along Interstate 70. (Courtesy of the Denver, South Park & Pacific Historical Society.)

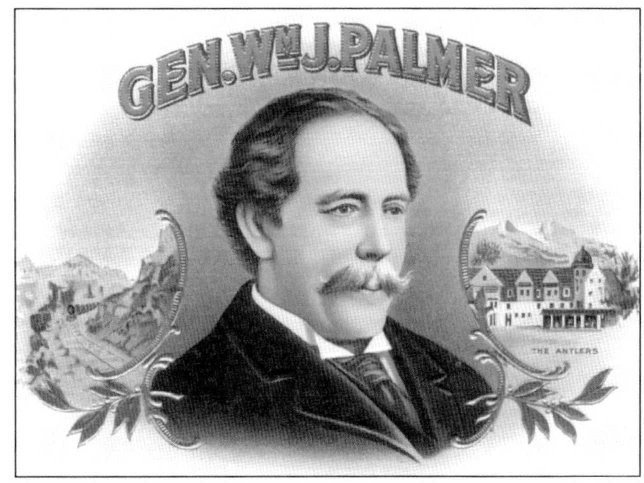

WILLIAM JACKSON PALMER. William Jackson Palmer, the president of the Denver & Rio Grande, felt that "a population engaged in mining is by far the most profitable of any for a railroad." He built the Leadville, Ten Mile & Breckenridge Railroad (officially the Leadville & Ten Mile Narrow-Gauge Railroad), which ran from Leadville through the Ten Mile Canyon to Dillon, a distance of 36 miles. (Courtesy of the Denver, South Park & Pacific Historical Society.)

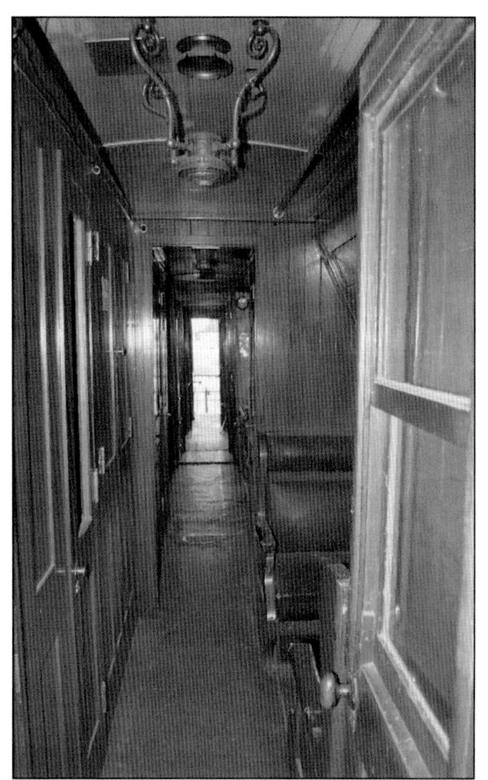

INTERIOR OPULENCE. This interior view of the Denver & Rio Grande business car B-1 conveys the level of opulence enjoyed by the railroad's "brass hats" on their journeys over the line. Fancy oil lamps hung from the ceiling. Day seats converted into lower and drop-down upper berths to accommodate overnight travel, as seen in the opening to the first compartment on the right. (Courtesy of the Denver, South Park & Pacific Historical Society.)

INTERIOR LIGHTING. Adams & Westlake lamps, such as this, provided interior illumination on Denver & Rio Grande passenger coaches. Although usually constructed of shiny brass, some were nickel plated. This example features four ceiling mounting legs, one large fuel canister, and two chimneys. Three or four of these lamps provided light in each narrow-gauge passenger car. Although many companies provided lamps for railroads, Adams & Westlake, based in Chicago, lighted the most cars. (Courtesy of the Denver, South Park & Pacific Historical Society.)

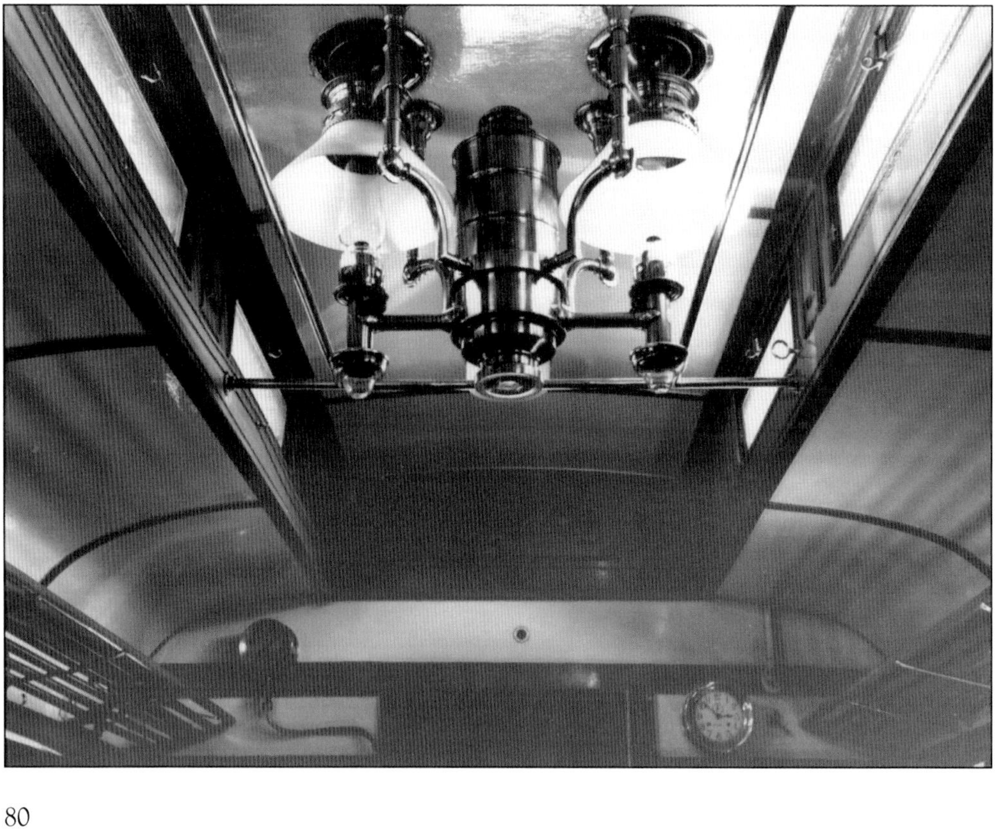

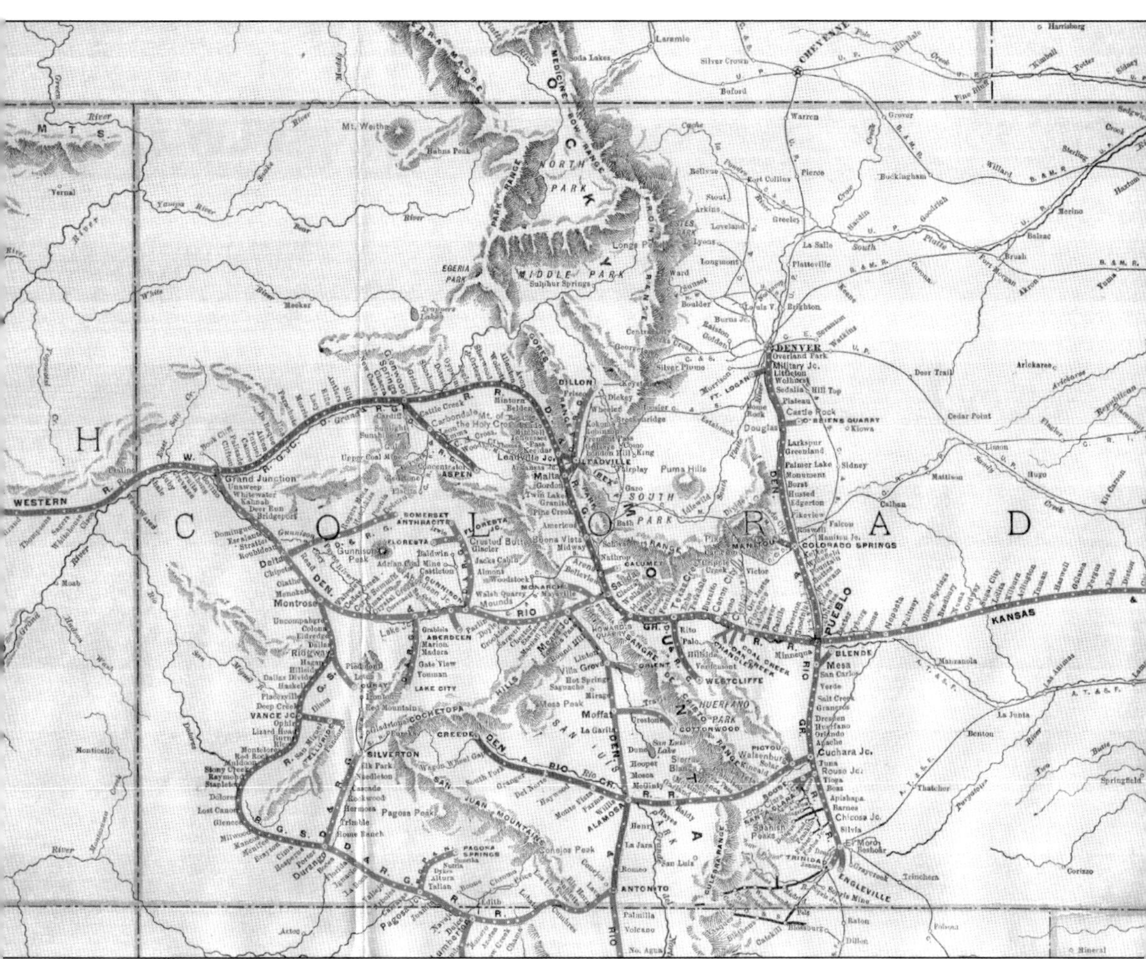

Map of the Denver & Rio Grande Railroad System. The Denver & Rio Grande system had more track miles in Colorado than any other railroad. Crews worked through very difficult weather laying the track through the canyon but finally reached Dillon in November 1882. The company considered extending its service south to Breckenridge and north to Kremmling but did not complete the projects. (Courtesy of the Denver, South Park & Pacific Historical Society.)

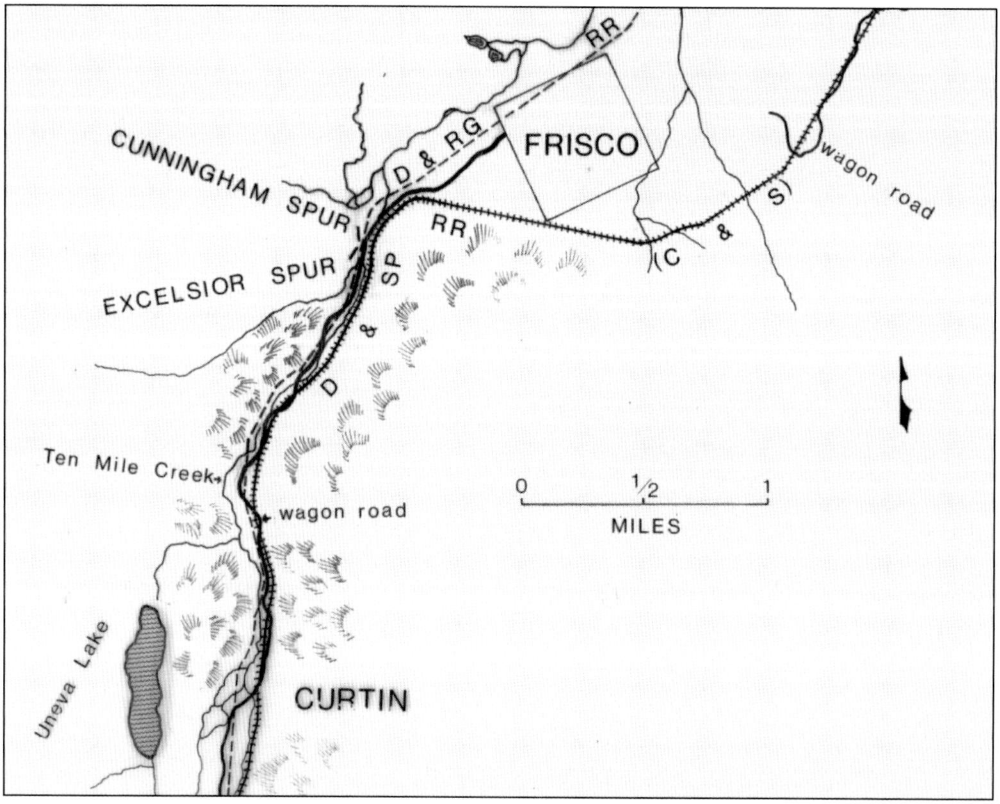

Transportation Network in the Northern and Middle Ten Mile Canyon. Two railroad rights-of-way, a wagon road, and the meandering Ten Mile Creek lay side-by-side in the narrow canyon on this undated map. The railroads built spurs and sidings to serve mining and lumbering interests along the route. Above is northern Ten Mile Canyon; below is middle Ten Mile Canyon. (Both reproductions by Sandra F. Pritchard Mather.)

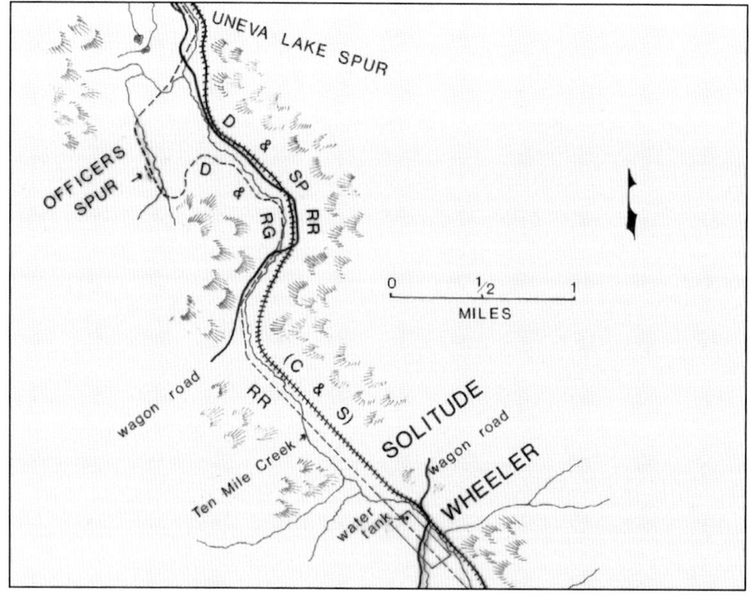

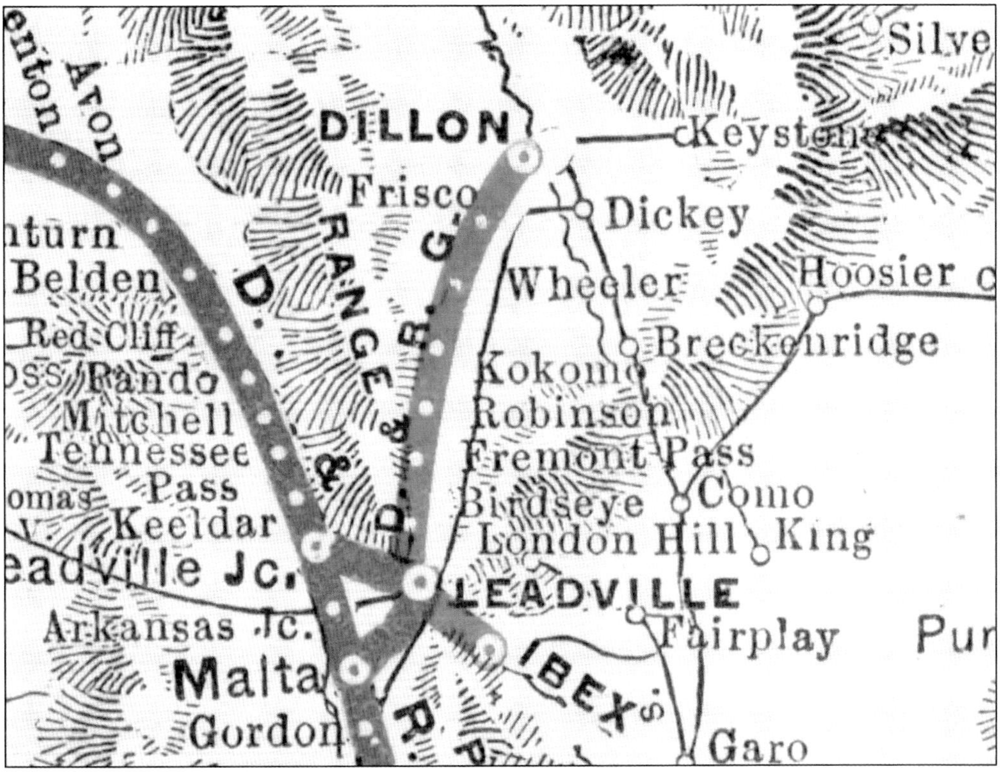

THE DENVER & RIO GRANDE IN THE TEN MILE CANYON. The 1904 map shows the Denver & Rio Grande system throughout the Ten Mile Canyon from Leadville to Dillon. The company considered laying track to Breckenridge but never proceeded with the plan. Although crews did some grading and laid about a mile of track north of Dillon, the plan to serve the ranchers along the lower Blue River was abandoned as unprofitable. (Courtesy of the Denver, South Park & Pacific Historical Society.)

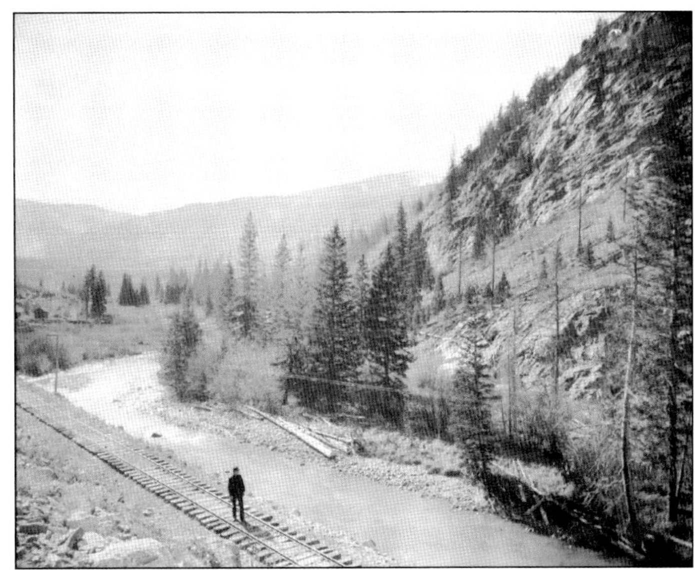

DENVER & RIO GRANDE GRADE NEAR FRISCO. Because it built first in the canyon, the Denver & Rio Grande claimed the higher, drier, and flatter west side of the canyon, thus avoiding the meandering Ten Mile Creek and some of the yearly spring-time floods. The Denver, South Park, relegated to the east side of the canyon, faced unstable slopes, wet conditions, and rough terrain as it laid its tracks. (Courtesy of the Denver, South Park & Pacific Historical Society.)

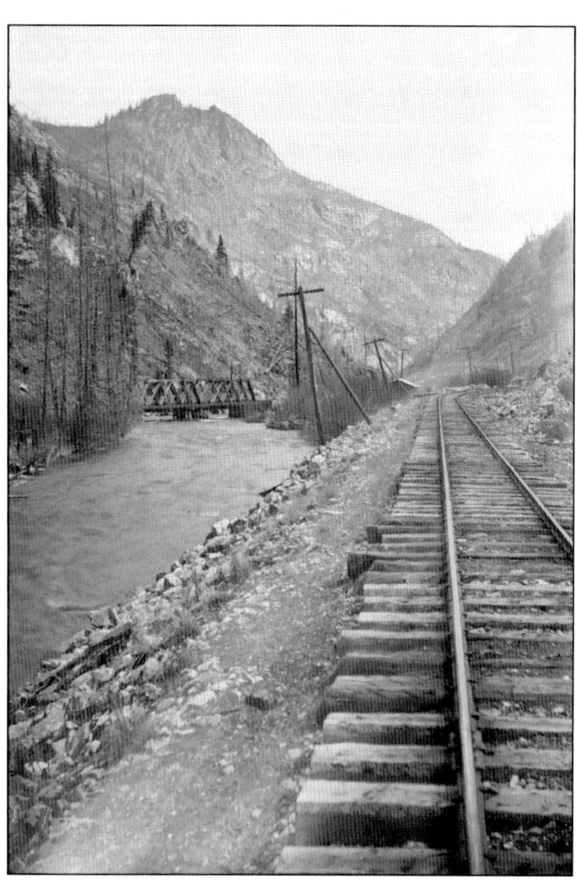

Denver, South Park & Pacific Grade in the Ten Mile Canyon. Between Kokomo and Solitude, today known as Copper Mountain, the Denver, South Park hugged the eastern side of the Ten Mile Canyon while the Denver & Rio Grande built on the higher and drier west side. In the distance, the Denver & Rio Grande tracks crossed the Ten Mile Creek on a two-span trestle bridge. (Photograph by Dr. Clinton H Scott, courtesy of the Ed and Nancy Bathke collection.)

Denver & Rio Grande Bridge Remnants. The two-span bridge seen in the distance in the previous photograph shows the ravages of time. The company removed the bridges many years ago. Only the bridge supports remain. The last of the supports for this bridge sits by the Ten Mile Creek on the east side of Colorado Route 91 just south of Copper Mountain. (Courtesy of the Denver, South Park & Pacific Historical Society.)

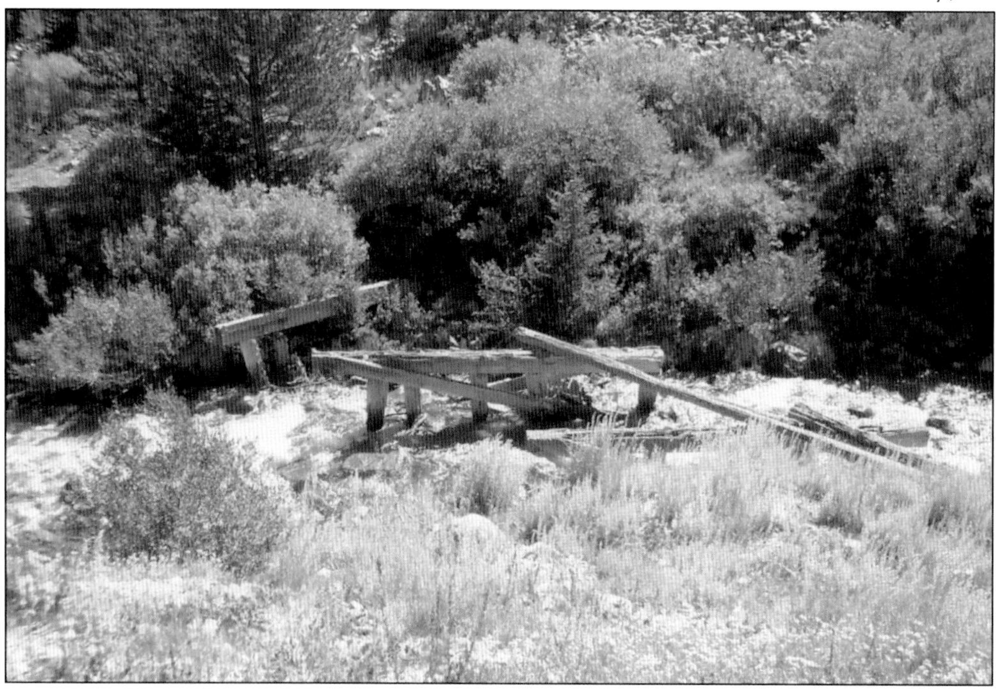

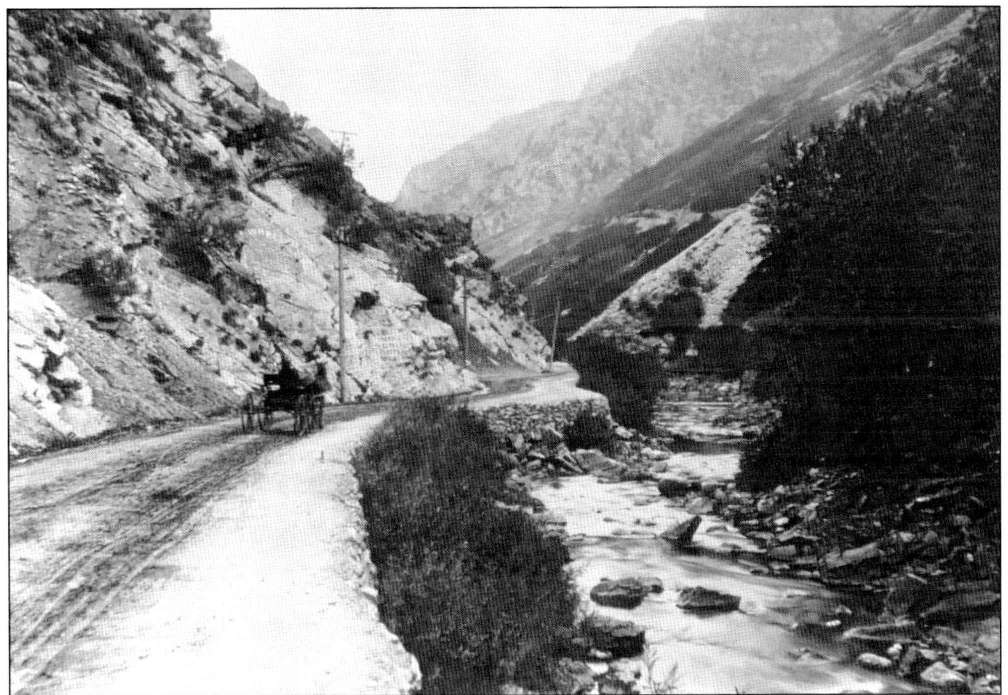

Dangerously Close to the Water. The Denver, South Park & Pacific faced many challenges in the narrow, flood-prone Ten Mile Canyon. Finding room in the canyon for the right-of-way proved difficult. Often the tracks could only be placed near the Ten Mile Creek, which flooded with snowmelt each spring, creating hazardous conditions for equipment, crew, and passengers. Throughout the year, avalanches, heavy snow, rock slides, and floods hurt the railroad's ability to earn a profit. (Courtesy of the Summit Historical Society.)

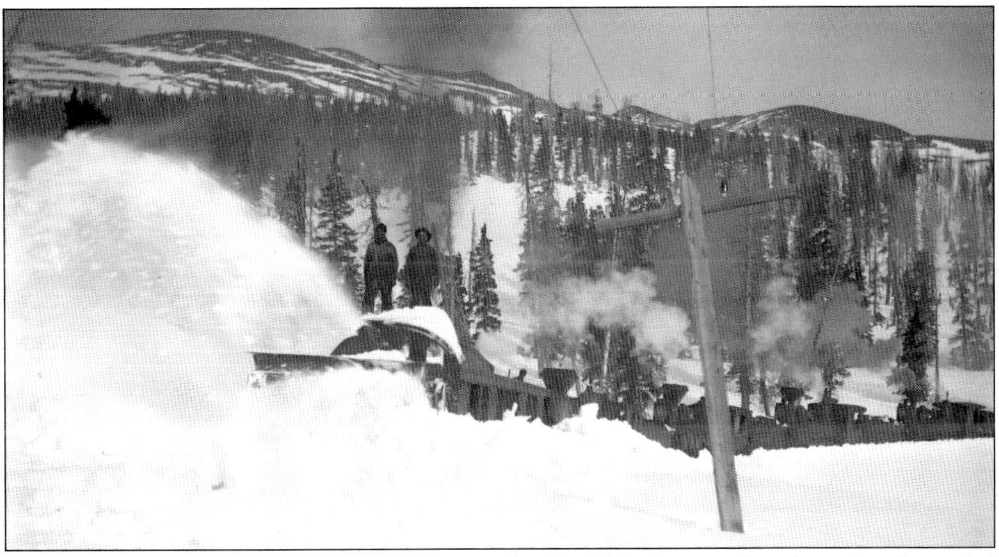

Rotary Snow Plow. Snow became so deep in the Ten Mile Canyon that the railroads needed rotary plows to clear the tracks. Working like a modern snow blower, the rotary plow chewed its way through a drift, throwing the snow up to 30 feet from the track. (Courtesy of the Denver, South Park & Pacific Historical Society.)

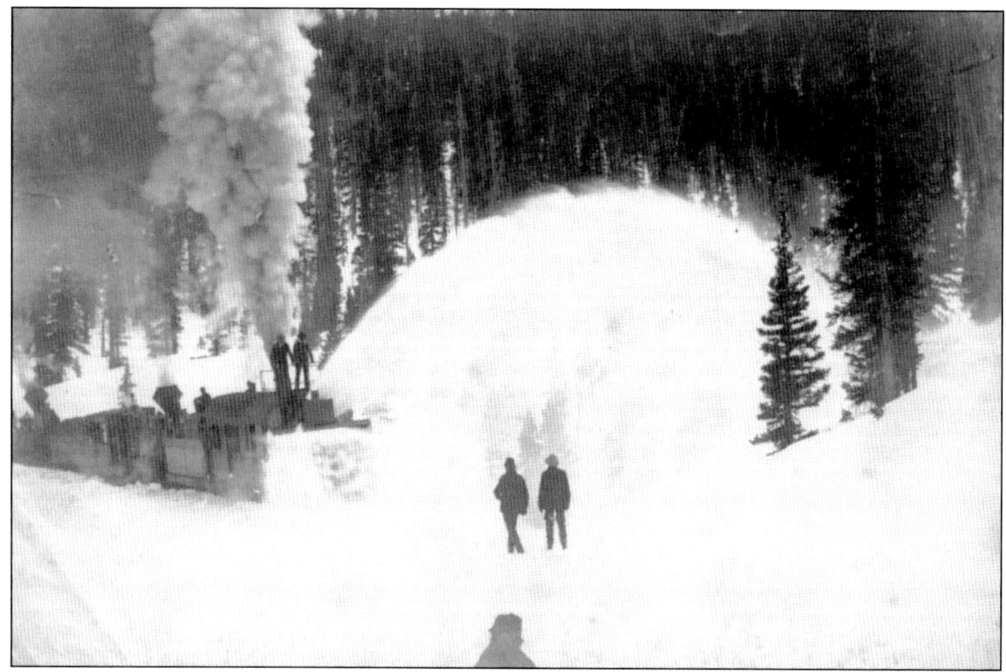

Throwing Snow. A rotary snow plow blew the snow either to the right or left, depending on the angle of the rotating blades. Naturally, downhill was the preferred direction, but if telephone or telegraph poles had been installed on the downhill side of the tracks, snow had to be blown uphill and could slide back down on the tracks. In this undated photograph, the rotary throws the snow uphill. (Courtesy of the Ed and Nancy Bathke collection.)

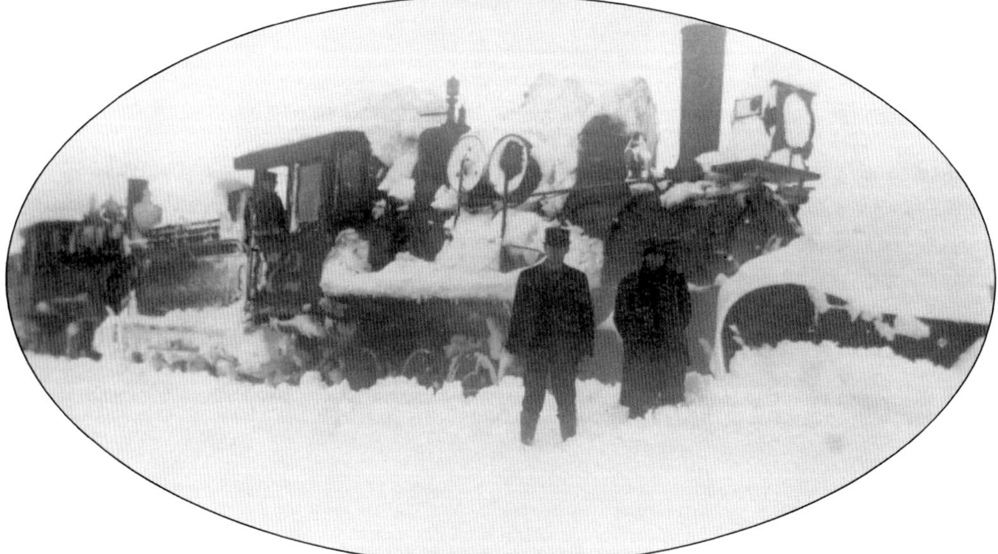

Snow-Covered Engine. The engineer and fireman worked with little protection from the weather. The cab on the fireman's side opened to the raging wind. A canvas curtain might have covered part of the opening. Ice formed on the walls of the cab, while snow covered the deck. Sometimes the ice built up so heavily on the outside of the cab that opening the cab door became impossible. (Courtesy of the Ed and Nancy Bathke collection.)

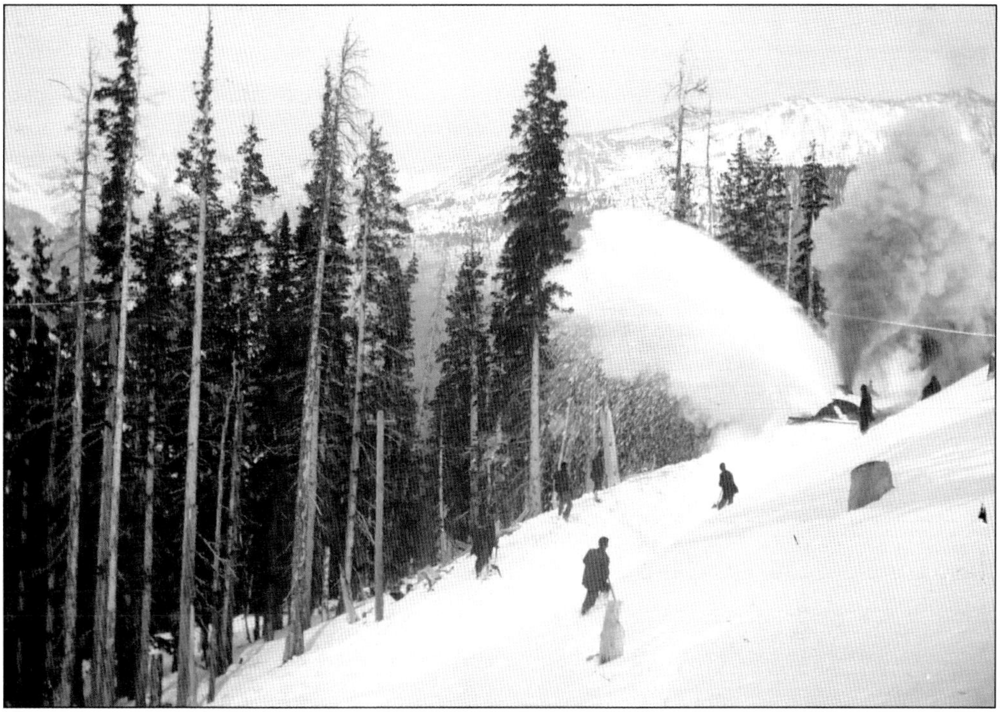

BATTLING SNOW DRIFTS. As the rotary plow blew snow from its path, strong winds swirled the snow around the rotary. The snow blew into the open cabs of the locomotives pushing the rotary snow plow, creating hazardous conditions for the crew. Though they wore multiple layers of clothing, the men experienced temperatures cold enough to cause frostbite on exposed skin. (Photograph by Dr. Clinton H Scott, courtesy of the Todd Hackett collection.)

HEAVY WINTER CLOTHING. To face the winter weather, with its winds strong enough to blow the coal off the shovel on its way into the fire box, men wore two sets of woolen underwear, two sets of pants, two shirts, two overalls, two sets of woolen socks, heavy leather boots, a heavy coat, two woolen scarves, a wool cap, and fur-lined gloves. (Courtesy of the Denver, South Park & Pacific Historical Society.)

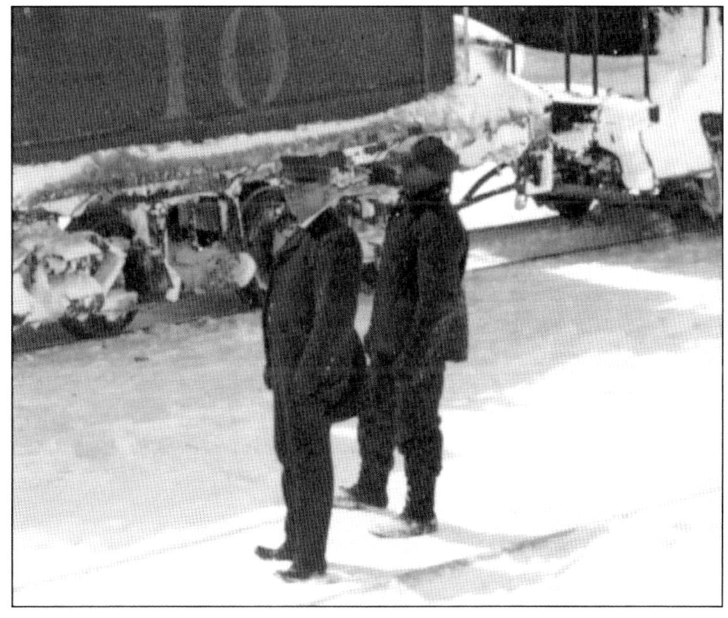

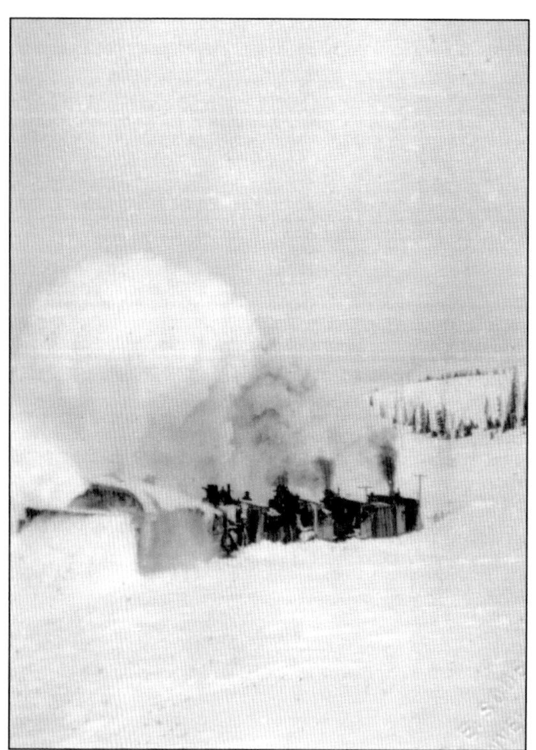

Heavy Snow. Deep snow required four engines to push this rotary snow plow. Sometimes the last engine faced backwards in case the rotary became stuck and the train had to back up through newly fallen snow. Shovelers lived in the boxcar outfitted for eating and sleeping seen between the third and fourth engines. The men rode the tracks all winter, going wherever needed. (Courtesy of the Summit Historical Society.)

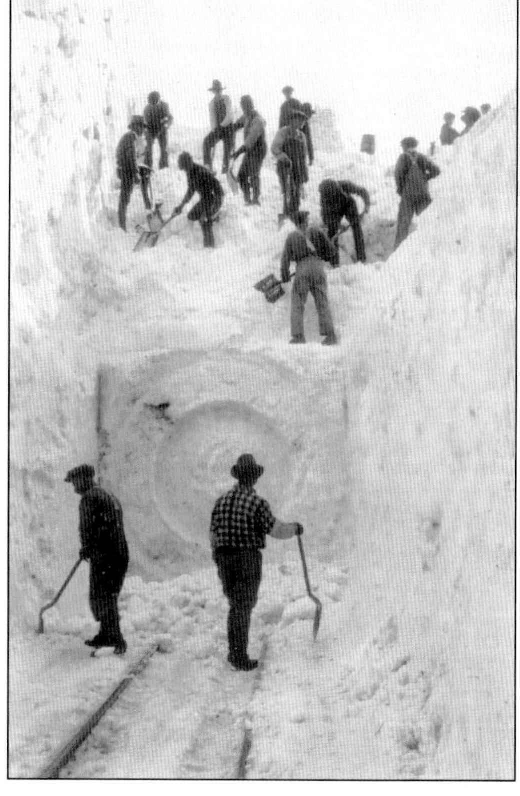

Deep Avalanche. When confronted with an avalanche, the rotary needed the help of the shovelers. The company hired as many as 60 men per year from the labor pool in Denver. The shovelers probed the avalanche, looking for boulders large enough to damage the blades. When it was safe to proceed, the rotary moved slowly through the avalanche while the shovelers continued to probe the snow in front of the rotary. (Courtesy of the Denver, South Park & Pacific Historical Society.)

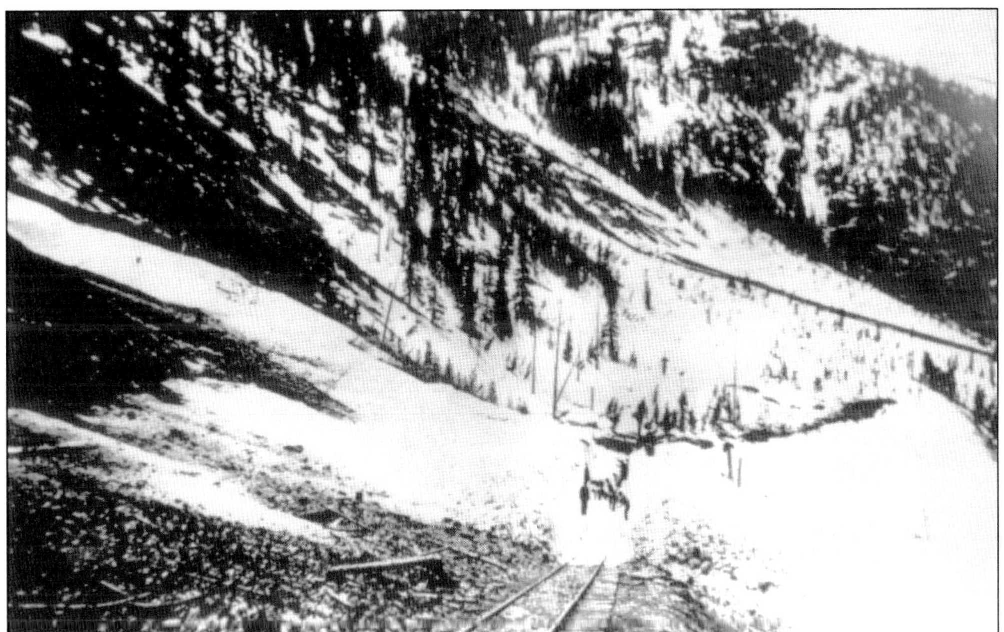

AVALANCHE IN THE TEN MILE CANYON. Bitter cold, howling wind, and blowing snow created hazardous travel conditions for trains and passengers. Avalanches, often caused by rumbling engines and shrill whistles, buried the tracks in snow, rocks, and uprooted trees. When clearing an avalanche required dynamite, crews had to replace the tracks damaged by the dynamite before the railroad could resume service. (Courtesy of the Bill Fountain collection.)

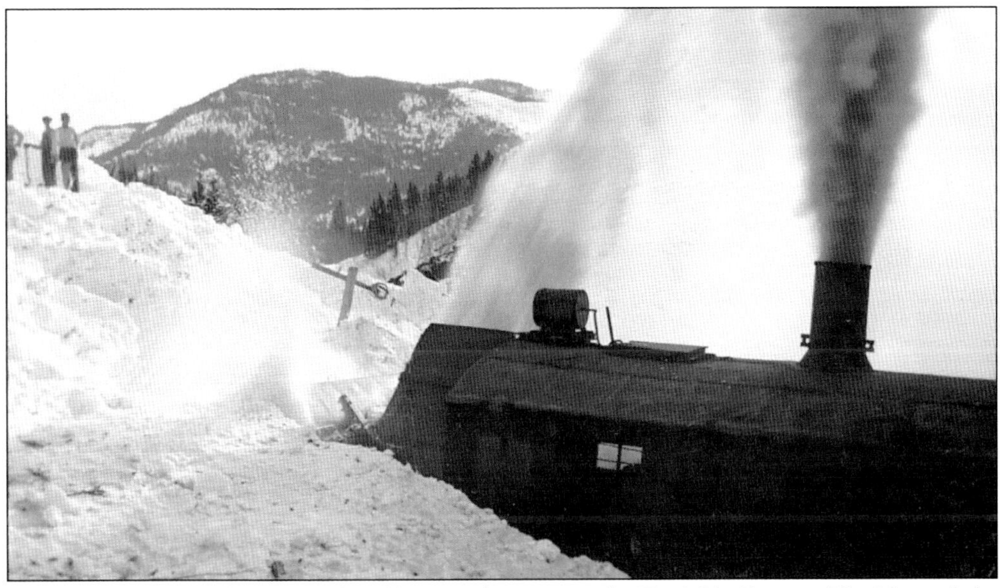

UNEVA SLIDE. Snow slides caused problems each winter in the Ten Mile Canyon. The Uneva Lake area near Curtin, west of Frisco, proved particularly troublesome each winter. Here, the rotary struggles to clear snow deeper than the top of its blades. When it goes as far as it can, it will back out and hand shovelers will shovel the top of the slide onto the cleared track. The rotary will move forward and throw that snow away from the rails. (Courtesy of the Denver, South Park & Pacific Historical Society.)

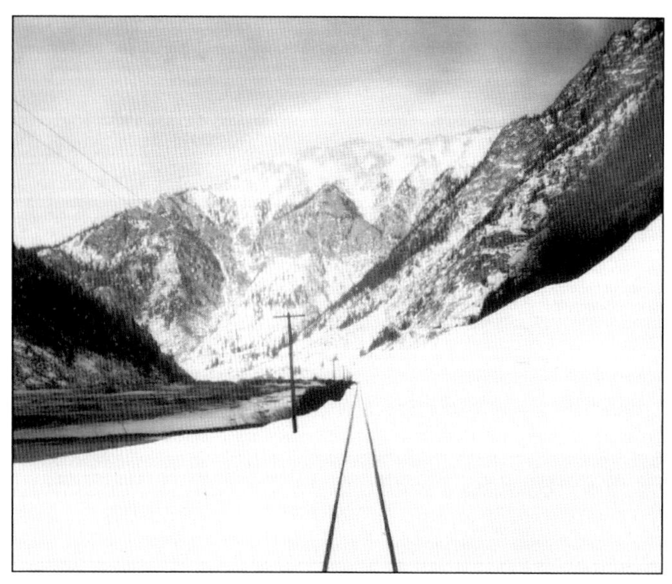

PRONE TO AVALANCHES. Many avalanches roared down the steep slopes in this section of the Ten Mile Canyon, near mile post 124.5, south of Solitude (Copper Mountain) and Curtin. Snow slides often buried the tracks to depths exceeding 25 feet, requiring herculean efforts from snow shovelers and the rotary snow plow. The abandoned Denver & Rio Grande tracks lie just beyond the Ten Mile Creek on the west side of the canyon. (Courtesy of the Denver, South Park & Pacific Historical Society.)

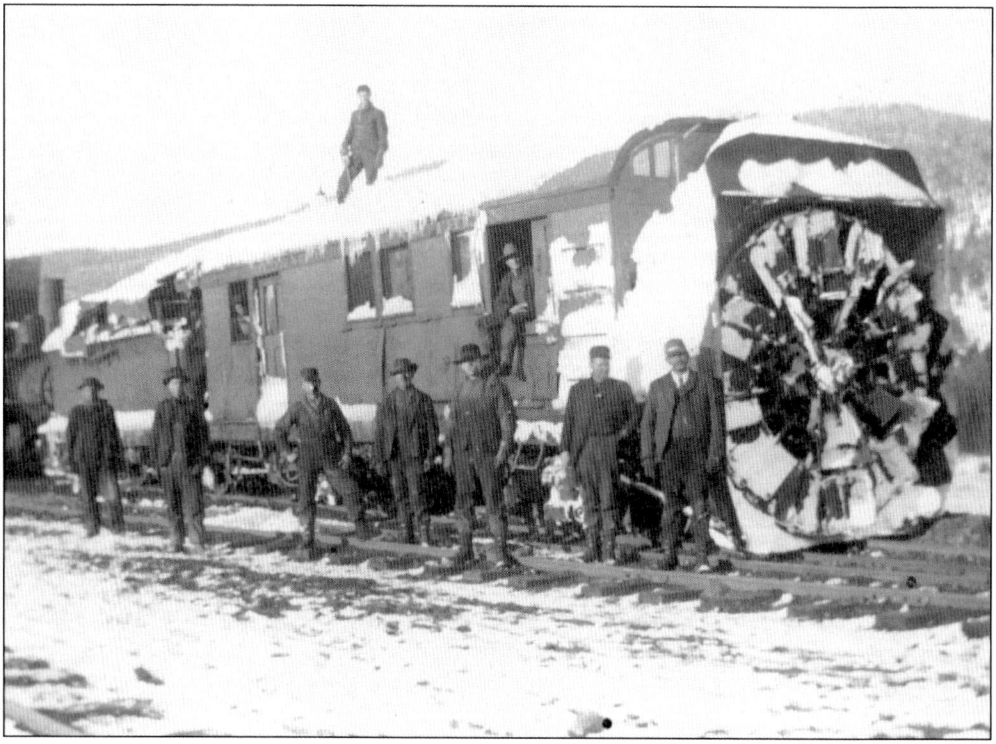

A HARSH WINTER. The winter of 1898 demanded the services of the rotary plow. Snow slides containing boulders and trees interrupted service in the Ten Mile Canyon. At one time in early February, three slides blocked the tracks. The first, 30 feet long and 8 feet deep, covered the tracks one mile west of Frisco. Another slide, near Curtin, measured 300 feet long and 10 feet deep. (Courtesy of the Ed and Nancy Bathke collection.)

Helping the Rotary. Shovelers worked hard in the Ten Mile Canyon, where the potential for slides and avalanches remained high. Several slides in 1886 between Kokomo and Frisco covered nearly 7,000 feet of track. The crippling slides in the canyon had names. One slide that occurred each year near the Uneva spur was named "Big Tim" or "Big Mike." (Courtesy of the Denver, South Park & Pacific Historical Society.)

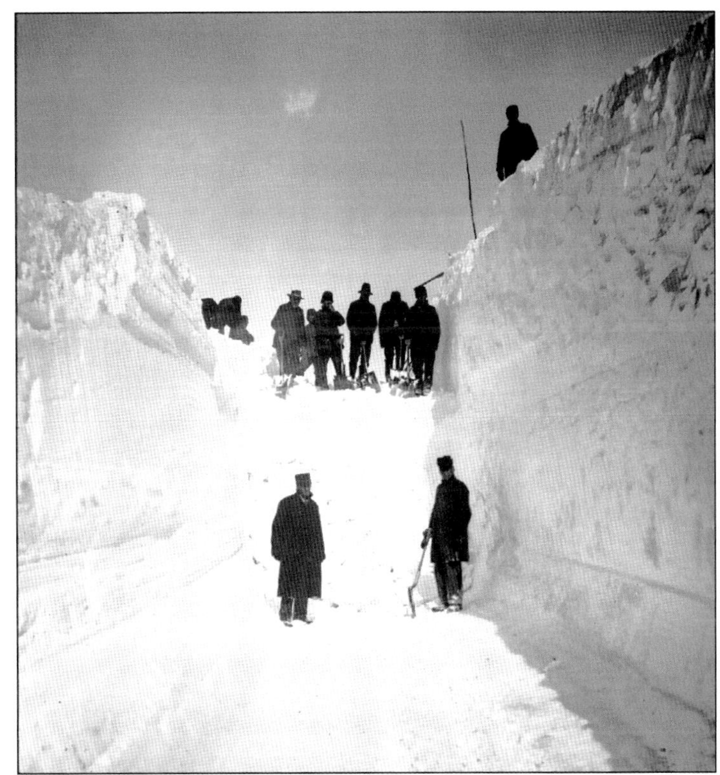

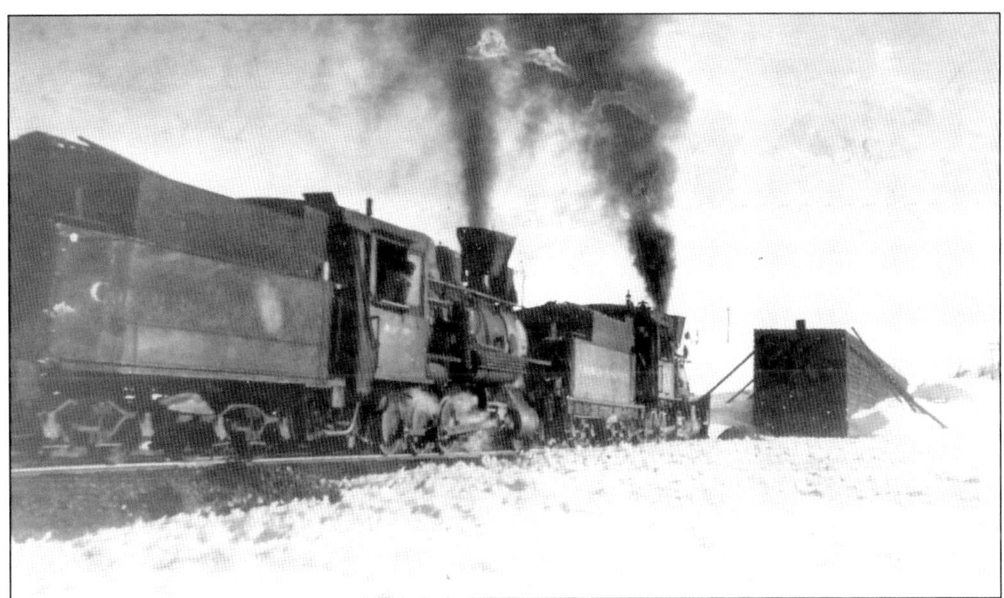

Winter Operations. Colorado & Southern engines 75 and 71 pull a westbound train through the Ten Mile Canyon to Kokomo. After leaving the Kokomo depot, the engines face a difficult climb to Fremont Pass. The train will enter the 544-foot-long snow shed just west of the depot and then cross the trestle over the Denver & Rio Grande track. Kokomo, Recen, and the Denver & Rio Grande depot are to the right. (Courtesy of the Denver, South Park & Pacific Historical Society.)

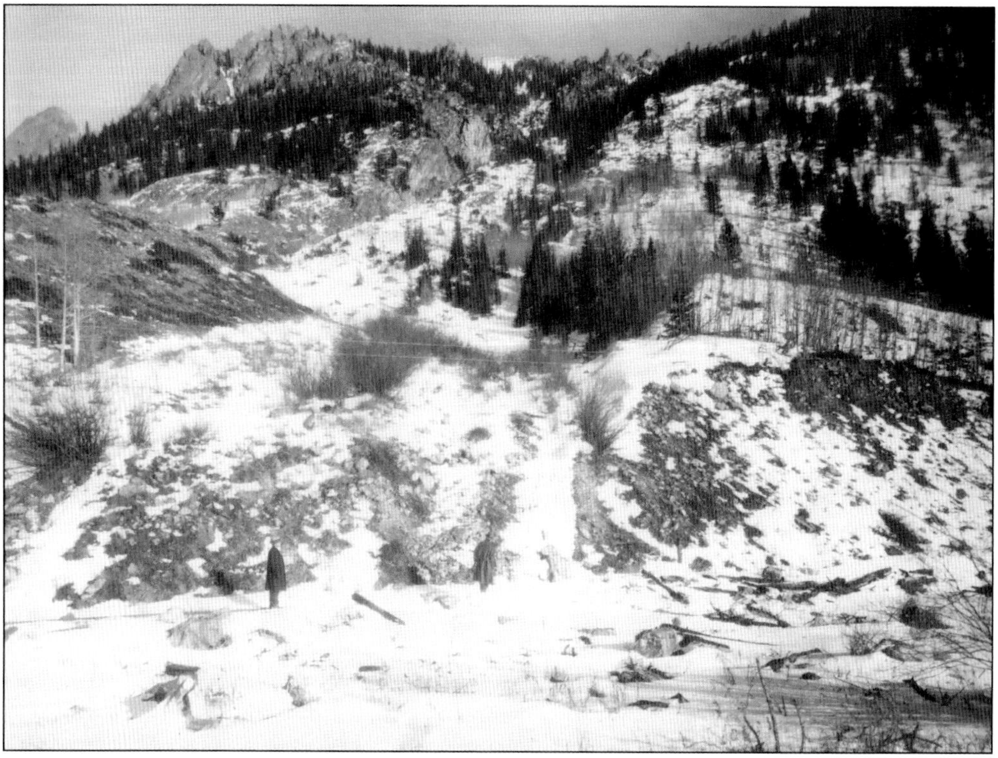

"Instant Flying Beef Steaks." The unstable, weathered rocks of the Ten Mile Canyon produced many avalanches over the years. An avalanche does not contain only snow; boulders and tree trunks can also be part of the rapidly moving mass. One tall tale describes how a rotary plow produced "instant flying beef steaks" as it cut through an avalanche that swept away a herd of cattle. (Courtesy of the Denver, South Park & Pacific Historical Society.)

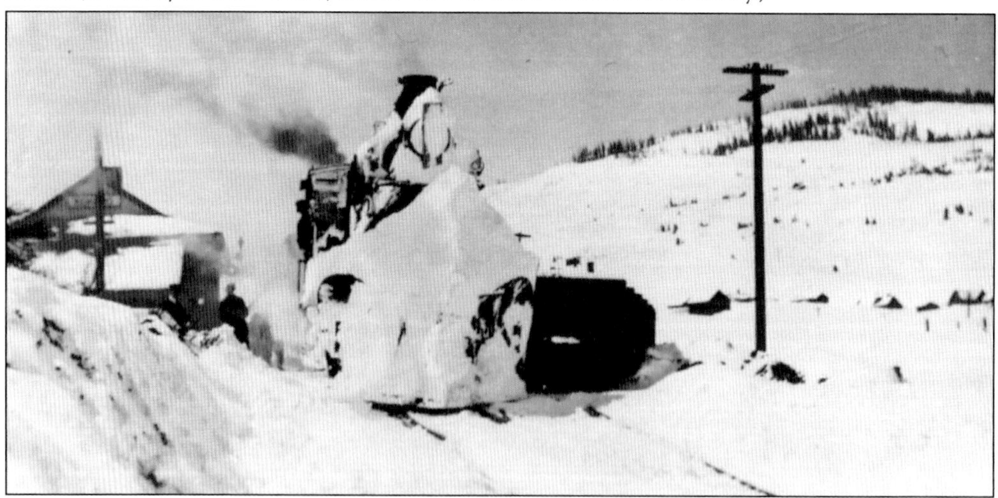

Bucking Plow at Kokomo. Bucking plows, some so large they hid the engine pushing them, spent hours clearing the tracks. With a full head of steam, the engine pushed through the drift until it could go no farther. It backed up and tried again until it broke through the drift, hence the term "bucking plow." A board covers the headlight above this plow to keep it from breaking. (Courtesy of the Bill Fountain collection.)

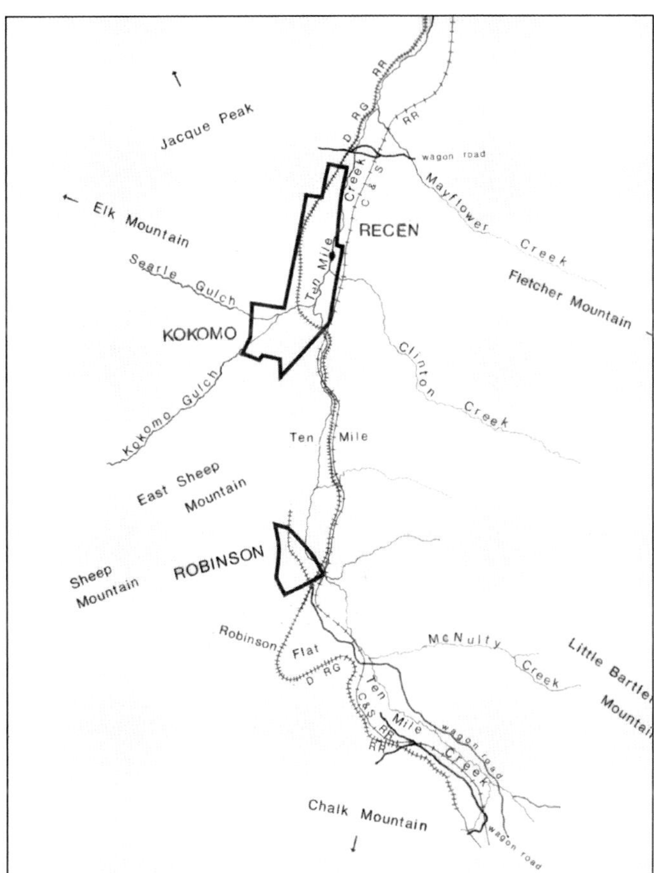

Transportation Network in the Southern Ten Mile Canyon. This map shows Recen, Kokomo, and Robinson after 1898. By order of the US Circuit Court, the Denver, South Park & Pacific crossed the Denver & Rio Grande tracks twice on trestles in the narrow canyon near Kokomo in order to reach Leadville. (Reproduction by Sandra F. Pritchard Mather.)

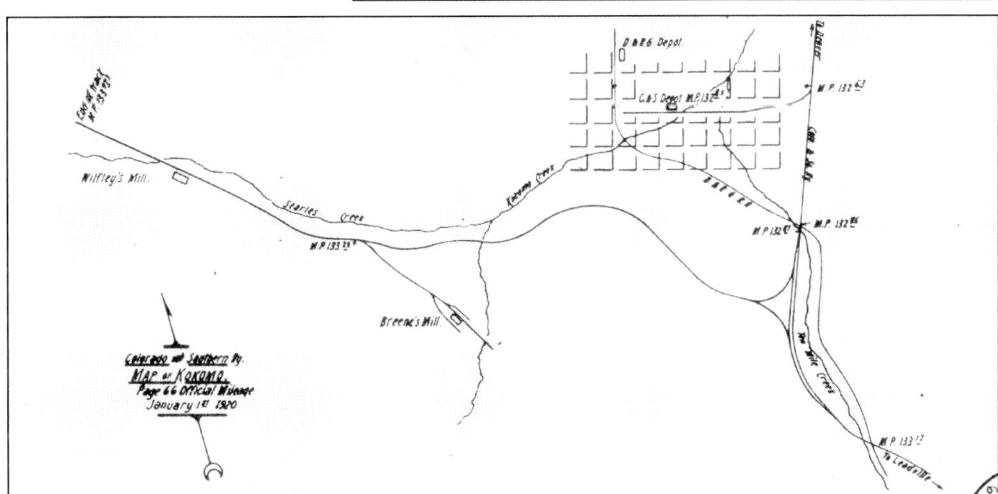

Colorado & Southern Map of Kokomo. The Colorado & Southern railroad built several spurs in Kokomo. One, built in 1895, led to Wilfley's Mill; another, built in 1908, led to Breene's Mill. Workers constructed a wye for turning engines as part of the Wilfley spur. The Colorado & Southern depot sat beside the downtown spur. The spurs to the two mills have not been covered by the Climax molybdenum mine's tailings ponds. (Courtesy of the Denver, South Park & Pacific Historical Society.)

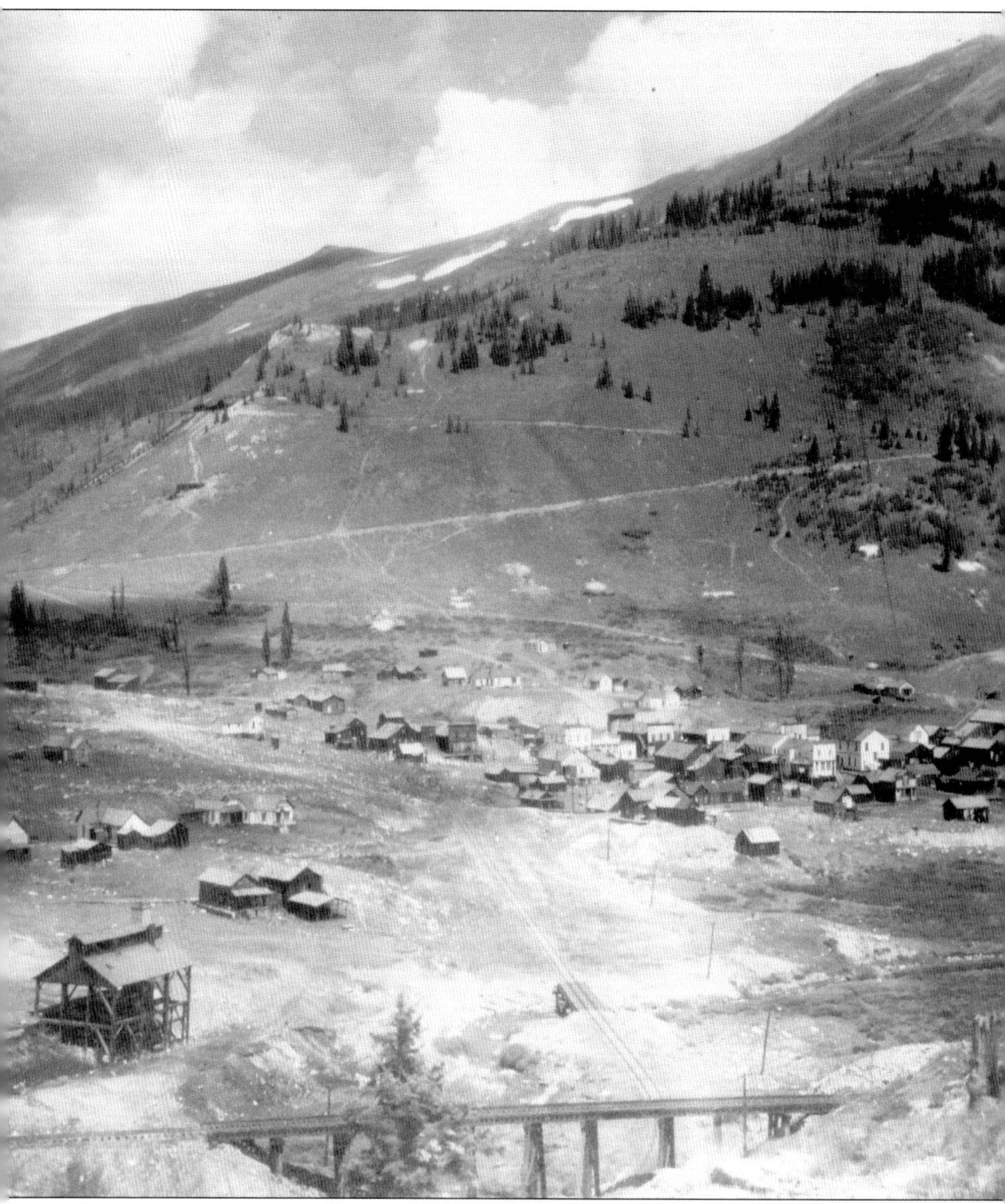

LOOKING NORTHWEST OVER KOKOMO. The Denver & Rio Grande hindered the construction of the Denver, South Park facilities in many ways. In September 1883, at the instigation of the Denver & Rio Grande, several owners of unproductive placers filed injunctions to prevent the railroad from building on their land. To continue construction, the Denver, South Park & Pacific bought one of the worthless claims for $11,000. (Courtesy of the Ed and Nancy Bathke collection.)

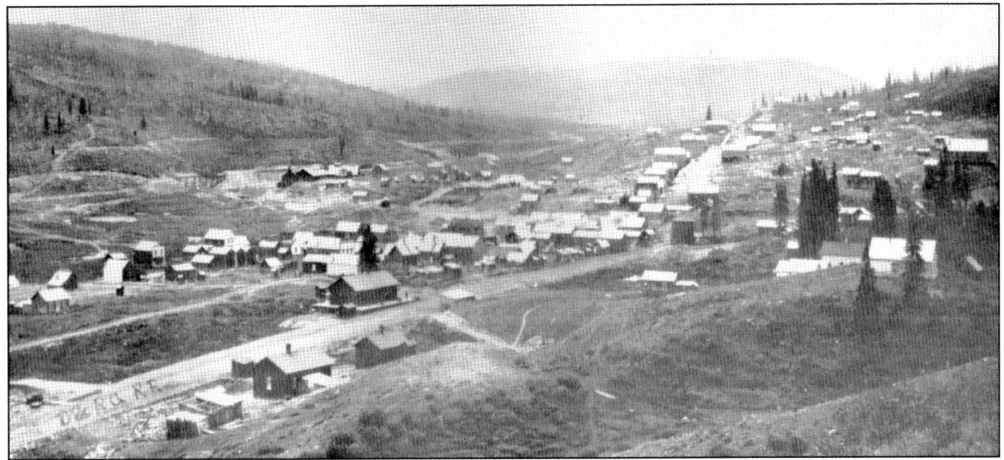

Kokomo Looking Southwest, c. 1885. The Denver & Rio Grande depot, built on the main line running through town, appears just left of center and east of the tracks. The two Denver, South Park & Pacific trestles crossing over the Denver & Rio Grande tracks appear in the distance. The White Quail mining complex stood between the two trestles. (Courtesy of the Denver, South Park & Pacific Historical Society.)

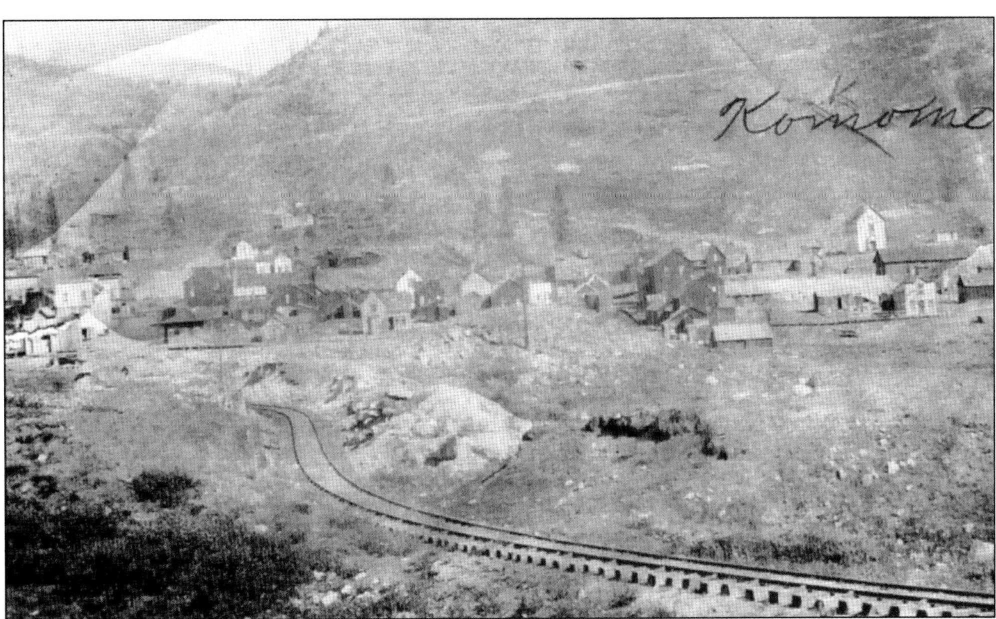

Kokomo and Recen, Early 1900s. The photographer stood on the Colorado & Southern main line to take the photograph. In the foreground, a spur leads to the C&S depot, seen in the left center distance. Around 1915, the company moved the depot to the spot where the spur joined the main line. The Denver & Rio Grande tracks lie behind the buildings. (Courtesy of the Denver, South Park & Pacific Historical Society.)

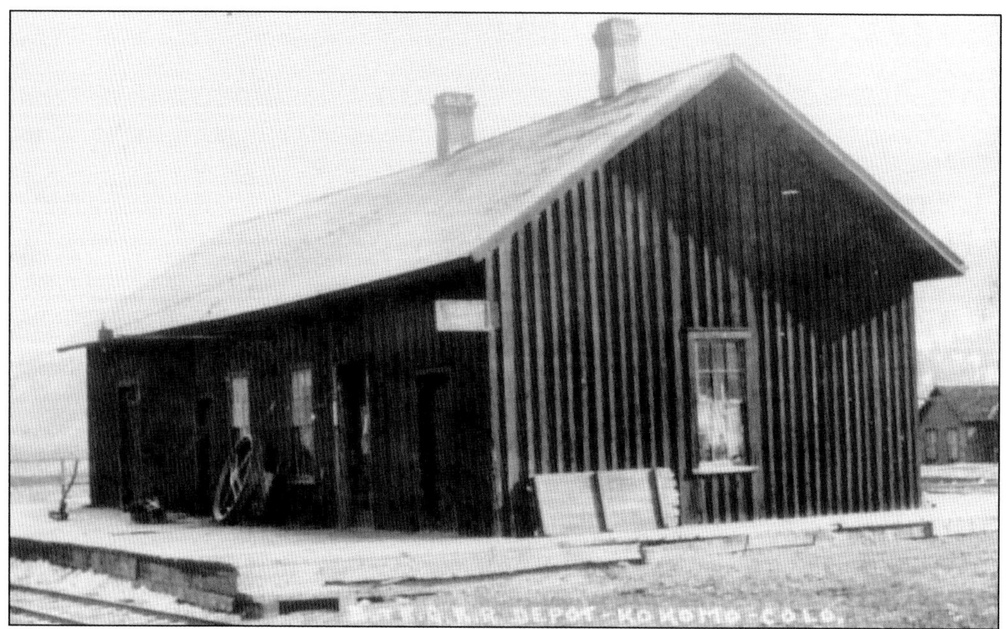

THE DENVER & RIO GRANDE DEPOT IN KOKOMO. Built in 1881 and sitting on the boundary between Kokomo and Recen, the board-and-batten wooden building served both communities until the Denver & Rio Grande abandoned its Blue River line in 1911. A large gear, probably destined for a mining operation, sits on the depot's platform. (Courtesy of the Denver, South Park & Pacific Historical Society.)

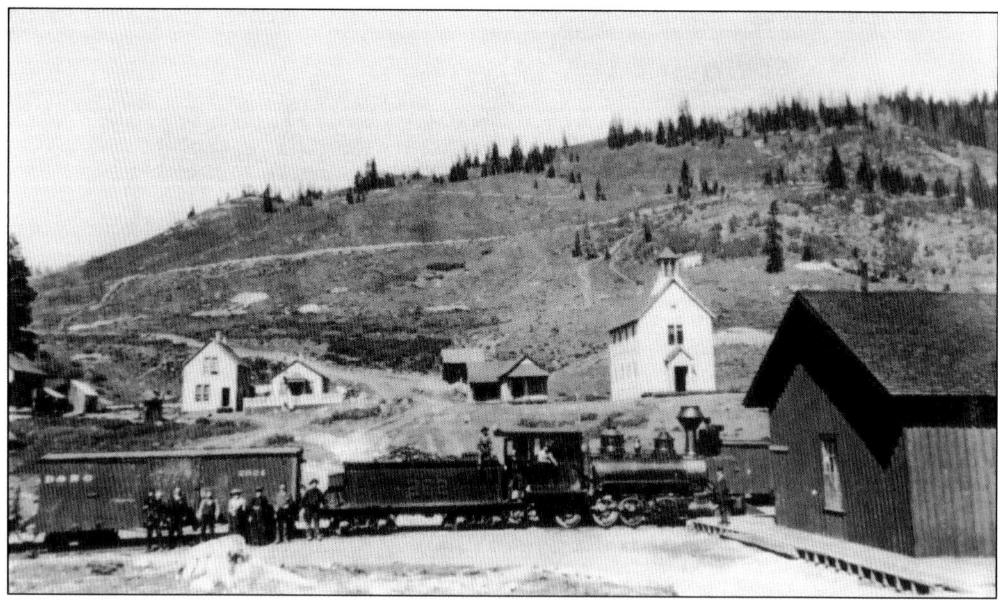

DENVER & RIO GRANDE TRAIN BESIDE KOKOMO DEPOT. Miners and others generally welcomed both railroads in the Ten Mile Canyon. They felt that competition would reduce prices. The newspaper editor in Breckenridge remarked that competition would increase trade, cut travel time to Denver, open markets for ores at reasonable rates, stimulate prosperity, and hasten development. The legal battles between the two companies created little sympathy among residents. (Courtesy of the Frisco Historic Park & Museum.)

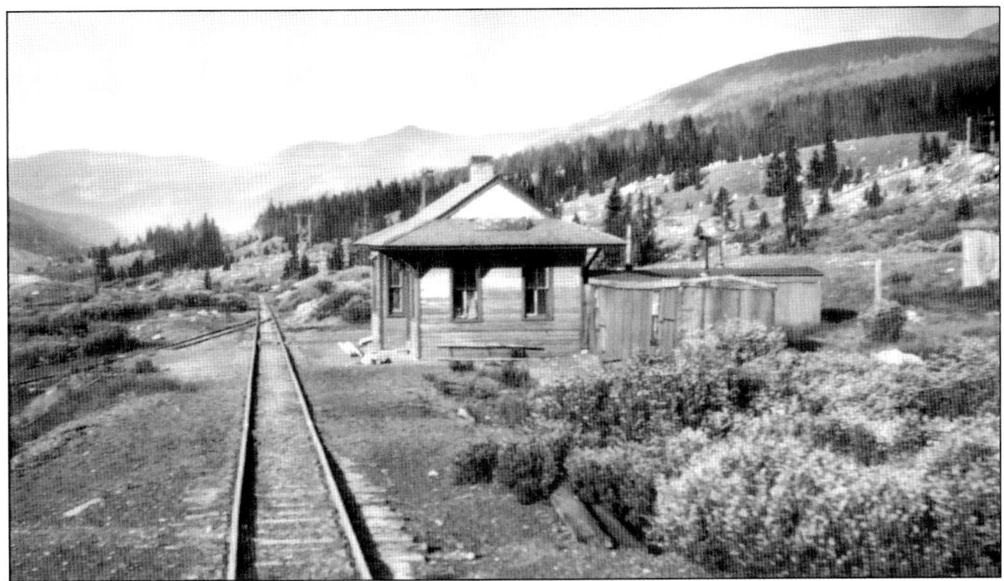

The Colorado & Southern Depot in Kokomo. In this photograph, taken looking northeast, the depot, which had been moved to this location from downtown around 1915, sits on the main track leading to Wheeler (today's Copper Mountain). The downtown spur joins the main line just beyond the depot. On the hill, tall tree stumps indicate that lumbering occurred when deep snow covered the ground. (Courtesy of the Denver, South Park & Pacific Historical Society.)

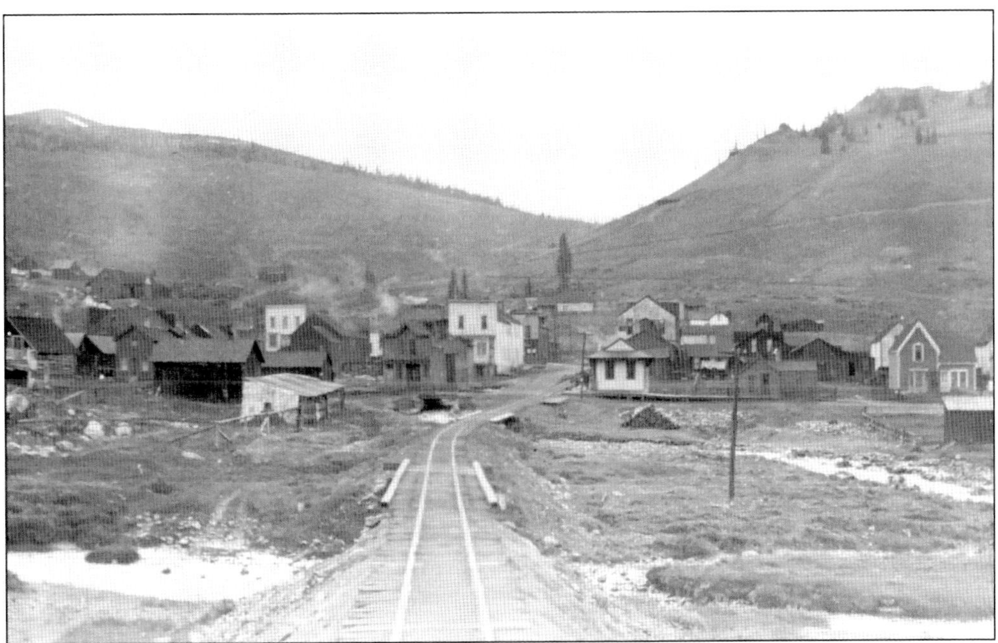

Light Gray with Green Trim. The South Park's depot, built in 1895, sits beside the spur in downtown Kokomo. The spur ended just beyond the depot, within a few feet of the Denver & Rio Grande main line. The company painted its buildings light gray with green trim. The depot would be moved to a new location on the main line that ran through the Ten Mile Canyon. (Courtesy of the Denver, South Park & Pacific Historical Society.)

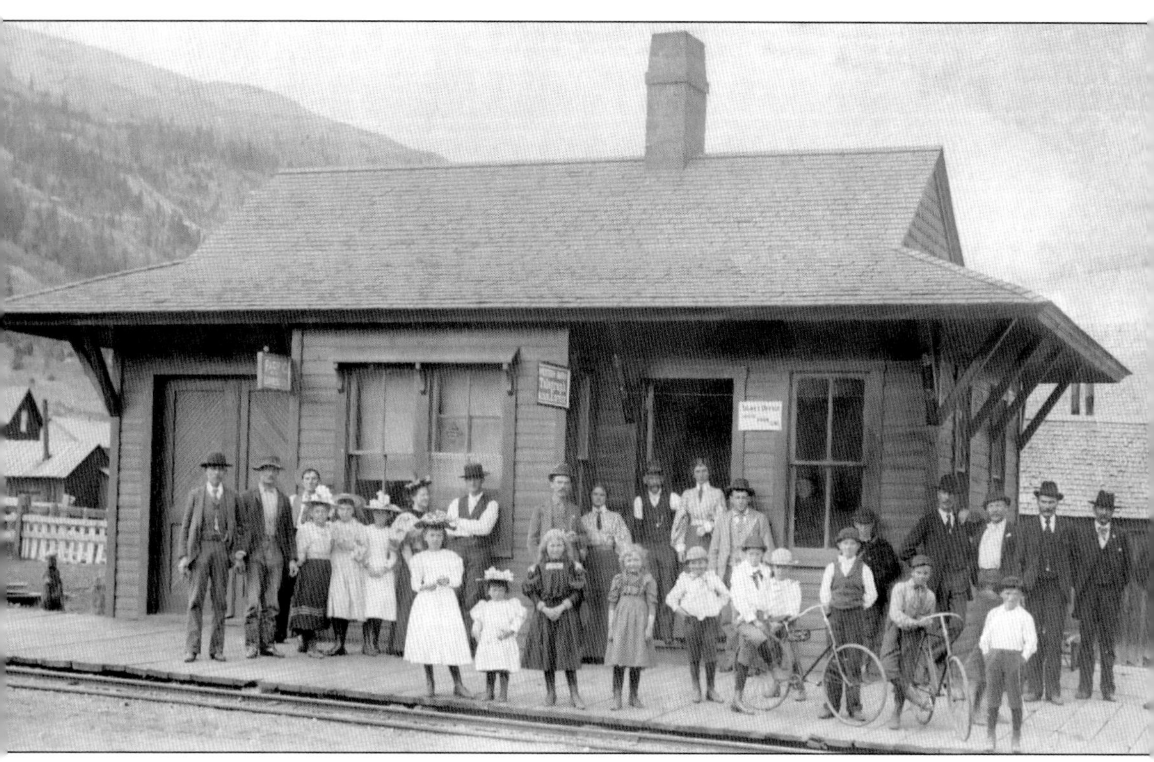

THE 1895 DENVER, LEADVILLE & GUNNISON DEPOT IN KOKOMO. Dressed in their finest clothing, these residents of Kokomo pose on the loading platform of the former Denver, South Park & Pacific (later the Colorado & Southern) depot on a summer day. The stationmaster stands in the doorway. The men at right wear lapel jewelry identifying them as members of a fraternal organization such as the Odd Fellows or Masons. (Courtesy of the Dave Cattani collection.)

TRESTLE IN KOKOMO IN 1893. Towns such as Kokomo, dependent on the railroad to overcome isolation, felt the brunt of high shipping rates. High prices to ship ore to smelters cut into profits; goods brought for residents became very expensive. As rates rose, fewer passengers rode the rails and trains carried less freight, resulting in a greater financial loss for the railroads. (Courtesy of the Denver, South Park & Pacific Historical Society.)

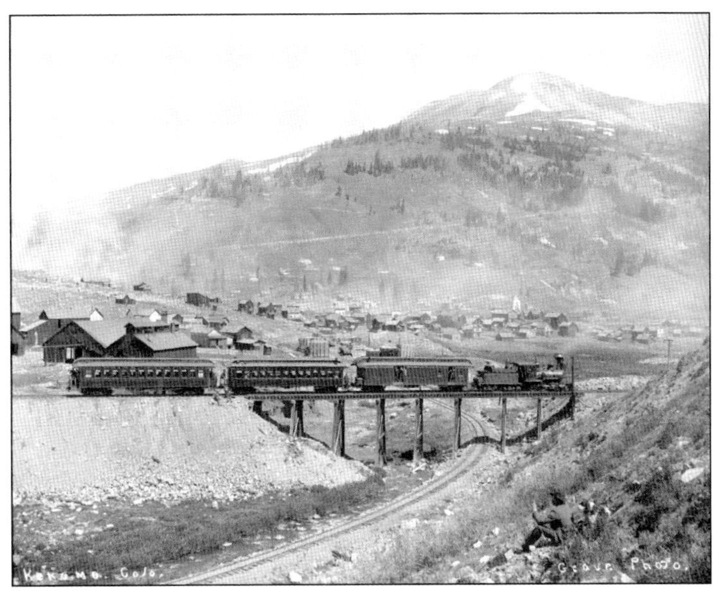

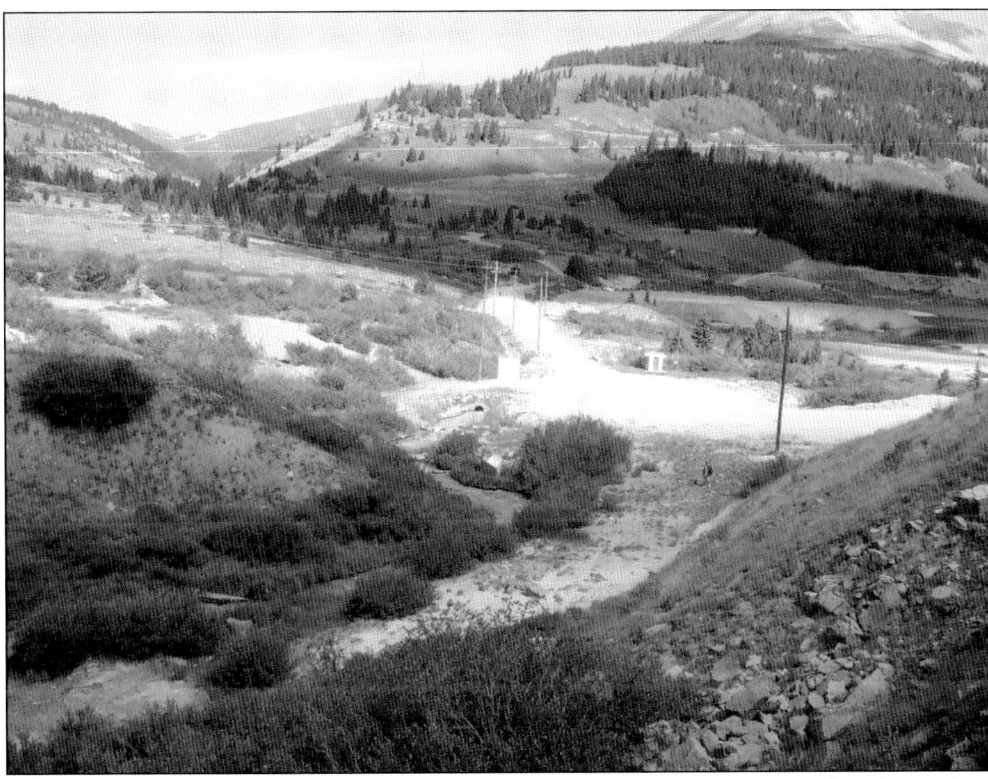

LOCATION OF TRESTLE REMAINS IN 2010. Nothing remains of the trestle except for a few timbers. This part of the town of Kokomo has not yet been covered with tailings from the Climax molybdenum mine. A greatly reduced Ten Mile Creek flows beneath the road. Vegetation has slowly reclaimed the slopes once stripped bare by timbermen. (Courtesy of the Denver, South Park & Pacific Historical Society.)

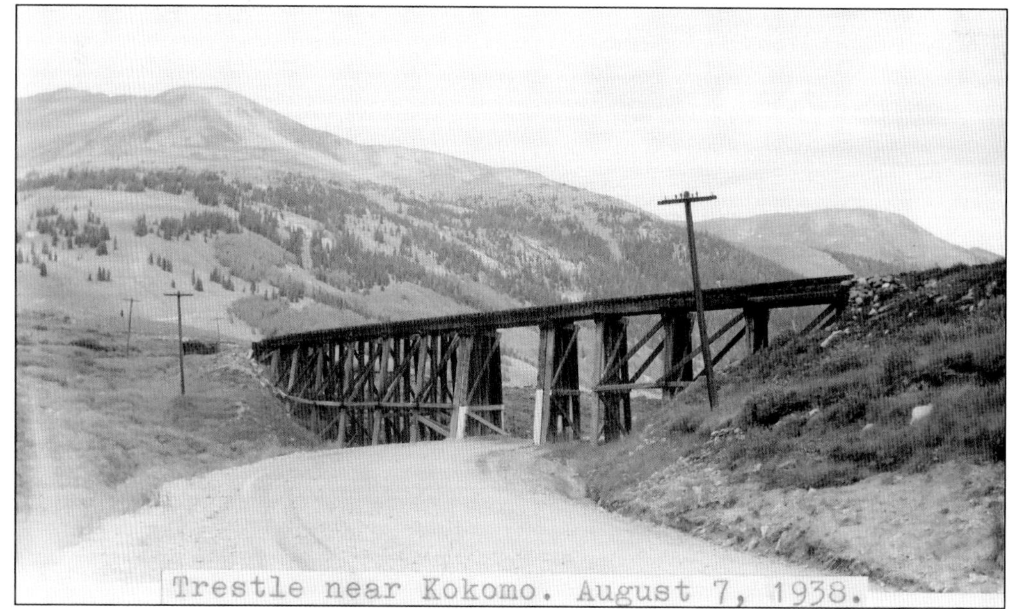

Second Trestle in Kokomo. Just a short distance west of the trestle in the previous photograph, the DSP&P built a second trestle, allowing it to proceed through Kokomo uninterrupted. These two trestles eliminated an inefficient switchback arrangement. The second trestle remained after both railroads curtailed service in the Ten Mile Canyon and throughout the county. (Courtesy of the Denver, South Park & Pacific Historical Society.)

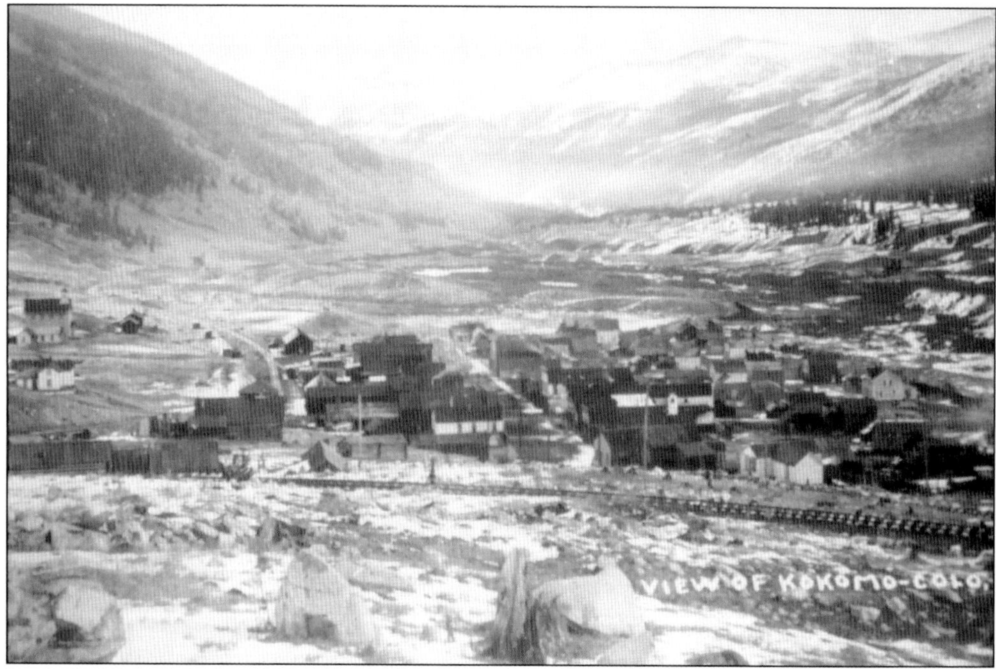

Kokomo Townsite, Late 1890s. The Denver & Rio Grande spur leading to the Summit mill cuts across the foreground of the photograph. The Denver & Rio Grande track and depot appear to the left of center. Compare the rocks in the foreground to those in the following photograph, taken in 2009. (Courtesy of the Denver, South Park & Pacific Historical Society.)

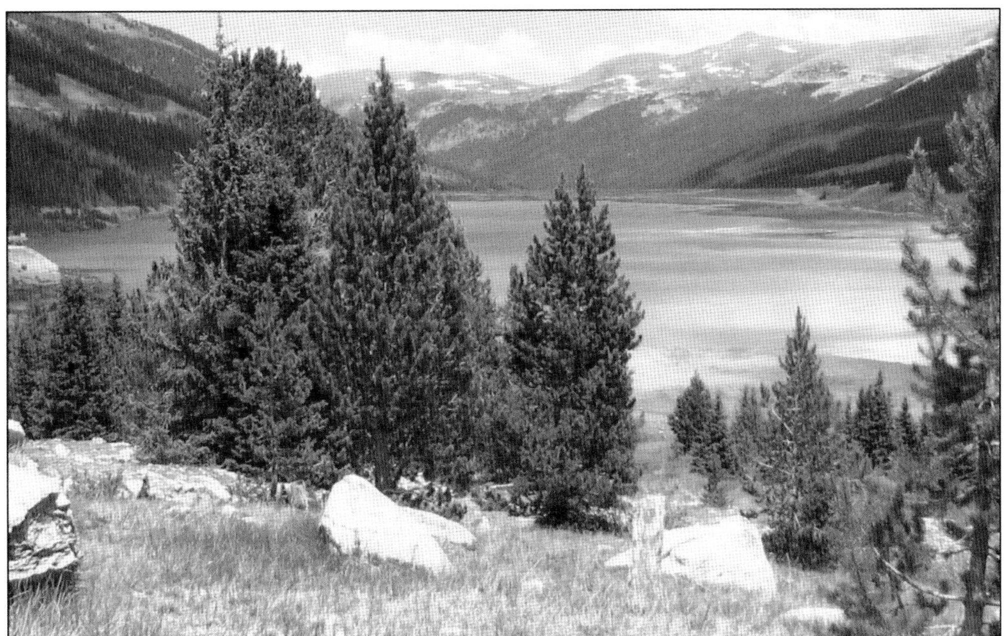

Kokomo Townsite in 2009. The owners of the Climax molybdenum mine purchased the entire upper Ten Mile valley for their tailings ponds in 1959. The company bought private land, mining claims, and public property such as streets and school grounds. To obtain additional acreage, the company engaged in land swaps with the US Forest Service. Tailings and water in the ponds almost completely cover the town site. (Courtesy of the Denver, South Park & Pacific Historical Society.)

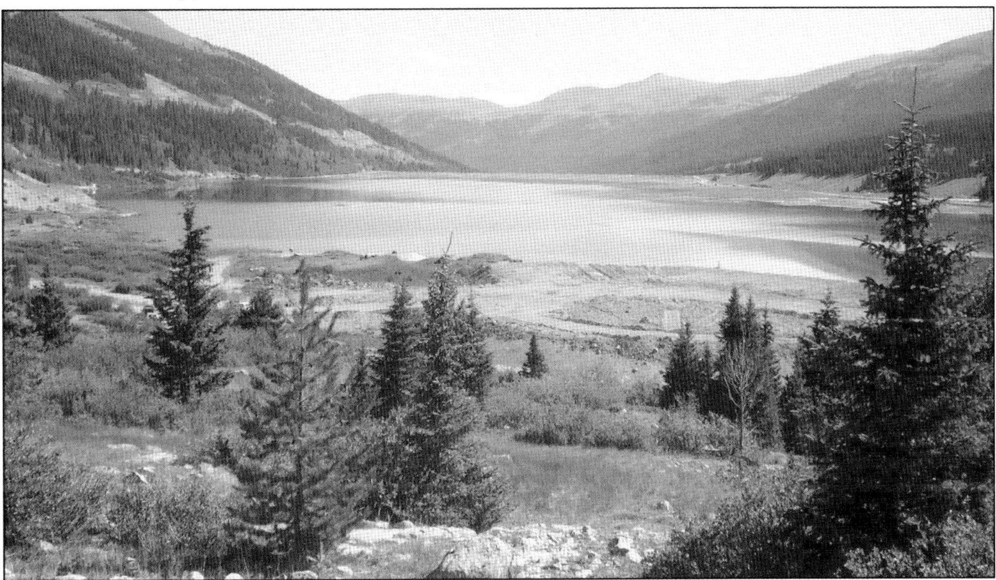

Kokomo Townsite in 2015. Tailings from the Climax molybdenum mine continue to fill the valley. A pipeline brings a slurry of water and tailings to the ponds, which fill from front to back. In essence reverse dams, water enters the pond from the front rather than collecting behind the dam. Each pond abuts the next terrace/dam uphill. (Courtesy of the Denver, South Park & Pacific Historical Society.)

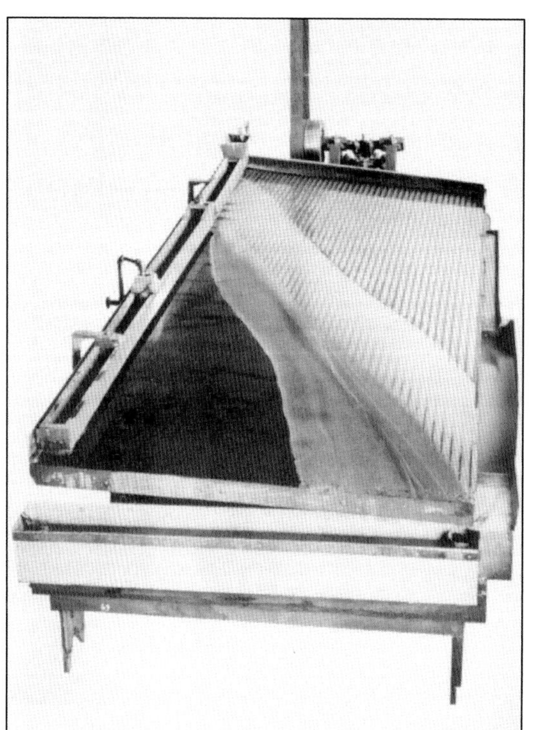

The Wilfley Concentrating Table. In the 1890s, Arthur Redman Wilfley developed his highly successful transversely inclined vibrating table, which concentrated the low-grade ores of the Ten Mile Canyon. The 12-foot-by-5-foot tables cost $450. The size of the tables allowed them to be carried by the two railroads to mining sites throughout the county, thus helping to assure the success of Wilfley's invention. (Courtesy of the Denver, South Park & Pacific Historical Society.)

The Wilfley Mill. Despite Wilfley's success as a mining entrepreneur and developer of numerous innovative mining inventions, the Wilfley mill rarely operated at a profit. Later known as the Kimberly mill, it sat in Searle Gulch close to the Wilfley mine. The track in front, laid in 1895, became known as the Wilfley spur. (Courtesy of the Denver, South Park & Pacific Historical Society.)

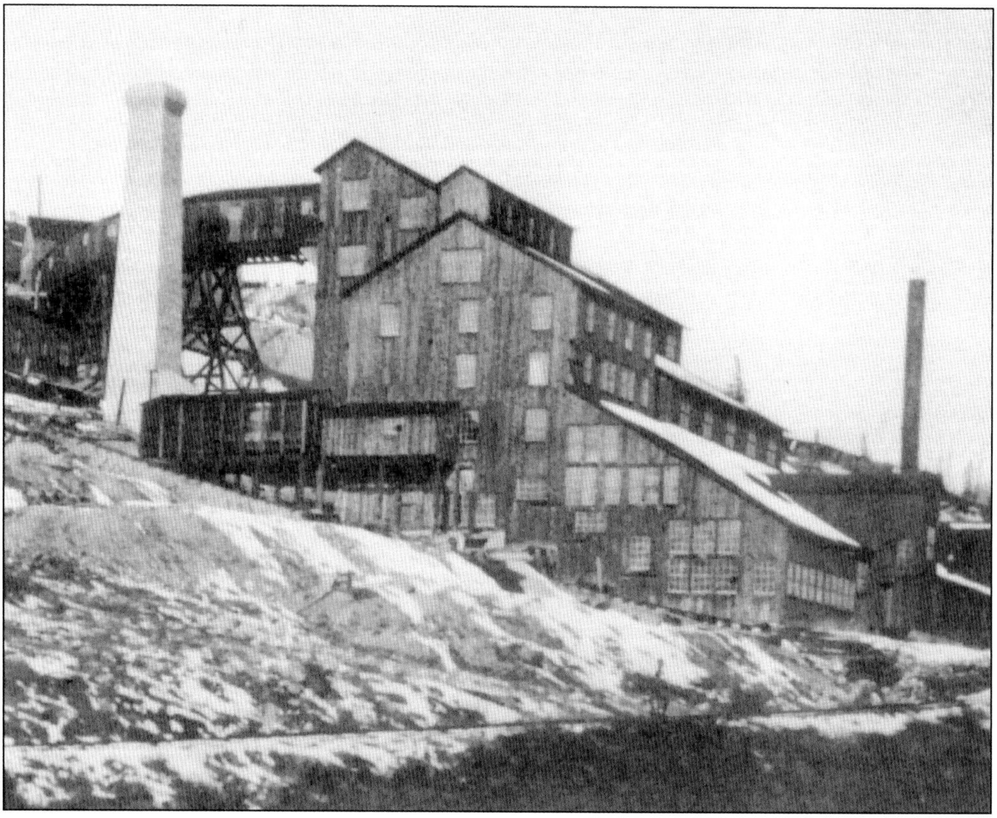

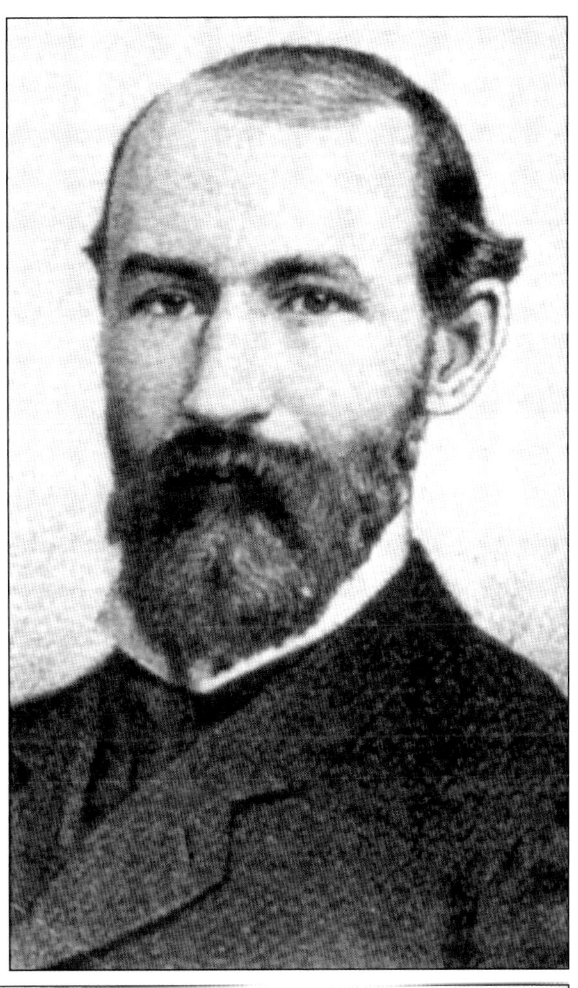

George Robinson. The town of Robinson, named for George Robinson, a successful businessman, sat in the upper Ten Mile Canyon between Kokomo and Fremont Pass. Tragically, armed guards at Robinson's mine killed him in a case of mistaken identity on a dark night. Today, Climax mine tailings cover the townsite, a process that began immediately after the Colorado & Southern abandoned its tracks in 1937. (Courtesy of the Denver, South Park & Pacific Historical Society.)

The Town of Robinson. Also called Robinson's Camp, Ten Mile City, Summit, and Summit City, Robinson grew rapidly to as many as 800 people because of its proximity to the rich Robinson mine. The town housed the hard rock or lode miners who worked in the mine, merchants, and tradesmen as well as their families. The population fluctuated before declining to 250 in 1889, when the mine played out. (Courtesy of the Ed and Nancy Bathke collection.)

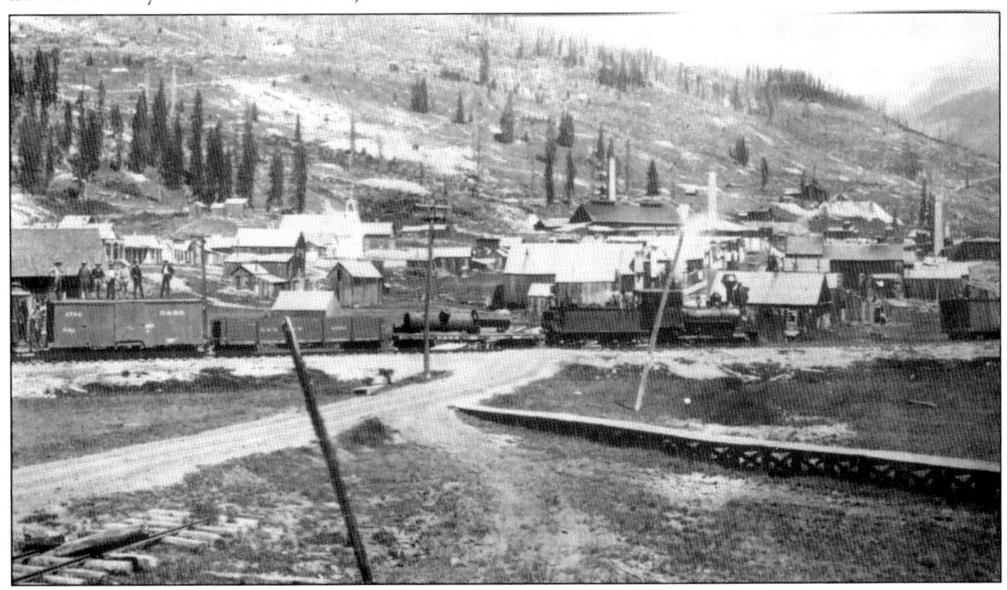

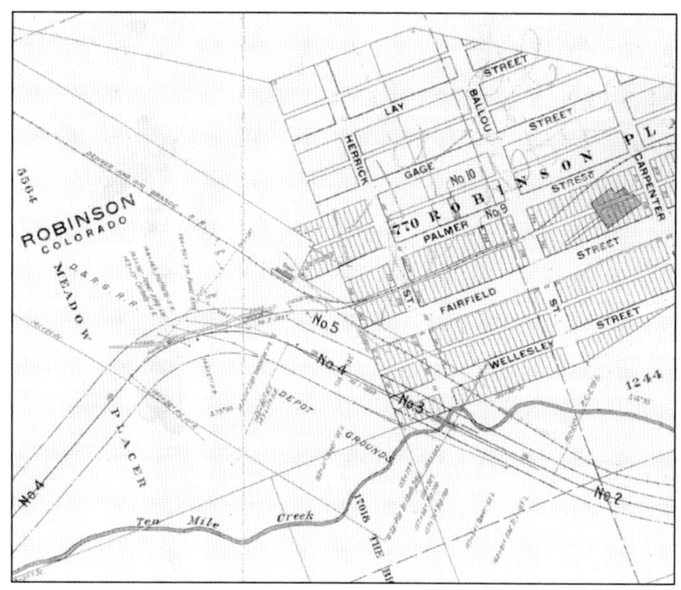

Map of the Denver & Rio Grande Tracks in Robinson. The Interstate Commerce Commission map shows that the tracks skirted the southeastern section of town, with a spur leading northwest through alleys and along streets. The two buildings at the depot site sat beside the main track, just southwest of where the spur joined the main line. The map also shows the Colorado & Southern tracks. (Courtesy of the Denver, South Park & Pacific Historical Society.)

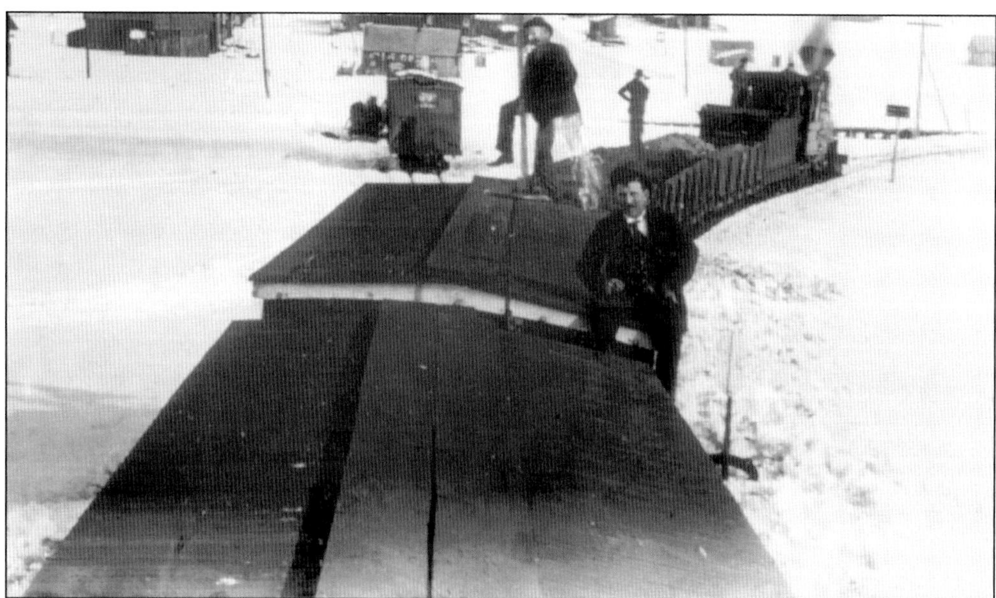

Freight Entering Robinson. In this 1896 photograph, men pose on the tops of a Denver, Leadville & Gunnison freight train entering Robinson. Brakemen, who regularly walked on the tops of the cars setting brakes, held some of the most dangerous railroad jobs, especially in winter, when snow and ice covered the roofs. To the left of the first man is the brake wheel that the brakemen would turn to set the brakes on a boxcar. (Courtesy of the Denver, South Park & Pacific Historical Society.)

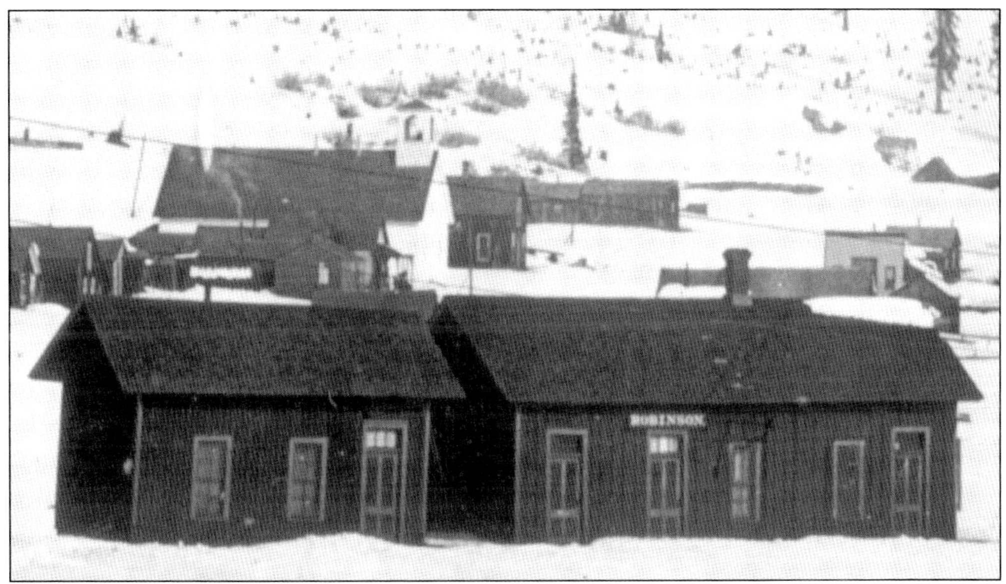

Denver & Rio Grande Depot, Late 1890s. The Denver & Rio Grande arrived first in Robinson in 1880, building eastbound from Leadville. The Denver, South Park line did not arrive until 1884, building westbound toward Leadville. The building next to the depot might be a section house. A nearby smelter treated the ore produced by the mines surrounding the town. (Courtesy of the Denver, South Park & Pacific Historical Society.)

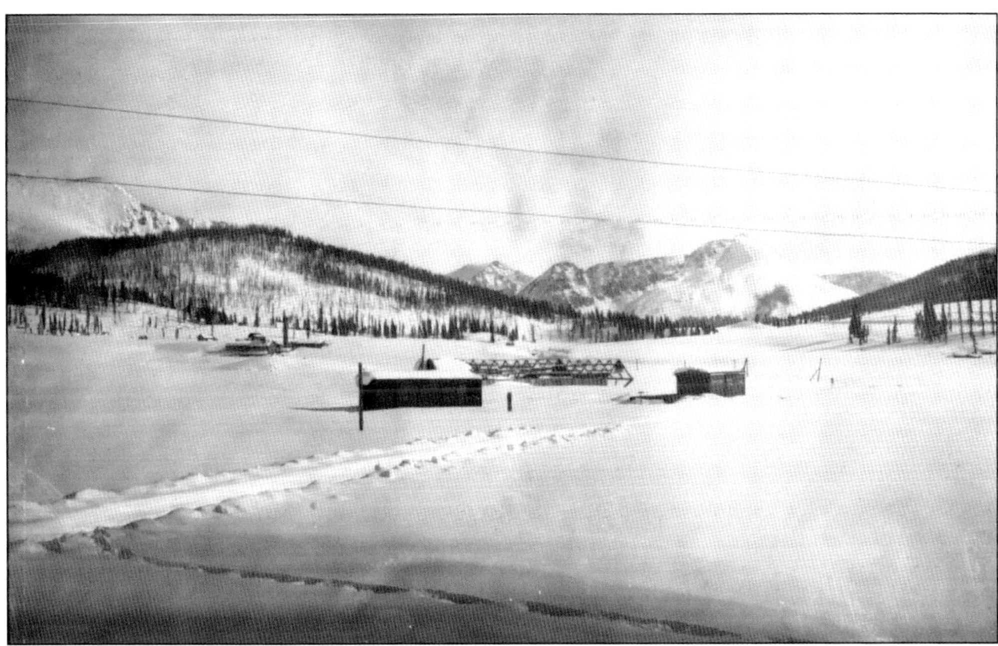

The Town of Carbonateville. In the late 1880s, William Henry Jackson captured this image of the remains of Carbonateville, the first settlement on the east side of Fremont Pass. The South Park "boxcar" depot sits in the center of the photograph. In the distance, smoke from a Denver & Rio Grande train rises in the cold air. (Photograph by William Henry Jackson, courtesy of the Denver, South Park & Pacific Historical Society.)

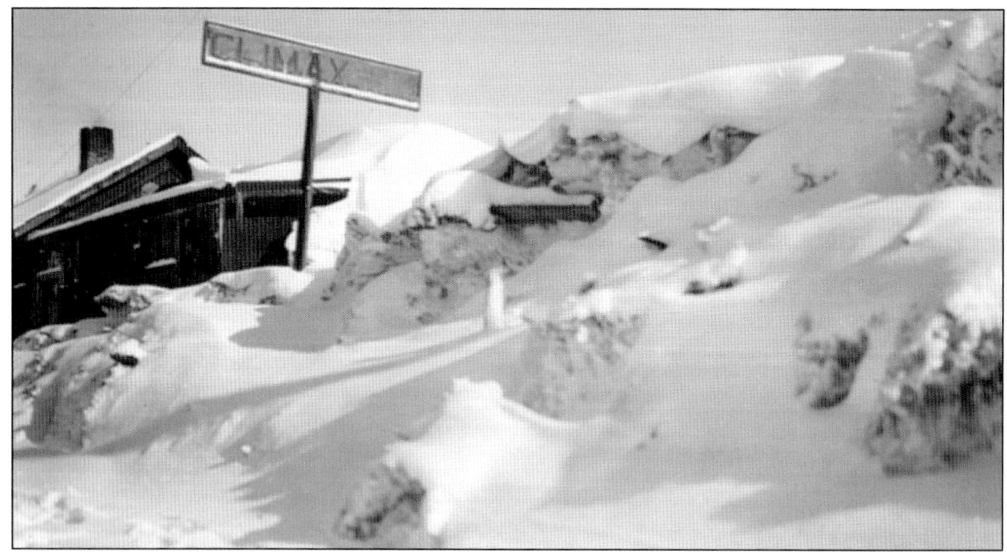

Snow at Climax. Snow hastened the financial ruin of the Denver, South Park & Pacific as well as its successor, the Denver, Leadville & Gunnison. It has been estimated that over half of the income of the railroads had to be spent on maintenance of the tracks and rights-of-way. Heavy snow at Climax on Fremont Pass, in the Ten Mile Canyon, and over Boreas Pass necessitated the expenditure. (Courtesy of the Denver, South Park & Pacific Historical Society.)

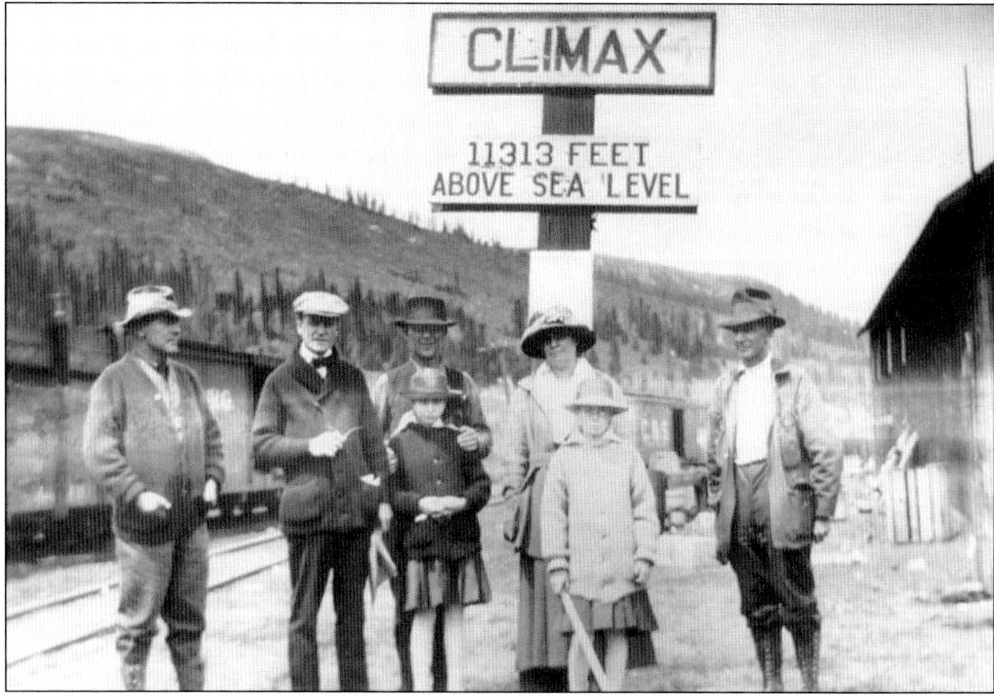

Waiting at the Climax Depot. Looking north, this group stands by the sign indicating that the Climax depot stood at over two miles above sea level. The C&S engine house stands to the right; its track is seen on the left. The Denver & Rio Grande tracks are to the far left. Today, Colorado Route 91 has replaced the tracks of both railroads. (Courtesy of the Denver, South Park & Pacific Historical Society.)

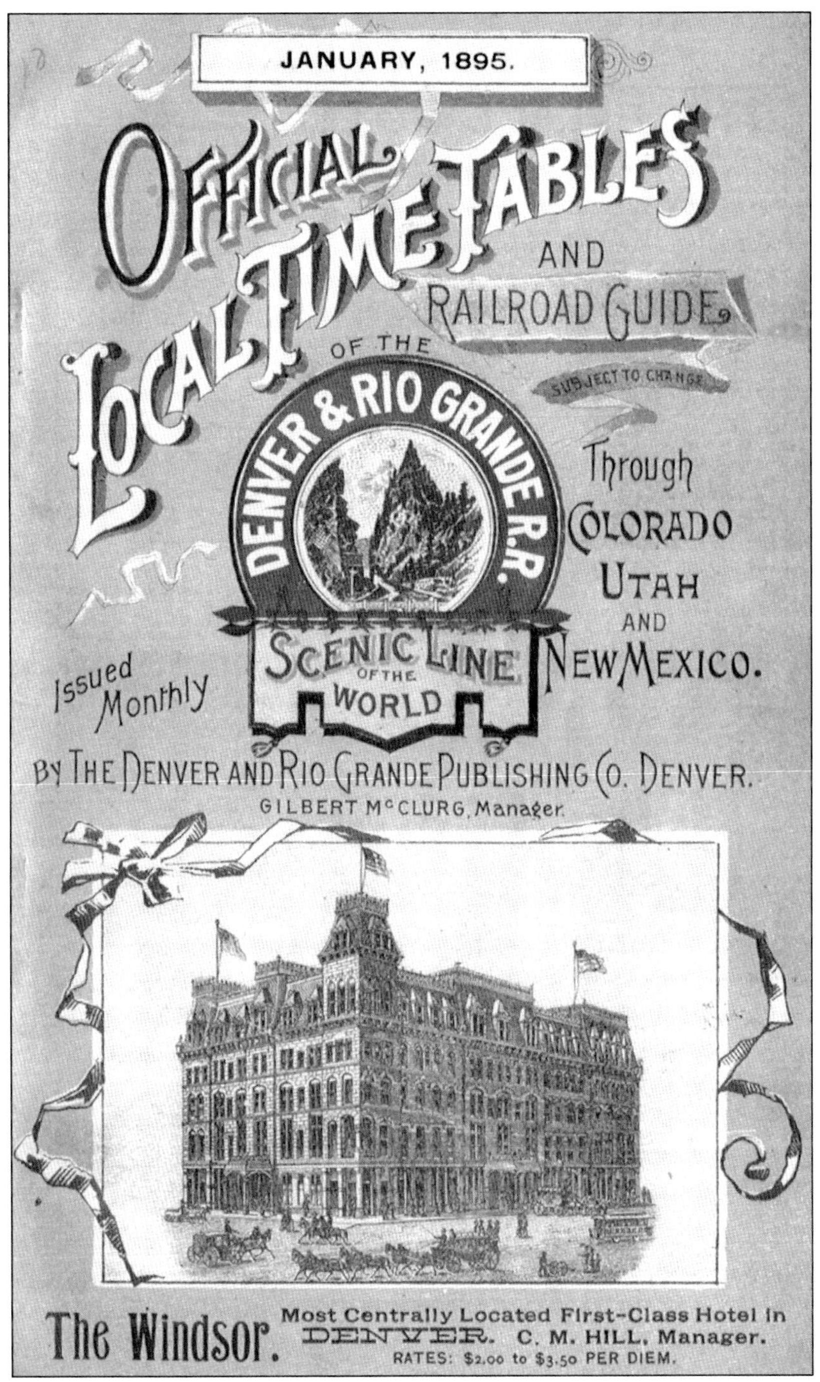

Denver & Rio Grande Timetable. The Denver & Rio Grande Railroad extended far beyond its short line in Summit County, from Denver to the southern border of Colorado and from the high plains of Kansas to Utah, tapping the mining areas of the state. Calling itself the Scenic Line of the World, it promoted tourism. The company issued official local time tables and railroad guides to help tourists plan their travels on the railroad. (Courtesy of the Denver, South Park & Pacific Historical Society.)

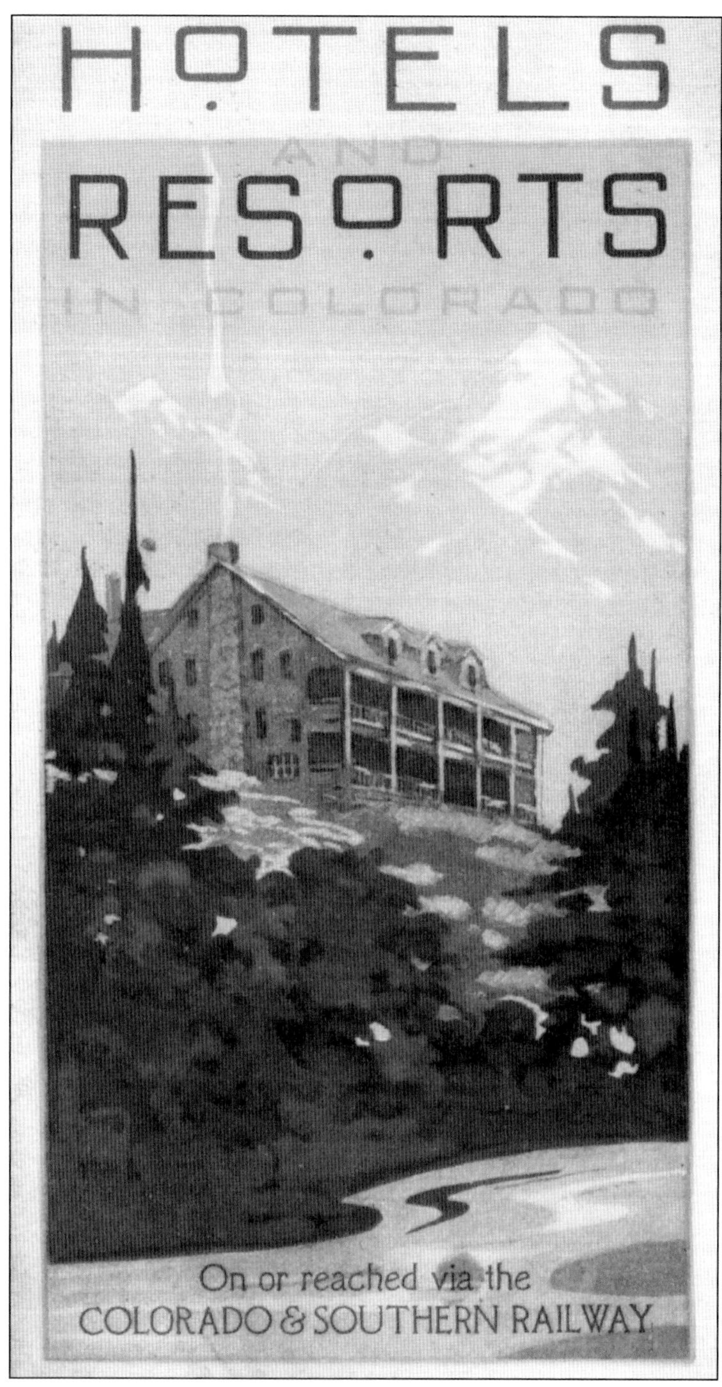

Tourist Brochures. Not to be outdone, the Colorado & Southern line issued its own set of brochures with schedules, area industry, tourist attractions, and in this instance, hotel and resort information. In some cases, the railroads built and operated destination resorts to draw tourists to them. In this 1915 brochure, the Colorado & Southern listed all lodging found along the line with rates and other pertinent information. (Courtesy of the Denver, South Park & Pacific Historical Society.)

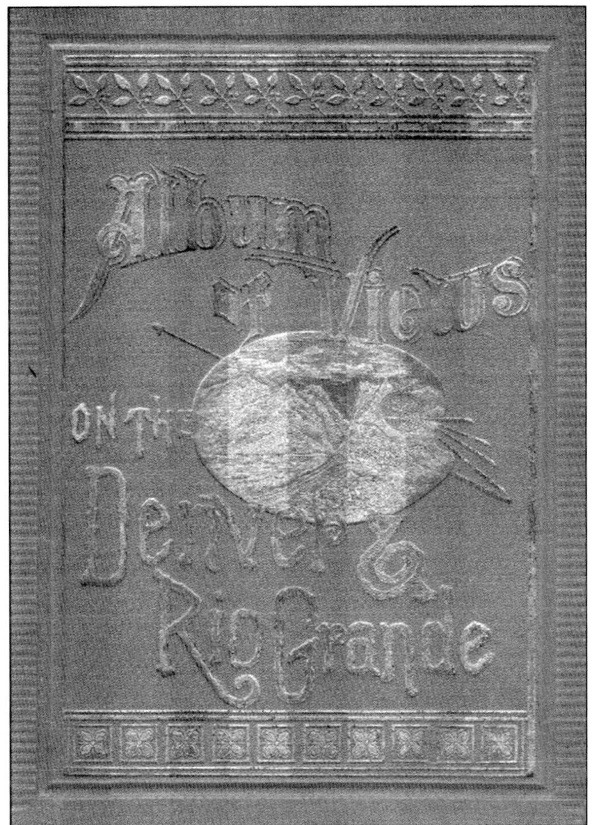

EXCURSION BOOK. The Denver & Rio Grande advertised Sunday excursions through the Ten Mile Canyon on a regular basis in the Breckenridge newspaper. Guests were encouraged to spend the afternoon enjoying the spectacular sites as they rode through the canyon. To remember their trip, tourists bought albums such as this one from vendors. Not to be outdone, the South Park line offered similar trips and souvenirs. (Courtesy of the Denver, South Park & Pacific Historical Society.)

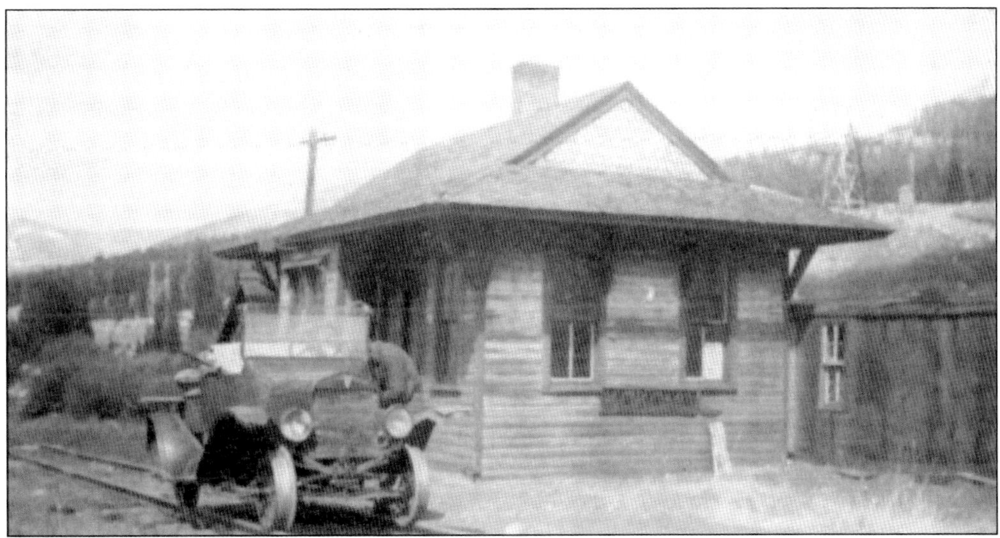

SOUTH PARK ZEPHYR AT KOKOMO. Built by three residents of Como (see page 18), this converted Ford Model T traveled the abandoned trackage from Como almost to Fremont Pass, where tailings from the Climax molybdenum mine blocked the way. Because the railroad had abandoned the tracks the prior year, the "crew" had the entire line to itself. Going east from Como, they traveled to Bailey, over 40 miles away in the Platte Canyon. (Courtesy of the Denver, South Park & Pacific Historical Society.)

LEADVILLE TO DILLON.

MILES. From Pueblo.	From Leadville.	Between Stations.	NAMES OF STATIONS.	Elevation.	Average Grade Per Mile. Ascending.	Descending.	Maximum Grade Per Mile. Ascending.	Descending.	Maximum Curvature, Per 100 Feet.	Length of Side Track.	Iron or Steel and Weight. Per Yard.	Grading and Bridging Completed.	Date When Track Laid.	Iron or Steel and Weight, per yard.	Open For Business.	REMARKS.
157,8			Leadville	10199,6												
			West End Leadville Yard													
162,9	5,1	4,8	Bird's Eye	10183,2		3,2′	52,8′	52,8′	15°	1,197	30 lb Steel	Sept. 1, 1880	Sept. 10, 1880	30 lb Steel	Sept. 10, 1880	
169,5	11.7	6,6	Alicante	11170	149,5′			186′	15°			" 15, 1880	" 25, 1880	" "	" 25, 1880	
170.8	13	1 3	Summit	11328.5	121,9′			180′	15°	798	" "	Nov. 1, 1880	Nov. 15, 1880	" "	Nov. 15, 1880	Continental Divide.
174.	16,2	3,2	**Robinson**	10870.9		143.′		180′	15°	2,334	" "	" 15, 1880	" 25, 1880	" "	" 25, 1880	
176.	18,2	2.	**Kokomo**	10630,9		120.′		180′	15°	3,600	" "	" 27, 1880	Dec. 27, 1880	" "	Dec. 27, 1880	
176,2	18.4	,2	Recen	10610.9		100.′		132′	20°	3,737	" "	Aug. 1, 1881	Aug. 17, 1881	" "	Aug. 17, 1881	
182,3	24.5	6.1	**Wheeler's**	9780,9		136.1′		180′	15°	4,045	" "	Sept. 1, 1881	Sept. 18, 1881	" "	Sept. 18, 1881	End of Track.
187,2	29.4		Mincio	9340,9		89,8′		180′	13°							
189 9	32.1		Frisco	9085,9		94,4′		148′	12°							Grading completed and ties laid to ready for iron.
193,4	35,6		Breckenridge Jc. or Dillon	8873,9		58,8′		88′	8°							

Total, 24.2 Miles Main Track.

Total, 15,711 Feet -- 3 Miles Side Track.

1 Miles Main and Side Track, 27.2.

Denver & Rio Grande Timetable. This 1881 Denver & Rio Grande timetable shows the schedule for the not-yet-finished track of the Blue River Line, which would eventually run from Leadville to Dillon. The schedule shows that track crews had completed the line to Wheeler (Copper Mountain) by September 1881. The tracks would reach Dillon by November 1882. (Courtesy of the Denver, South Park & Pacific Historical Society.)

Six

On to Leadville

Statistics tell of the uniqueness of the Denver, South Park & Pacific line from Como to its terminus in Leadville. Beginning at Como with an elevation of 9,796 feet (2,985 meters), the railroad crossed Boreas Pass at 11,481 feet (3,499 meters), dropped to 9,004 feet (2,744 meters) at Dickey, and climbed back to 11,108 feet (3,385 meters) at Fremont Pass. Almost 63 miles of track covered a distance of 23 miles. From Boreas to Breckenridge, a distance of six and one-half miles, crews laid slightly over 11 miles of track. Trains rounded 108 curves of between one and 25 degrees; 82 percent of the 11 miles had a four-percent grade, meaning a drop or rise in elevation of four feet for every 100 feet of horizontal distance.

From Breckenridge to Leadville, 234 curves made over 16 complete circles. The maximum grade to Leadville was 4.3 percent, while maximum curves measured 15 to 25 degrees. If the curves had not been incorporated, the engines would have faced far steeper grades than they could have climbed. Even in the best of weather, the trip through the canyon proved difficult for the engines. At Solitude Station near Wheeler (Copper Mountain), trains took on water, using it completely by the time the train reached Kokomo, six miles away and 800 feet higher. After a refill, the trains continued on to Robinson, two miles away and 94 feet higher. Fremont Pass, three miles away, meant another climb of 460 feet. Waiting at the top of the pass was the combination passenger and freight depot completed in 1884.

The first Denver & Rio Grande train arrived in Leadville around 10:00 p.m. on July 22, 1880, amid great hoopla. Despite the late hour and heavy rain, five bands, two cavalry companies, five infantry companies, and a 100-gun salute welcomed the train. Pres. Ulysses S. and Julia Grant were passengers on that first train and spent five days in Leadville as part of their "around the world" tour. The railroad truly changed the economic landscape in the area. While mines benefitted from lower rates and shorter times to concentrators and smelters and residents enjoyed the ability to order luxury items such as fine perfume, wines, and laces, the freighting industry suffered.

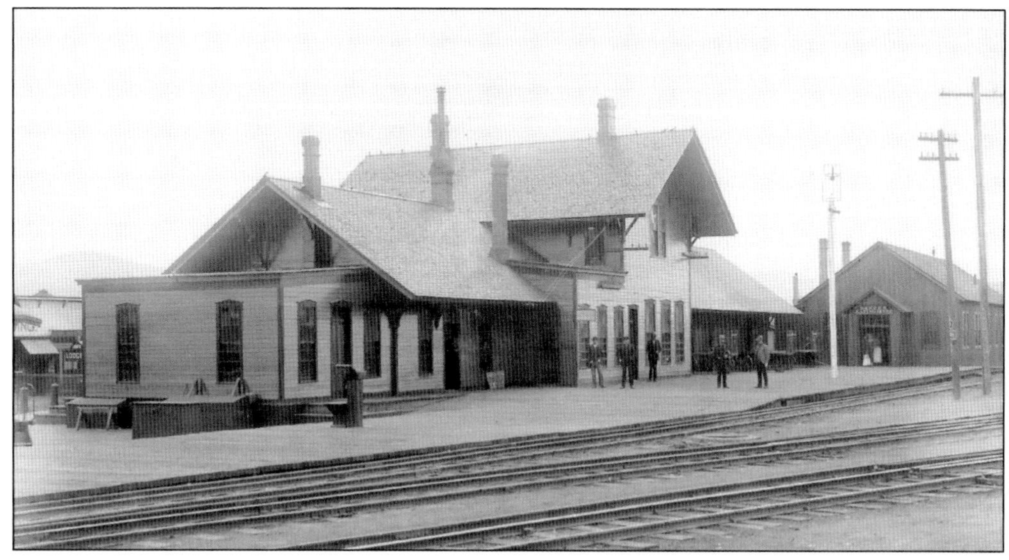

Leadville Denver & Rio Grande Depot. The Denver & Rio Grande depot in Leadville, an impressive structure, featured a very long wooden platform and large waiting room to accommodate a great number of passengers. An eating house adjacent to the depot served hungry passengers. At this location, the narrow-gauge Blue River Line to Dillon met the standard-gauge Tennessee Pass Line with connections to Denver and Salt Lake City. (Courtesy of the Denver, South Park & Pacific Historical Society.)

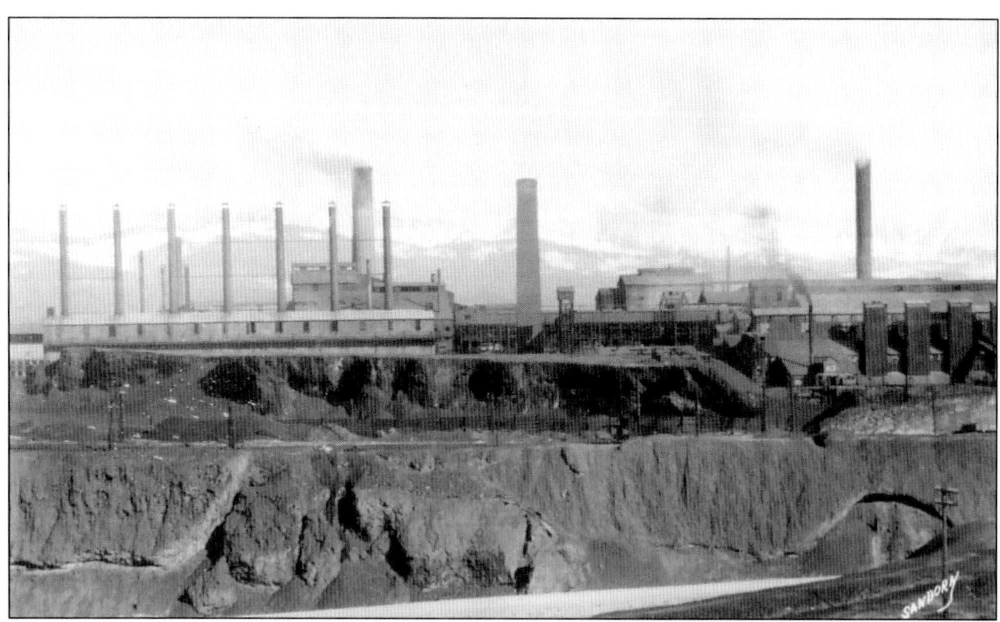

Smelter in Leadville. Sydney Dillon and Frederick L. Ames, large stockholders in the Omaha Smelting and Refining Company in Nebraska, decided to merge the company with the Grant Smelting Company in Denver, creating a monopoly in smelting. They hoped to drive the local smelters such as this one in Leadville out of business and take profits away from the Denver & Rio Grande. (Courtesy of the Denver, South Park & Pacific Historical Society.)

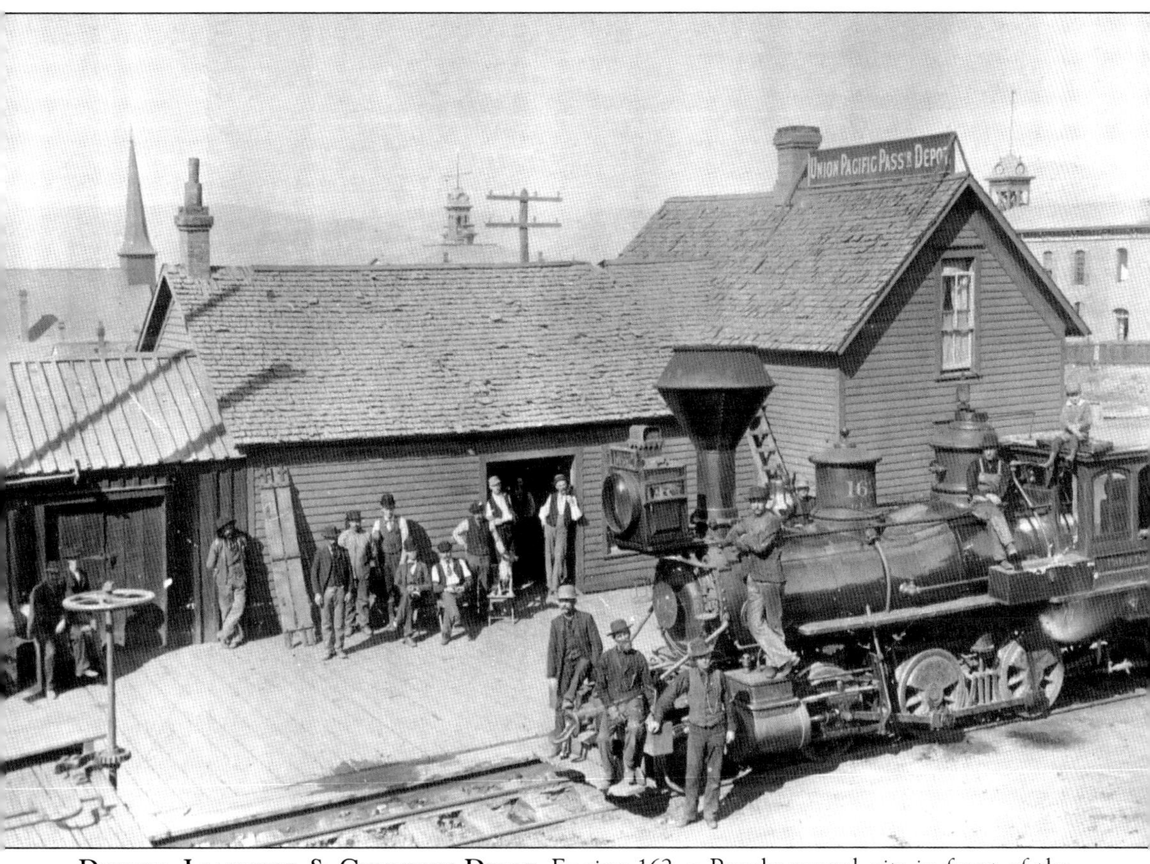

DENVER, LEADVILLE & GUNNISON DEPOT. Engine 162, a Brooks mogul, sits in front of the original Denver, South Park depot soon after the 1889 reorganization into the Denver, Leadville & Gunnison, which occurred while Union Pacific still controlled the company. The Brooks-built mogul has a 2-6-0 type of wheel arrangement. As business improved, a larger depot replaced this one that sat just north of the later brick depot. (Courtesy of the Denver, South Park & Pacific Historical Society.)

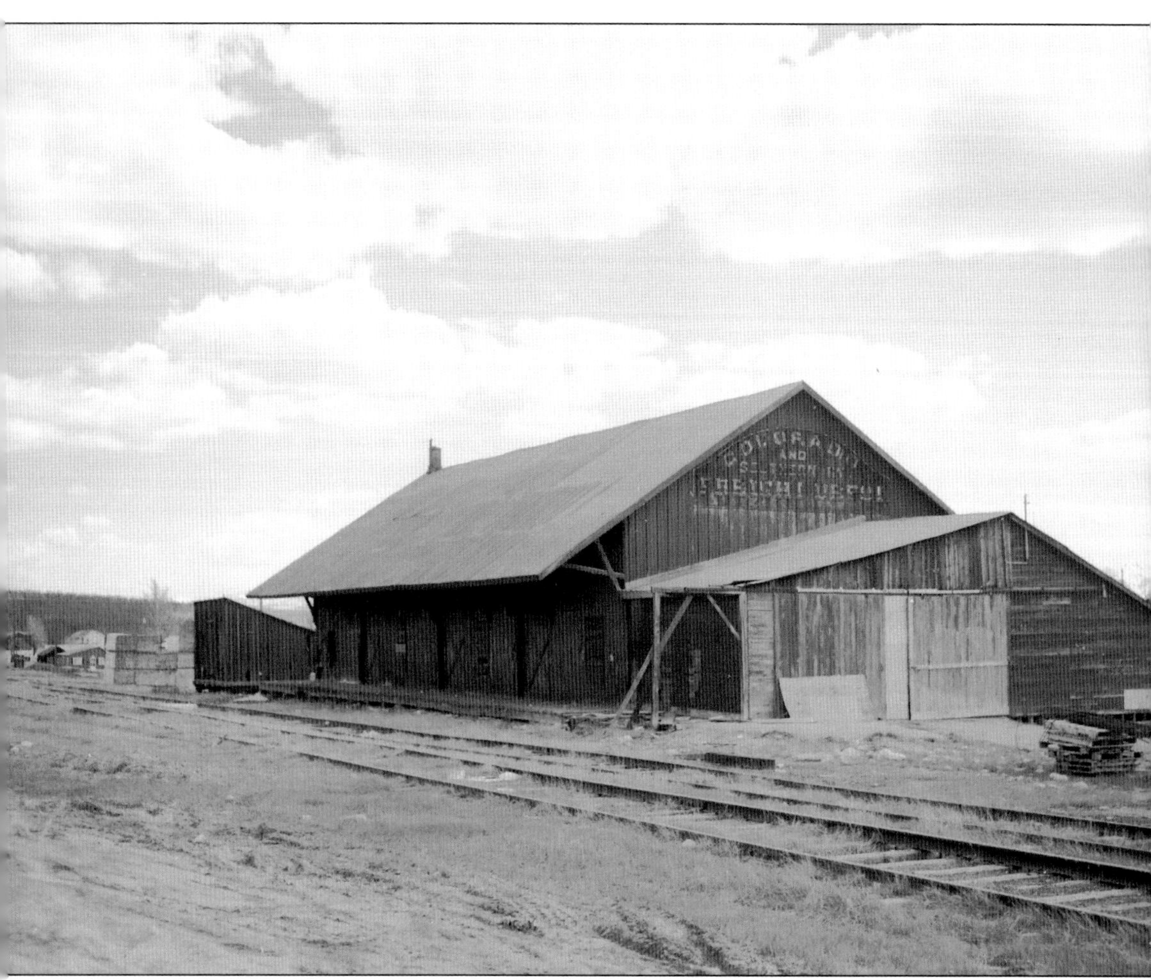

LEADVILLE COLORADO & SOUTHERN FREIGHT HOUSE. Many tons of freight have passed through the Colorado & Southern freight house, a Leadville landmark for well over 100 years. Still in excellent condition, the structure today houses a Leadville lumber company. An overhead beam in the freight house bears the signature of W.G. Nymerick, the contractor who built the freight house in 1884. (Courtesy of the Denver, South Park & Pacific Historical Society.)

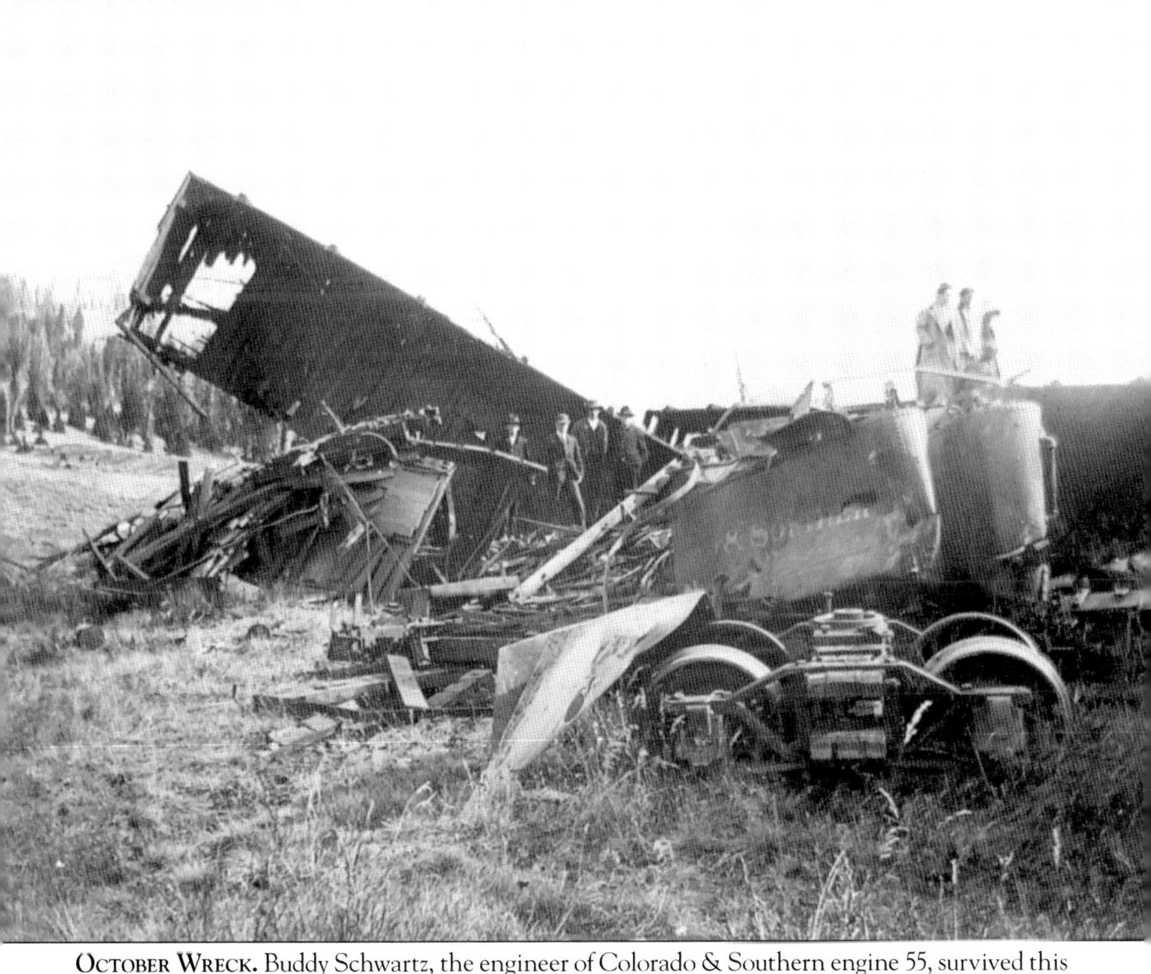

October Wreck. Buddy Schwartz, the engineer of Colorado & Southern engine 55, survived this October 1907 wreck on Fremont Pass between Climax and Kokomo. One month later, two fully loaded freight cars with their brakes not set rolled downhill from Kokomo to Frisco, derailing and spilling clothing along the right-of-way. (Courtesy of the Clair Dungan collection.)

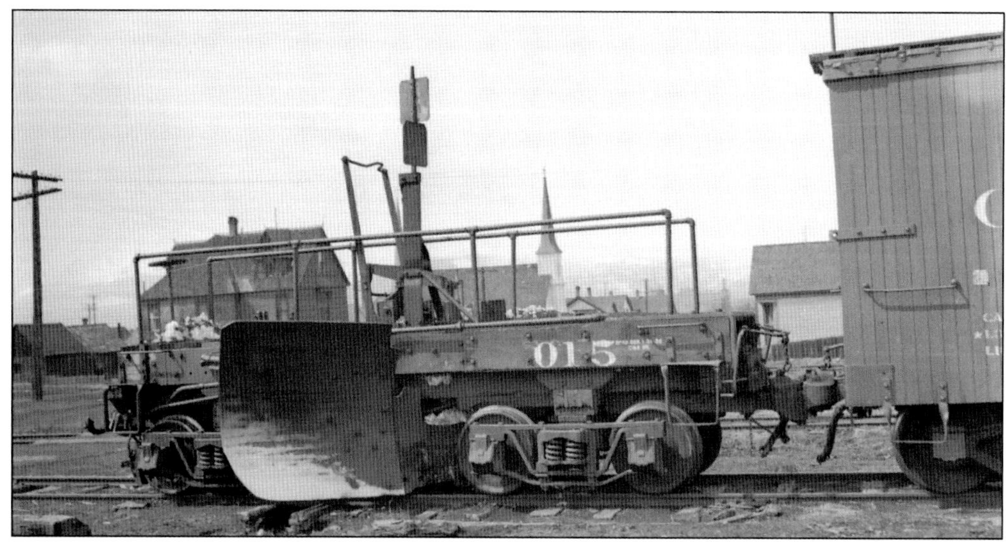

Leadville Flanger Plow. Flanger plows, heavily weighted cars with adjustable snow plow sides, helped clear snow from the tracks. Normally these cars sat just behind the lead engine or between the locomotives on double-headed trains. As long as snow drifts remained small, flanger plows such as flanger 015, seen here behind a boxcar in Leadville, could clear the tracks. For deep snow, only the rotary would suffice. (Courtesy of the Denver, South Park & Pacific Historical Society.)

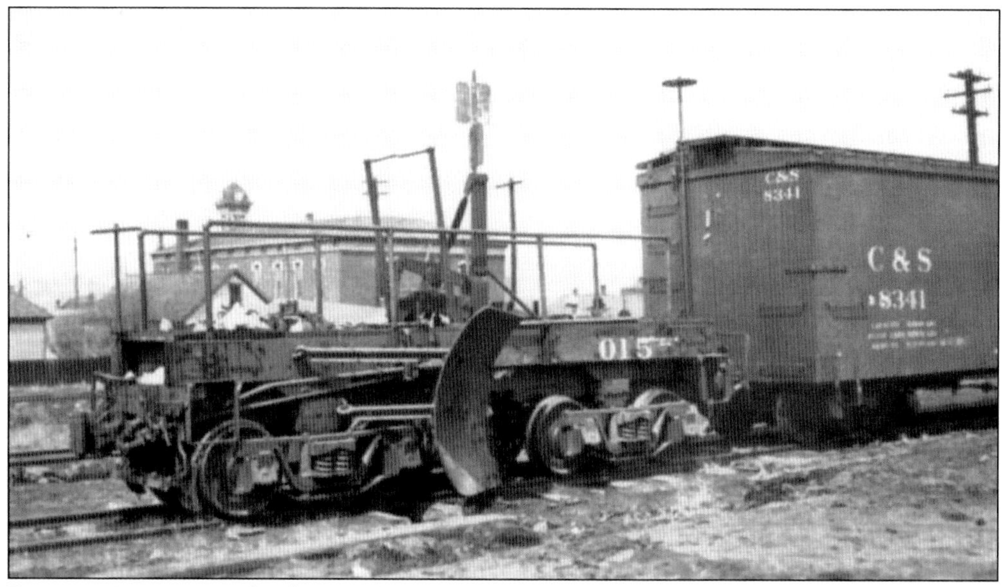

Flanger Plow 015. The flanger plow blade could be raised and lowered by air with controls in the locomotive. Fastened to the sides of the flanger plows were two large blades extending outward and backward from the sides of the car. With this configuration, the flanger plow cleaned the rails, and with the blades locked in a spread position, threw snow upward and away from the tracks. (Courtesy of the Denver, South Park & Pacific Historical Society.)

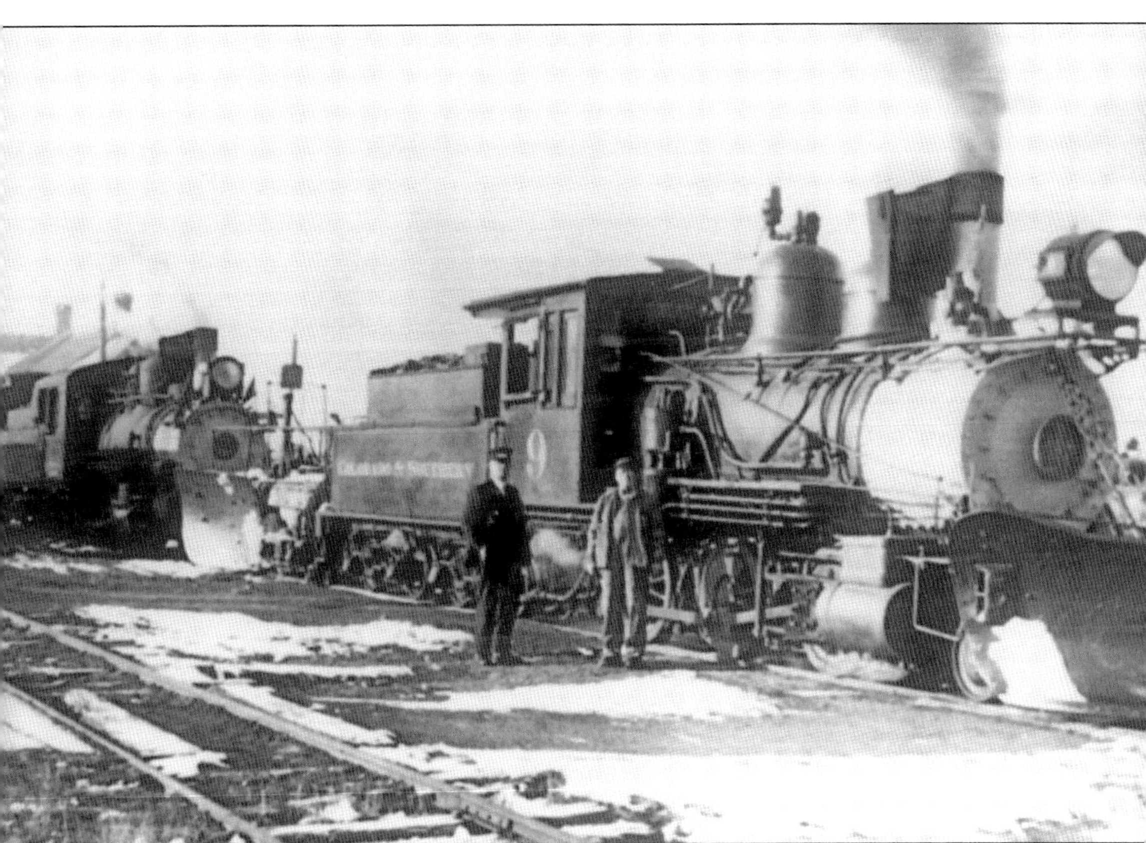

ENGINE 9 AT LEADVILLE. Engine 9, built in 1884 by the Cooke Locomotive Works, sits in the Leadville yards ready to attack deep snow. Coupled to engine 9 are a flanger plow and another locomotive. The snowplow on the front and the flanger behind clear ice and snow from the tracks. Curley Colligan, the engineer, stands beside the locomotive. (Courtesy of the Denver, South Park & Pacific Historical Society.)

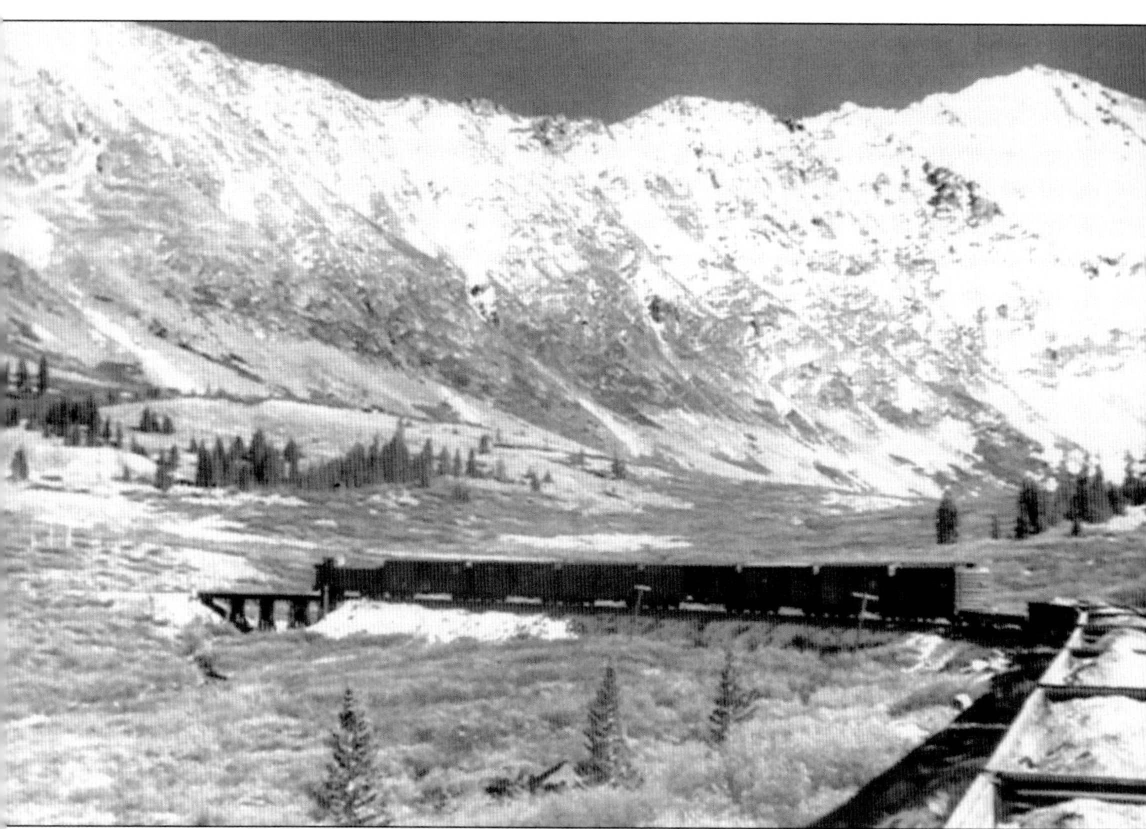

WORTMAN'S CURVE. Colorado & Southern replaced the narrow-gauge tracks with standard gauge in 1943 in order to increase its capacity and thus meet the demands of the burgeoning war effort. This freight train rounds a section of track known as Wortman's curve on its way from Climax to Leadville. C&S owned the only rail line available between the rail stops, because the Denver & Rio Grande removed its tracks in 1924. (Courtesy of the Denver, South Park & Pacific Historical Society.)

Seven

PRESERVING THE LEGACY

Although smoke no longer billows into the cloudless sky and screaming whistles no longer pierce the quiet, the legacy of the narrow-gauge railroads remains. Cars and trucks drive along Interstate 70 on the former Denver & Rio Grande right-of-way through the Ten Mile Canyon, bicycles and walkers use the recreational path on the east side of the canyon, the former Denver, South Park & Pacific right-of-way to enjoy the spectacular scenery, and recreationalists of all kinds travel from Breckenridge to Como on the Denver, South Park & Pacific right-of-way over Boreas Pass.

Those who care make sure the story of the narrow-gauge railroads is told to succeeding generations. While youngsters play among the railroad-themed playground equipment in the High Line Railroad Park in Breckenridge, older visitors learn about the railroad and its contributions to Summit County and its residents. Displays tell about the life of the men working on the railroads, the families that waited for them at the end of a run, and the importance of the railroads to the economy of Summit County from the 1880s until the 1930s. The rotary snow plow, built in 1900 by the Cooke Locomotive and Machine Works of Paterson, New Jersey, and engine 9, built in 1884 by the same company, hold the attention and grab the imagination of everyone who sees them.

With financial help from History Colorado, Colorado Department of Transportation, and private donors, volunteers from the Denver, South Park & Pacific Historical Society completed the restoration of the long-neglected Como depot and held a grand opening on August 22, 2015. The building, constructed in 1879, served passengers on the Denver, South Park & Pacific for 58 years. Restoration included raising the structure, rebuilding the foundation and chimneys, and reshingling the roof. Photographic exhibits and historic artifacts such as railroad lanterns, a depot clock, and a potbellied stove tell the story of the railroad and those who lived and worked in Como.

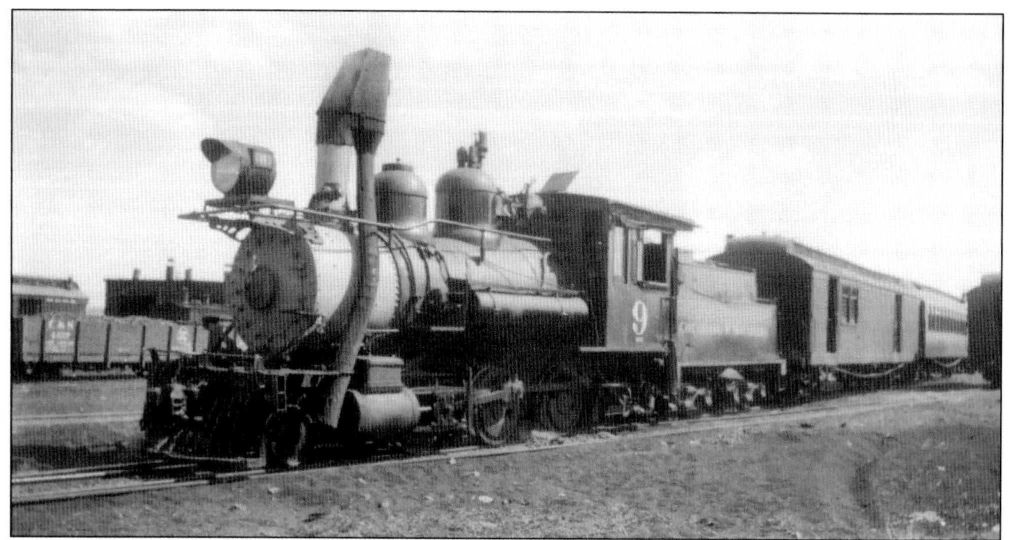

Engine 9 in Como. One of eight identical engines built by the Cooke Locomotive and Machine Works of Paterson, New Jersey, in 1884, engine 9 burned coal to create steam for power. Behind the engine is the tender that carried coal and water. The company installed the "bear trap," or Ridgeway smokestack, in 1917 or 1918 to catch sparks and prevent fires along the tracks. (Courtesy of the Denver, South Park & Pacific Historical Society.)

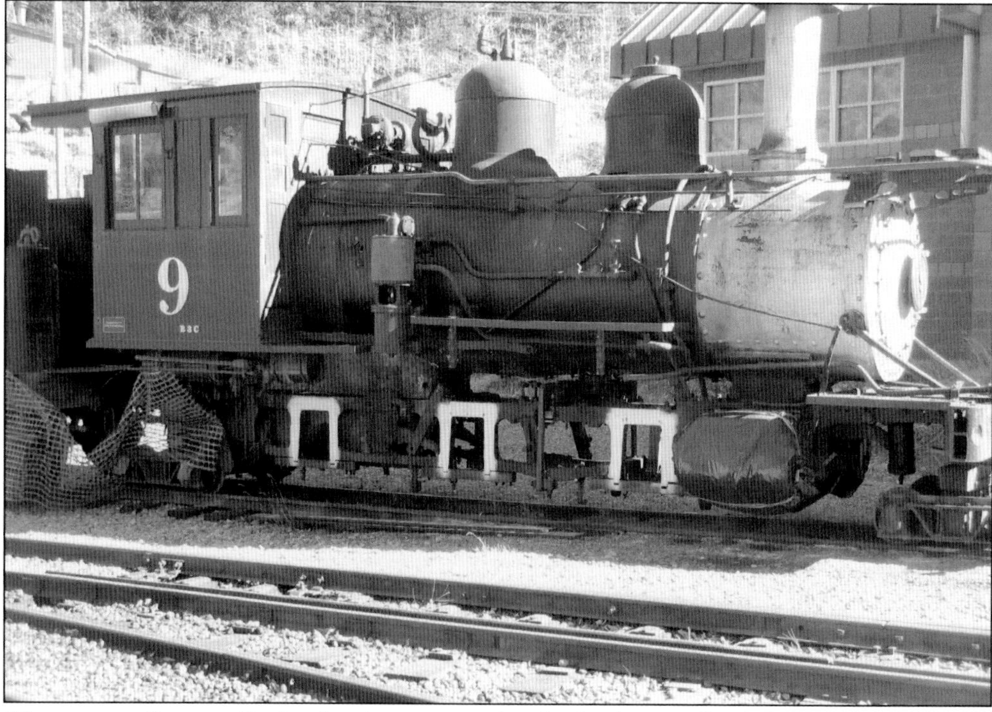

Waiting for Repairs. Engine 9 enjoyed years of work after leaving Summit County. It appeared at the New York World's Fair in 1939 and the Chicago Railroad Fair in 1948. Later, it carried passengers on the Black Hills Central Railroad in South Dakota. Purchased by History Colorado, it began working on the Georgetown Loop in 2006. Its working days ended soon after because of numerous mechanical problems. (Courtesy of Rick Hague.)

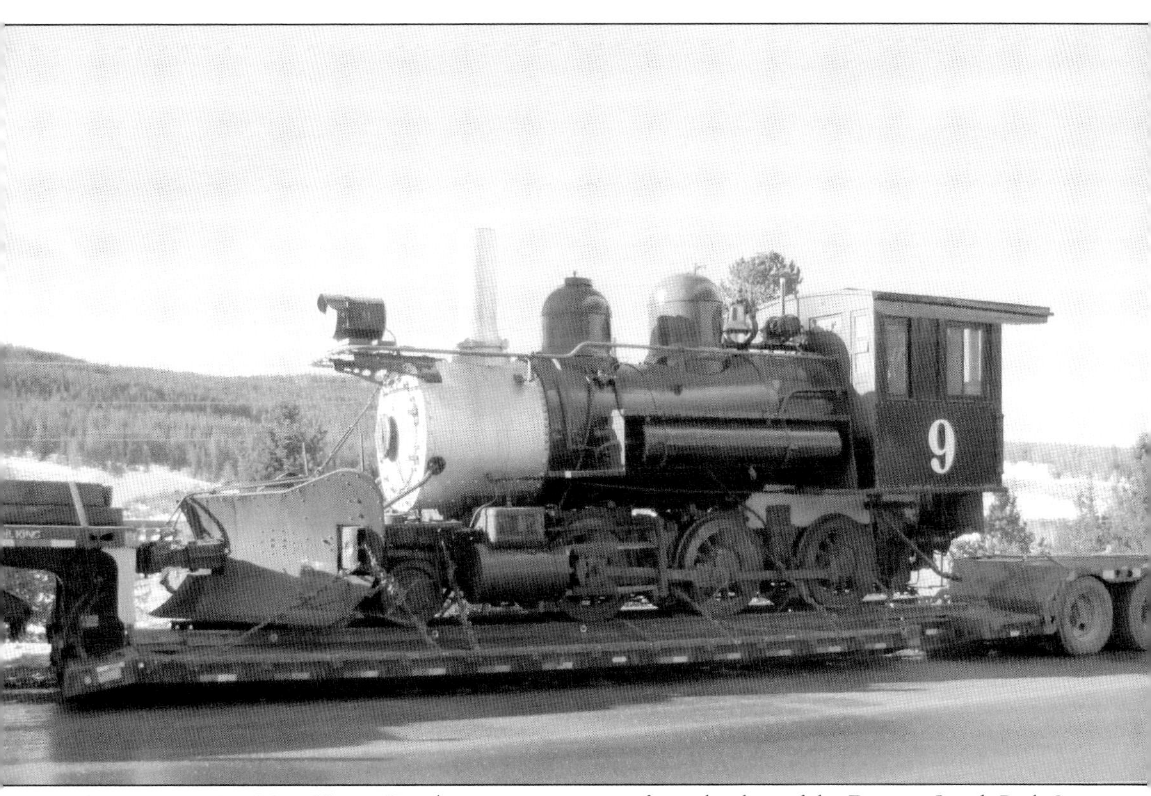

Arriving at Its New Home. Two locomotives remain from the days of the Denver, South Park & Pacific. Engine 9 is one of them. Restored by Mammoth Locomotive Works in Palisade, Colorado, and on long-term loan to the Town of Breckenridge from History Colorado, engine 9, weighing 35 to 40 tons, arrived at its new home in December 2010. The company modified the truck's trailer bed for the journey by welding railroad tracks to it. (Courtesy of Rick Hague.)

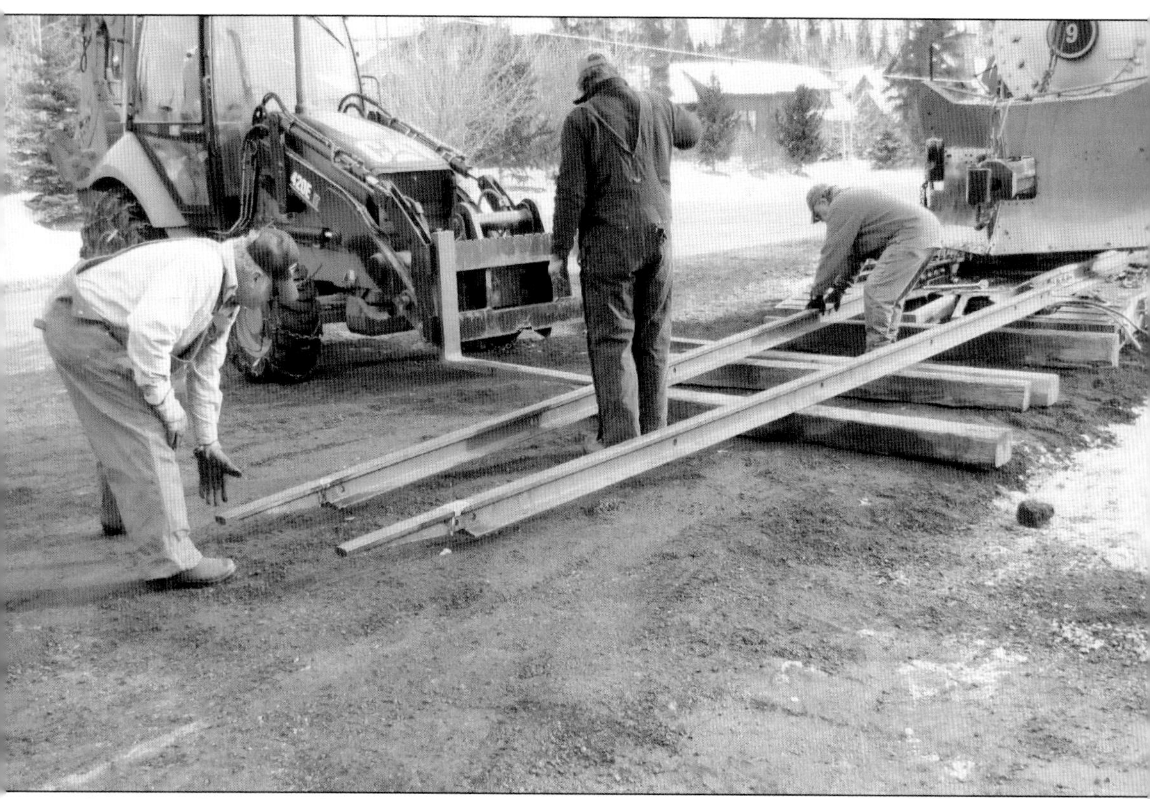

INCLINED TRACKAGE. On December 14, the truck and trailer maneuvered into a position exactly aligned with the tracks on the ground. The position needed to be exact, because the engine would roll off the tracks welded to the truck bed directly onto the tracks on the ground. A short inclined track segment, roughly 20 to 25 feet long, connected the rails on the truck bed with the rails on the ground. (Courtesy of Rick Hague.)

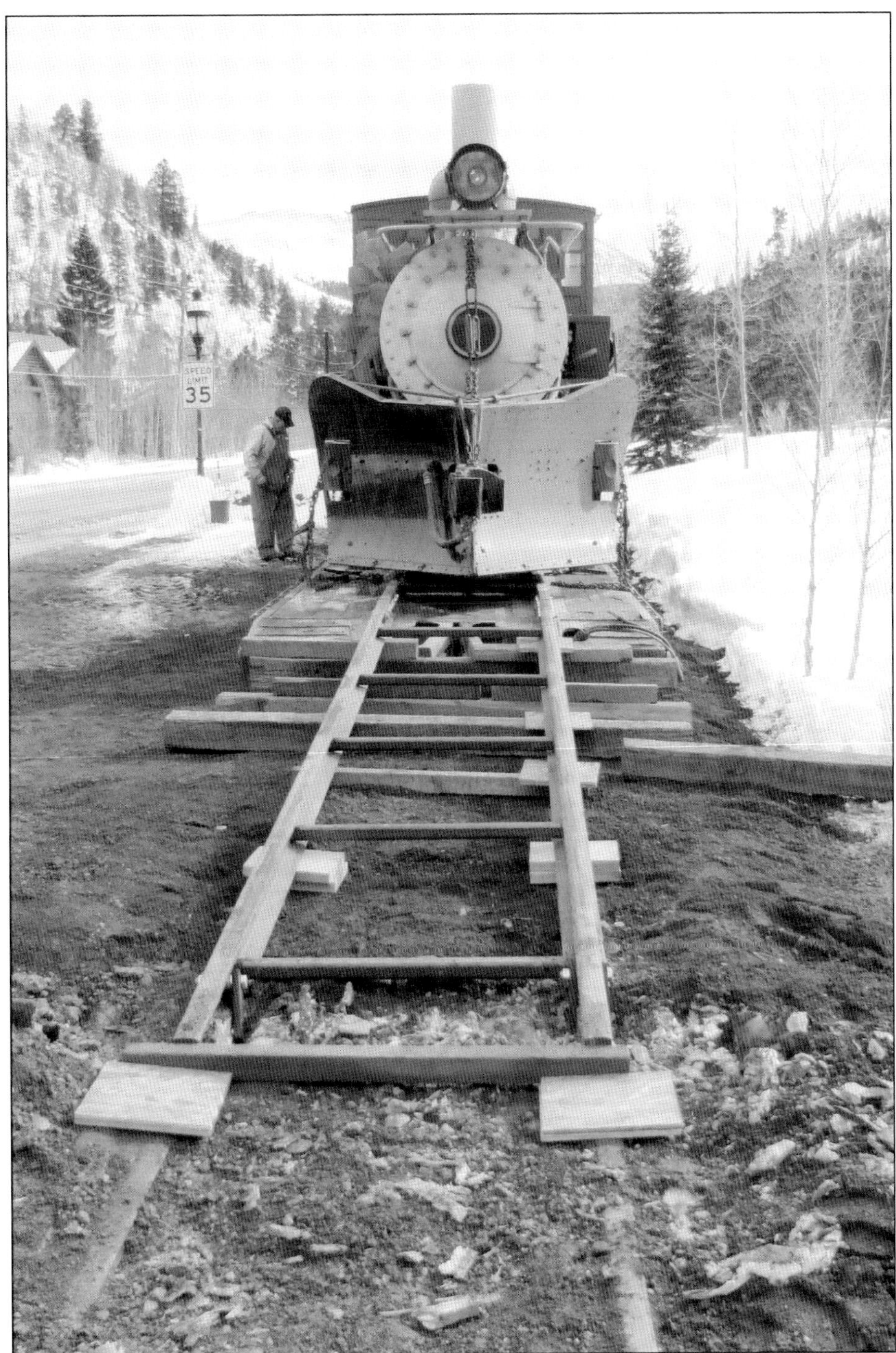

Metal Blocking Bar. Once the truck was aligned with the engine facing its new home, workers attached the winch cable of a truck-towing wrecker positioned behind the engine. Because the engine would roll off the trailer by gravity, the wrecker was necessary to control the speed of engine 9 as it rolled down the inclined track. A metal blocking bar, welded across the track on the ground, would stop the engine in case it got away from the wrecker. (Courtesy of Rick Hague.)

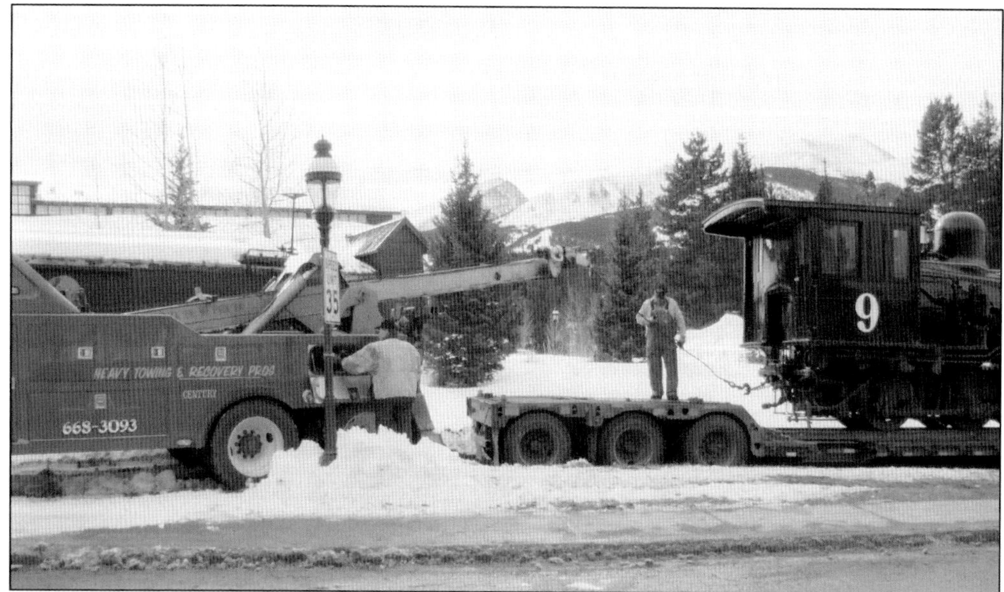

Moving by Gravity. With the engine held in place by the wrecker, the front end of the specially designed trailer was lowered to the ground. Engine 9 rolled by gravity down the inclined track. Because the track on the ground was relatively flat, a backhoe, attached by cable to the front of the engine, pulled the engine into place under its shelter. (Courtesy of Rick Hague.)

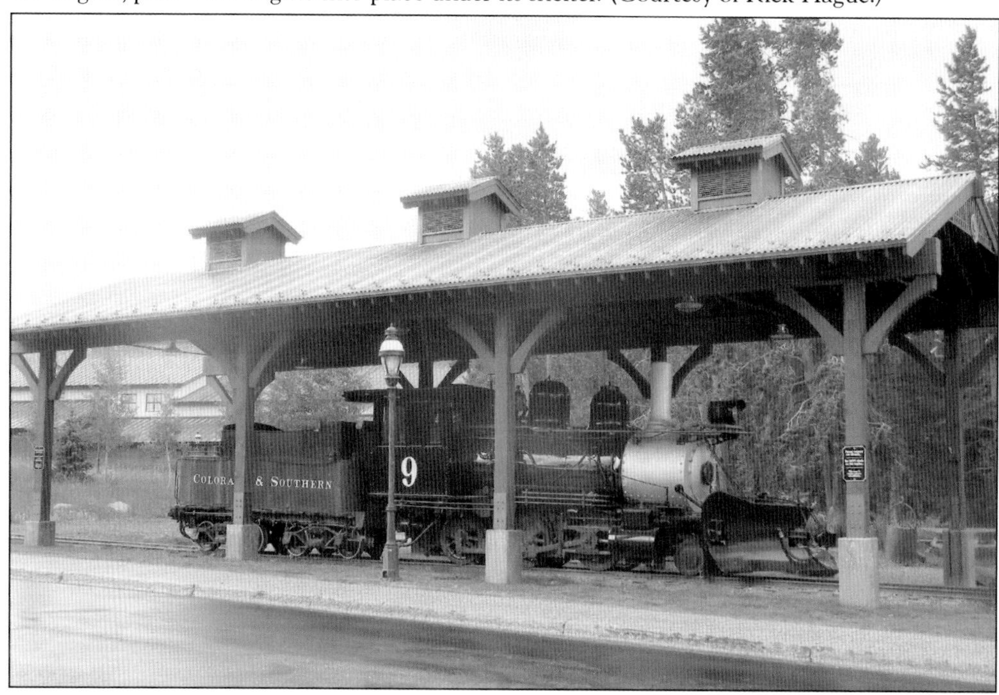

Protective Covering. The Town of Breckenridge designed and constructed a protective covering for engine 9 in 2010. Local contractors and businesses provided more than $40,000 of in-kind support for the shelter. The tender for engine 9, also on loan from History Colorado, arrived at the park in 2011 from Strasburg, Colorado. Local contractors completed the restoration of the tender in 2012. (Courtesy of the Breckenridge Heritage Alliance.)

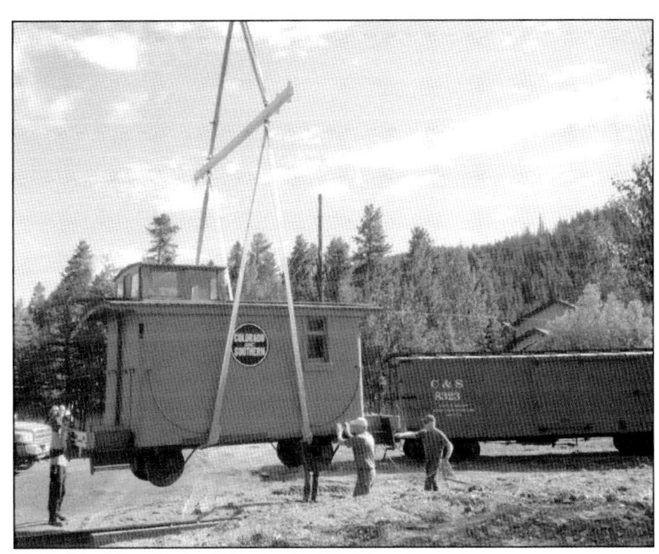

Placing the Caboose on the Tracks. Men carefully guide the caboose onto the tracks. This caboose, a replica, was constructed in McKinleyville, California, from measurements of Colorado & Southern caboose 1006, on display in Silver Plume, Colorado. The original 1006 served on Clear Creek narrow-gauge lines. The railroad originally painted cabooses rust red, because it was the cheapest paint available. Later, it painted cabooses bright red for safety. (Courtesy of the Breckenridge Heritage Alliance.)

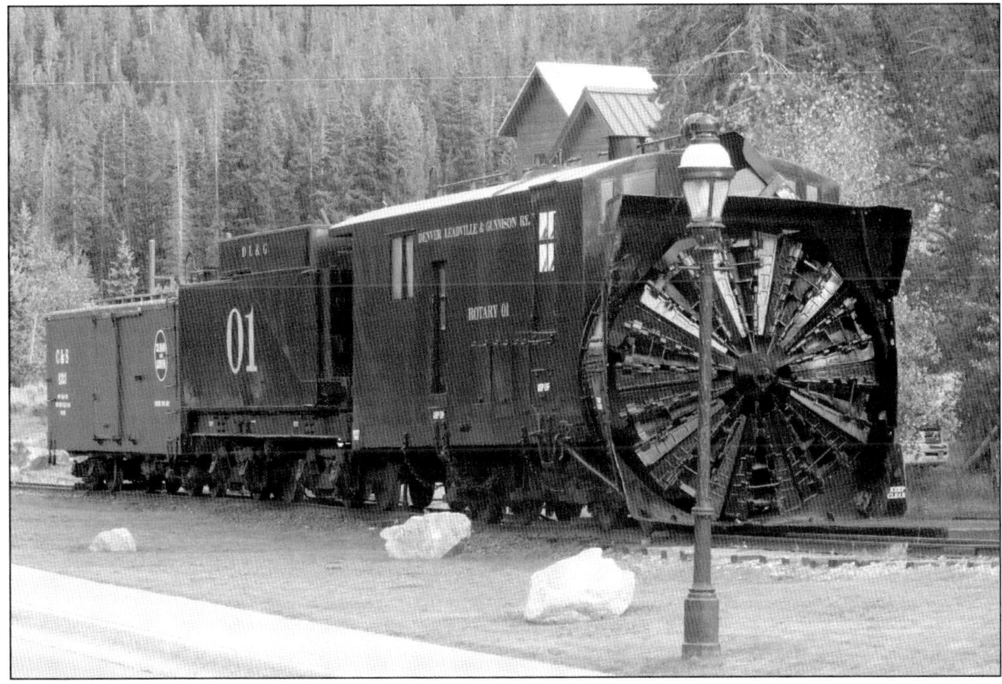

Rotary Snow Plow. The rotary snowplow at the High Line Railroad Park cleared the rails of Alaska's White Pass and Yukon Route until 1963. Put in storage in Skagway until 1977, it was purchased by Sumpter Valley Railroad Restoration, Inc., and moved to Oregon. Subsequently bought by the Denver, Leadville & Gunnison Railway in 1988 and renamed rotary 01, it was repaired and restored in Denver before arriving in Breckenridge in 1989. (Courtesy of the Breckenridge Heritage Alliance.)

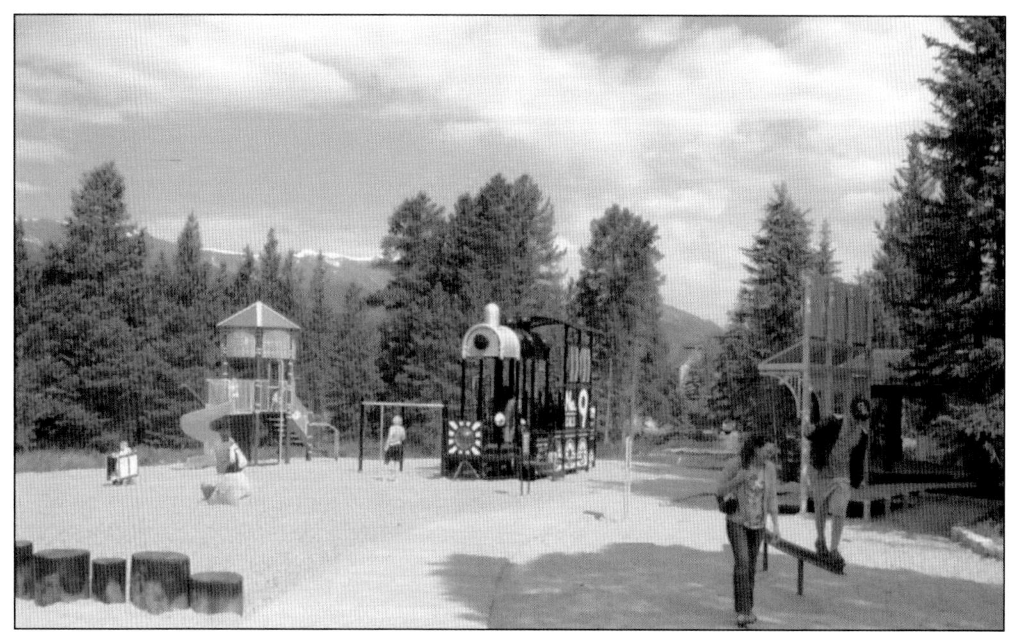

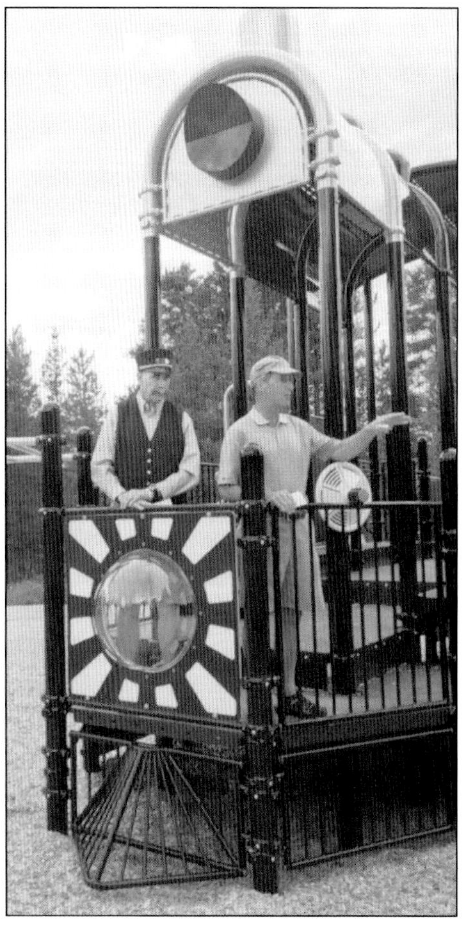

Dedicating the Playground at the High Line Railroad Park. While Mayor John Warner (left in the image to the left) and Jerry Dziedzic, president of the Breckenridge Heritage Alliance, gave their speeches dedicating the playground in summer 2014, two boys played in the gravel beneath them. The former Rotary Snow Plow Park, renamed the High Line Railroad Park in 2014, includes a variety of playground equipment for children and a model railroad display in the depot. (Above, courtesy of the Breckenridge Heritage Alliance; left, courtesy of the Town of Breckenridge.)

About the Organizations

The Denver, South Park & Pacific Historical Society was established to promote the preservation of the history and artifacts of all the predecessor lines that became the narrow-gauge portion of the Colorado & Southern Railway. The society encourages artifact and equipment acquisition as well as dissemination of knowledge about these railroads and their effect on the history of Colorado and the nation.

The Summit Historical Society is dedicated to the discovery, preservation, interpretation, and exhibition of the rich heritage and history of Summit County. The all-volunteer society, incorporated on October 25, 1966, as a private, nonprofit organization, provides tours of historic buildings such as the 1883 Dillon Schoolhouse, the Myers Cabin, and Honeymoon Cabin; maintains a collection of historic artifacts; and conducts interesting educational programs throughout the year for residents and visitors of all ages.

The Frisco Historic Park & Museum, operated by the Town of Frisco, helps visitors learn about Frisco's historical and cultural heritage. The schoolhouse, still on its original site and now listed in the National Register of Historic Places, opened its doors to the public as a museum in 1983. During the ensuing years, the town added 11 other restored historic structures, each displaying artifacts from Frisco's past.

The Breckenridge Heritage Alliance is a nonprofit organization founded in December 2006 to promote and protect Breckenridge's unique heritage. Through a collection of historic sites, guided tours and hikes, as well as programs and events for all ages, the alliance encourages residents and guests to experience what life was like in historic Breckenridge. The alliance maintains the Mather Archive Room, which houses the Summit Historical Society's collection of photographs, maps, newspapers, and documents.

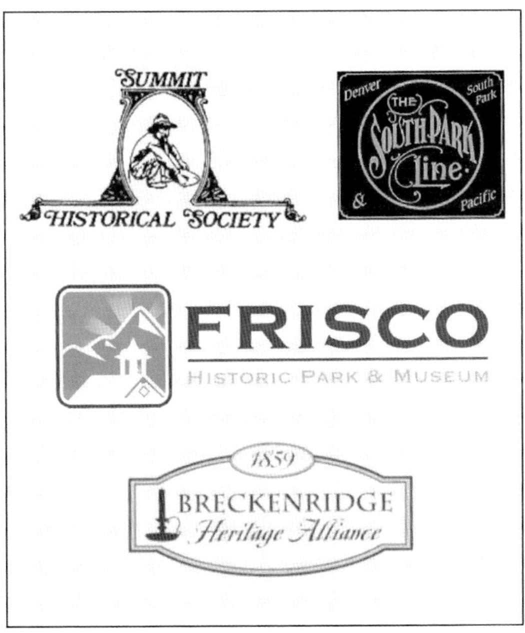

Consistent with our mission to preserve history on a local level, this book was printed in South Carolina on American-made paper and manufactured entirely in the United States. Products carrying the accredited Forest Stewardship Council (FSC) label are printed on 100 percent FSC-certified paper.

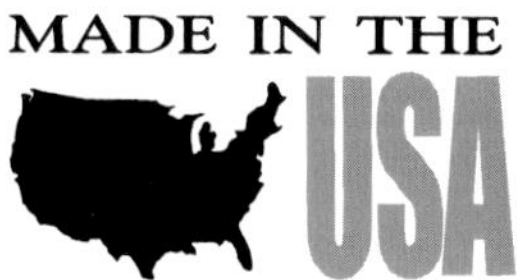